HIDDEN MESSAGES
IN CULTURE-CENTERED COUNSELING

*To the small flying phoenix
who migrates so easily back and forth from East to West.*

HIDDEN MESSAGES
IN CULTURE-CENTERED COUNSELING

A Triad Training Model

PAUL B. PEDERSEN

Sage Publications, Inc.
International Educational and Professional Publisher
Thousand Oaks ▪ London ▪ New Delhi

For information:

Sage Publications, Inc.
2455 Teller Road
Thousand Oaks, California 91320
E-mail: order@sagepub.com

Sage Publications Ltd.
6 Bonhill Street
London EC2A 4PU
United Kingdom

Sage Publications India Pvt. Ltd.
M-32 Market
Greater Kailash I
New Delhi 110 048 India

Printed in the United States of America

Library of Congress Cataloging-in-Publication Data

Pedersen, Paul, 1936–
        Hidden messages in culture-centered counseling: A triad training
    model / by Paul Pedersen.
            p. cm.
        Includes bibliographical references and index.
        ISBN 0-7619-1806-X (cloth) — ISBN 0-7619-1807-8 (pbk.)
        1. Cross-cultural counseling. 2. Intercultural communication. I. Title.
        BF637.C6 P337 1999
        158′.3—dc21
                                                99-006837

00   01   02   03   10 9 8 7 6 5 4 3 2 1

Acquiring Editor: Jim Nageotte
Editorial Assistant: Anna Howland
Production Editor: Diana E. Axelsen
Editorial Assistant: Patricia Zeman
TypesetterDesigner: Christina M. Hill
Indexer: Virgil Diodato
Cover Designer: Kristi White

Contents

Foreword   vii

    Edward T. Hall

Preface   ix

PART I: The Psychological Research Foundation   1

1. The Psychological Foundation of Counseling Relationships   3

2. The "Problem" as a Counseling Metaphor   19

3. The Relational Self   39

4. Hearing the Hidden Messages   53

PART II: The Triad Training Model   69

5. Positive and Negative Internal Dialogue in Counseling   71

6. Training Implications of Hidden Messages   84

7. Developing Multicultural Competencies With the
   Triad Training Model   101

PART III: Transcript Applications of the Triad Training Model 115

8. Sexual Harassment, Juvenile Delinquency, Political Affiliation, and Lesbian Lifestyle as Multicultural Issues and International Applications of the Triad Training Model 117

9. Transcript Examples of the Triad Training Model 132

10. Other Internal Dialogue Training Models 144

11. The Intrapersonal Context of Counseling 161

Appendix A: Self-Assessment in Using the Triad Training Model 165

Appendix B: Workshop Assessment 178

References 181

Index 195

About the Author 207

Foreword

There is nothing more fundamental than information and nothing more important to the future of the planet than the role of information gained from the transactions between human beings. This book centers on the essentials of communicating in the counseling relationship.

For openers, the generally accepted view of a conversation is that it is a "singular" process—a connecting link or channel between two or more individuals. Pedersen adds to this formula (as well as the practice of counseling) by broadening our view and by making the point that these everyday verbal exchanges constitute not one but *three or more simultaneous conversations, layered one on top of the other.* Furthermore, two of them are unspoken and carried in the interlocutors' heads. All this becomes increasingly complex when the counselor-client dyad is made up of individuals of different cultures or even different backgrounds in the same culture. This leads us to another point: namely, when the tacit rules of the "languages of encounters" are not followed or understood, are overly complex, or require specialized knowledge, the message becomes either garbled, obscured, or both, and the entire process begins to collapse.

What makes this book especially relevant to counselors is that it is built around one of the most important aspects of communication. By treating communication as a transaction, the author frees himself to describe the *hidden* dialogues of both sides during counseling and provides the reader with a coherent, readily understood statement of some of the most important variables inherent in verbal communication. Professional counselors will be reassured not only by how realistically rooted in experience Pedersen's descriptions are but also by their clarity. Particularly relevant is his decoding of the tacit processes based on patterns rooted in daily usage. For the essence of Pedersen's message is the more differences—explicit as well as implicit—between counselor and client, the more *hidden messages* there are to be attended to. Pedersen stresses the point that, as the number of hidden messages increases, the greater the counselor's need is to know how to read them. This book is designed to reinforce what the counselor has already learned from the client's hidden messages. In that, one of the principal reasons underlying the ambiguity associated with intercultural encounters can be traced to situations in which the words are understood but the tacit meanings on which they are based are not.

It is in these terms that the counselor must comprehend the need for mastery of the complexities, not just of what has been said but, particularly, of the *underlying assumptions* of the interlocutors. These heretofore overlooked aspects of counseling apply not only when the two sides of the equation share cultures but, particularly, when two different cultures are involved. Pedersen's book is so basic and so clearly stated that one might easily minimize the fundamental nature of his message. All that follows in this book is built on his dedication to making explicit the important aspects of what can be acquired only after years of experience.

—Edward T. Hall

Preface

When a counselor meets a client, there are three conversations going on at the same time. The first conversation is the verbal exchange between the client and the counselor, which is heard by both persons. The second conversation is going on inside the counselor's mind, analyzing what is and/or is not happening and what that might mean. The counselor also hears the second conversation. The third conversation is going on inside the client's mind, analyzing what is and/or is not happening and what that might mean. The counselor cannot hear that third conversation and is forced to guess or speculate on what the client's internal dialogue might be "saying." This *three-way* dialogue is the basis of the Triad Training Model. The more culturally different a client is from the counselor, the more difficult it will be for a counselor to guess accurately about what the client is thinking but not saying.

The more differences there are between the counselor and the client, the more "hidden messages" there will be in the counseling interview. Competence in counseling begins with the ability to respond appropriately to these hidden messages. That means, first, recognizing that some of the messages the client is sending are hidden from the counselor; second, recognizing that some of those messages will be negative and some positive; third, becoming sensitive to the verbal and nonverbal cultural cues—in both what is said and what is not said—in the counseling interview; and, fourth, training counselors to monitor and mobilize their own internal dialogue as a valuable resource in counseling.

Psychology as a science began by focusing on the study of consciousness. In recent years, psychology, and particularly the areas of applied psychology such as counseling, have returned to that focus on insidethe individual variables. Gilbert, Fiske, and Lindzey (1998) focus on intrapersonal phenomena in

Part III of their *Handbook of Social Psychology,* examining attitude structure and function, attitude change, mental representation and memory, behavioral decision making, motivation, and emotions. Freud's intrapsychic dynamic between the id, ego, and superego has been translated into a variety of other internalized applications from the behavioral, humanistic, and multicultural perspectives, which will be reviewed in the following chapters. Allport (1961) described the self as a central organizing scheme of our personality, the key to one's inner nature, a "me" as we feel and know it. Allport called this core of the conscious self the *proprium,* almost as though it were a separate identity within one's identity. As Jung (1965) put it, a person looks for instruction and guidance from "internal conversations" with one's self, derived from cultural background or spontaneous generation of other real and imagined experiences. Jung named his own internal self *Philemon,* who was his *guru* or teacher and from whom Jung received guidance.

Hearing voices does not presume pathology. Liester (1996) points out that individuals who are not mentally ill may also hear voices, following a strong tradition of many respected leaders who reported benefits from hearing internal voices. Lazarus (1997) describes how he dealt with his own personal problems and interpersonal issues through cognitive restructuring and imagery techniques. Sheik and Sheik (1989) point out that Western approaches to counseling and therapy have sometimes pathologized the behavior of non-Western clients by presuming the hearing of voices to be a clear sign of psychological disorder. The hearing of voices, talking to one's self, and carrying on internal dialogues are not atypical in Western cultures as well. Among the more spiritual and religious populations, prayer may provide an example of internal dialogue to or with a personalized presence. This internalized spiritual-religious source has remained an underutilized resource as a formal aspect of counseling and counselor education. It may be that all counseling is mediated by the client's internal dialogues, and successful counseling depends as much on what the client is thinking, but not saying, as it does on the explicit verbal messages of the counselor (Braiker, 1989). Blachowicz (1997) examines the cognitive significance of talking to ourselves, rejecting the "reflection" model and the "social" model in favor of a third view that inner speech is a genuine dialogue between independent interests within the consciousness and not merely a monologue. The focus of this book will be to demonstrate specific ways to mobilize those internal dynamics to better understand the counseling process and to better understand ourselves through our own internal dialogue.

Robins, Gosling, and Craik (1999) examined trends in the most widely recognized psychological systems of psychoanalysis, behaviorism, cognitive psychology, and neuroscience. Cognitive psychology was the only system that sustained a steady upward trajectory, and it continues to be the most prominent school of scientific psychology. This shift in psychology has been described as part of a new paradigm shift in psychology (Robins et al., 1999), although the paradigm shift may be in a multiparadigmatic stage rather than featuring one school of psychology competing with others in a zero-sum game.

This book seeks to demonstrate the extensive psychological literature supporting the importance of internal dialogue for conceptualizing counseling theory, for training and educating counselors, for direct service, for research, and for increased self-awareness. Internal dialogue is especially important for counseling across cultures. One approach, the Triad Training Model, for hearing what culturally different clients are thinking but not saying will receive particular emphasis. The Triad Training Model matches a counselor from one culture with a three-person team of client, anticounselor, and procounselor from the same contrasting culture. This model allows the counselor trainee to receive immediate, continuous, and direct feedback from an anticounselor and a procounselor about what negative and positive messages the culturally different client might be thinking but not saying. The Triad Training Model provides a means of incorporating the client's internal dialogue into the process of counselor education and training.

The following chapters will build on one another to describe the intrapersonal context of counseling through inner dialogue as an underused resource in counseling and counselor training. The eleven chapters will be divided into three parts. The first part will highlight the psychological research foundation of internal dialogue training models. The second part will highlight the Triad Training Model. The third part will present transcript applications of the Triad Training Model and other internal dialogue training models.

The first chapter is focused on how social psychological research has provided a foundation for counseling at both the interpersonal and the intrapersonal levels. The fact that counseling theory has depended on interpersonal research from social psychology is well documented in the literature. However, the social psychological research on intrapersonal variables has been less widely applied to counseling.

The second chapter is focused on the "problem," as a metaphor in the counseling relationship, as the opponent of a counselor-client coalition. Social psychological research on coalition formation is applied to the counseling relationship, focusing on how it is formed and maintained as a temporary coalition between the counselor and client against the problem.

The third chapter is focused on the "relational self" as a network of relationships within the individual that compete and cooperate according to the changing context. By presenting the self as a relational phenomenon, the social psychological research can more easily be applied to the intrapersonal dynamics of counseling. The multiplicity of potential selves demonstrates how each counselor may be both culturally similar and culturally different from each client, although the degree of similarity and difference will vary.

The fourth chapter is focused on the variety of methods for revealing hidden messages in the client's internal dialogue through direct-service interventions. Techniques and strategies for incorporating internal dialogue into direct service have been well established in the counseling literature. Becoming more familiar with the client's internal dialogue in the simulated training context may increase a counselor's ability to monitor the client's hidden messages later in a direct-service setting.

The fifth chapter is focused more narrowly on hearing the client's hidden messages in terms of positive or negative emphasis. The notion of anticounselor and procounselor for articulating the client's negative and positive internal dialogue in counseling will be introduced with the Triad Training Model.

The sixth chapter continues to describe the Triad Training Model and present the implications of the model for counselor education and training. The advantages of the Triad Training Model are described, and suggestions for implementing the model are presented.

The seventh chapter reviews the research on the Triad Training Model as it relates to the development of multicultural competencies. The three-stage developmental sequence, beginning with increased *awareness* of a counselor's cultural assumptions, moving to increased *knowledge* about the cultural context of counseling, and finally to increased *skill* for demonstrating multicultural competence in counseling, will be discussed.

The eighth chapter will demonstrate the applications of the Triad Training Model to broadly defined cultural categories of sexual harassment, juvenile delinquency, political affiliation, and lesbian lifestyle. The importance of "salience" will be emphasized in the broad definition of culture to include demographic, status, and affiliation as well as ethnographic variables.

The ninth chapter will present transcript examples using the Triad Training Model. These transcripts will provide examples of what a procounselor and an anticounselor might actually say or do in the simulated counseling interview as they make explicit the otherwise hidden messages of the client.

The tenth chapter will present other models that have developed from the Triad Training Model to train counselors to better hear the hidden messages of a client's internal dialogue. These wide-ranging variations demonstrate the range of possibilities for training counselors to monitor their own and their client's internal dialogue.

The eleventh chapter will synthesize the previous ten chapters in an examination of the intrapersonal context of counseling. A series of questions will be raised that demonstrates the implication of counseling as primarily an intrapersonal process and a multicultural event.

A self-assessment measure and a workshop assessment measure will be presented as appendixes for those using the Triad Training Model in education and training.

The ideas presented in this book are based on three assumptions. First, all counseling, and perhaps all communication, is primarily an intrapersonal phenomenon, because we encode messages before sending them and decode messages we receive. Second, the rules for encoding and decoding messages are culturally learned, and different ethnographic, demographic, status, and affiliation groups will encode and/or decode messages differently. Third, the more cultural differences there are between two people or groups, the more their messages will be "hidden" from one another.

The ideas presented in this book are not yet finished; they demonstrate a "model" or method of counseling and of counselor education or training that is still in process. Although the research supporting the importance of internal dialogue is comprehensive and well documented, the research on how to incorporate internal dialogue into counselor education and training is still very preliminary. This book will suggest education and training strategies that will be important to counselor educators, particularly those training counselors to work in multicultural contexts.

"Everything you can imagine is real."
—Pablo Picasso

PART I

The Psychological Research Foundation

The first section of four chapters will review the foundation of psychological research, documenting the importance of interpersonal and intrapersonal dynamics to the practice of counseling. The first chapter will discuss the linkage between counseling psychology and social psychology, especially as it relates to interpersonal processes. The second chapter will focus on the "problem" as a metaphor for better linking research in interpersonal coalition formation to the intrapersonal dynamics of counseling. The third chapter will examine the implications of defining self as a "relational" entity networking a multiplicity of potentially salient cultural identities. The fourth chapter will discuss the implications of intrapersonal dynamics to direct-service counseling as a strategy and as a meaningful perspective.

The Psychological Foundation of Counseling Relationships

The functional role of internal dialogue in counseling is based on research from many fields, particularly from social psychology. The long-established partnership between social and counseling psychologies has resulted in productivity for both scientific theory and constructive practice over at least the last 30 years. Counseling has tested major ideas from social psychology theories and research by applying them to the counseling relationship (Stoltenberg, McNeil, & Elliott, 1995). Critics of the interface between social psychology and counseling point to the lack of research on ethnic diversity, the lack of research on competing theories relating to counseling, the lack of training of psychologists on the interface, and a lack of enthusiasm by social psychologists to research the interface with counseling psychology (Heesacker & Carroll, 1997). Although it is unlikely that the interface will be abandoned and it is nonproductive to argue about whether there is a constructive interface, it is important to sort out those specific areas in which the interface can contribute to both social and counseling psychologies. The sources cited provide excellent reviews of the social psychology literature, which this chapter will not attempt to duplicate (Giergrist, 1995). This book is an attempt to build on one example of how this interface can advance our understanding of the counseling relationship: the intrapersonal dynamics of the counseling relationship across cultures.

THE COOPERATION BETWEEN
SOCIAL PSYCHOLOGY AND COUNSELING

Forsyth and Leary (1997) identify seven domains in which counseling and social psychology have worked together. These areas include (a) educational learning, teaching, and training; (b) professional relationships between researchers and practitioners; (c) practical attempts to solve individual and societal problems; (d) methodological approaches to empirical procedures and standards; (e) the construction of conceptual and theoretical models that span disciplines; (f) metatheoretical assumptions about phenomena; and (g) epistemological assumptions about how knowledge is expanded. This transfer of technology has been largely one-directional, from social psychology to counseling.

> Most prior efforts have taken a concept or theory from social psychology and applied it to a process of interest to counseling psychologists. Rarely have issues of interest to counseling psychologists prompted social psychologists to develop or revise their theoretical viewpoints. (p. 181)

Few social psychology journals publish articles about counseling, and it is rare to find social psychologists working in counseling settings.

As both counseling and social psychology have tended to focus more on managing specific problems or social issues through a truly scientist-practitioner model, the need to differentiate social and counseling psychologies has diminished. Not only are the polarized stereotypes not accurate, but they are a luxury we can no longer afford in the face of serious shared social problems. From the viewpoint of the client or consumer of psychological services, the differences in professional labels are less significant than is the ability of either field of psychology to manage problems. With the increased attention to the reflective, interpretative, and constructivist view of human nature in psychology to complement the traditional positivist view based on a natural sciences model, both social and counseling psychologies are focusing more on subjective data as well as objective data as valuable resources.

During the past three decades, counseling psychologists have increasingly depended on principles of social psychological processes in counseling theories and research as a result of influences by the behavioral movement and the cognitive process (Strong, 1968, 1978). In part, this has been the result of the behavioral movement in clinical/counseling psychology leading to a convergence between social and clinical/counseling psychologies (Maddux, Stoltenberg, Rosenwein, & Leary, 1987). This convergence has destroyed three common myths: first, the false dichotomy that research is purely objective and clinical work is purely subjective; second, that social psychology research is focused on "normal" populations and clinicians work with "clinical" populations that differ so much that data from one do not apply to the other; and, third, that social psychological research is nomothetic and clinical/counseling is ideographic, and there is a clear impermeable boundary between these two perspectives. Strong, Welsh, Corcoran, and Hoyt (1992) document three propositions that have guided the social influence dynamics research across relationships and theories: First, successful counseling relationships depend on a convergence between the counselor and client over time. Second, change results from differences between the counselor's and the client's perspective. Third, clients respond to the counselor as a function of their dependence on the counselor.

Despite their shared agenda, there are also differences in the social psychology and counseling psychology perspectives. Social psychology has focused on the influence of social environments on behavior, whereas counseling psychology has emphasized personality and individual differences. Social psychologists have studied behavior in the laboratory, whereas counseling psychologists have focused on counselor-client relationships in the field. Social psychologists have emphasized manipulation and sometimes deception, whereas counseling psychologists have emphasized trust and authenticity. Social psychologists focus on brief encounters between strangers, whereas counseling psychologists study therapeutic influences over time.

Literature about the interface between social and counseling psychologies typically credits Jerome Frank (1961) with first building the bridge, followed by Arnold Goldstein's (cited in Goldstein, Heller, & Seechrest, 1966) recommendation that social psychology provide a basis for selecting therapy variables. In recent years, social psychology has emphasized close or personal relationships in the social reality people construct together to reinforce their place in the broader social context. This common understanding is forged through conversation and the exertion or acceptance of social influence in counseling. Success in counseling is a demonstration of psychological convergence between the counselor and the client.

Strong et al. (1992) cite three types of evidence that social influence converges with counseling theory. First, counselors and clients synchronize their use of language to describe their shared reality. Second, positive outcomes are associated with a correlation of the client's and the counselor's similar understanding. Third, positive outcomes in counseling are associated with a cooperative social influence process that evolves over time. Clients tend to view themselves as they perceive their counselors to view them (Quintana & Meara, 1990). Strong et al. (1992) suggest that

> successful counseling relationships begin with high agreement, pass through a period of disagreement, and end with high agreement. The studies provide evidence that the middle, disagreement stage is a result of the counselor's effort to generate change and the client's resistance to the changes the counselor proposes . . . and that the reemergence of agreement in the last stage of counseling is due to the client's adoption of the constructs of the counselor's treatment policy. (p. 145)

The social psychology of this process is central to our understanding of counseling.

Many of the central constructs in counseling are based in social psychology. Changes in the client's behavior over time are the result of constructing a new social reality in response to discrepant influences from the counselor. Semantic discrepancy, by providing labels for facts, differs from propositional discrepancy in which causal frameworks are constructed. Communicating discrepant ideas is an important element of the social influence process in successful counseling. Social dependence is the recognition that the other person controls resources needed by both parties. Responsiveness is illustrated by each person's coordinating his or her behavior with the other. It provides the opportunity for mutual influence through sharing power.

THE SOCIAL PSYCHOLOGY OF SELF

It is impossible to speak of the self outside a multicultural context. The social self is a complex and interacting system. Oetting and Beauvais (1991) demonstrate this complexity in their "orthogonal model" that recognizes that increased identification with any one sociocultural identity does not require decreased identification with other sociocultural identities at the same time. The five most frequently used alternative models are less complex. The dominant majority model simply imposes a dominant sociocultural identity on all majority and minority groups. The transitional model presumes a movement toward the dominant sociocultural identity along the adjustment continuum. The alienation model seeks to avoid stress from anomie by assisting persons in transition to make a successful adjustment to a dominant identity. The multidimensional model presumes transition on several dimensions at the same time, with a different degree and rate of change for each dimension. The bicultural model presumes that one can adapt to one culture without losing contact with earlier sociocultural identities.

The orthogonal model, however, suggests that identifying any one sociocultural identity is independent from adapting to many other cultural identities simultaneously, providing an unlimited combination of patterns that combine the preceding five alternative models. The orthogonal model presumes a higher level of complexity than the alternative models and a more comprehensive inclusion of cultural context. This results in several advantages:

1. Cultural groups may exist in association with one another without isolating themselves or competing with one another.
2. Minority cultures need not be eliminated or absorbed to coexist.
3. A permanent multicultural society that is multifaceted and multidimensional without becoming a "melting pot" may be possible.
4. Conflicts of value and belief do not present insurmountable barriers but may be combined in a realistic pluralism.
5. Cultural conflict may become a positive, rather than a negative, force from the perspective of shared common-ground expectations.
6. Members of minority groups may be less inclined toward militancy when their survival is not threatened.

7. Interaction between minority and majority cultures may be less destructive for all parties.
8. There are economic advantages of releasing resources previously consumed by cultural conflict.
9. There are already models of orthogonal relationships in healthy bicultural and multicultural social units.

Given that individuals respond differently to different social contexts at different times in different areas of their lives, the difficulty of coping with this complexity is apparent. There is a tendency to seek consistency and compartmentalize the rival ways of life that compete and cooperate with one another. Managing this complexity becomes the single most difficult challenge of the social psychology of self, resulting in a compartmentalization of the self. As Thompson, Ellis, and Wildavsky (1990) explain,

> We would expect that individuals will make significant efforts to bring consistency to their social environments. This strain to consistency explains why people are not randomly distributed in social contexts. Individuals often seek out social relationships that are compatible with their preferred bias and shun those relations in which they feel less at home. (p. 266)

In some examples, the individual may not perceive contradictions among and between competing biases or may find ways that the competing biases actually complement one another. In other cases, the individual may be unaware of any contradiction at all between behavior in one role and quite different behavior in another role.

Baumeister (1986) suggests that one reason self-presentation has only recently become a more popular topic in social psychology is because the field of social psychology is dominated by dependent variables:

> Ask a social psychologist what he or she studies, and the answer will tend to be a dependent variable, such as attitude change, aggression, attraction, helping, impression formation, and so forth. Self-presentation, however, is usually studied as an independent variable, as a comparison between public and private situations. (p. vii)

The definition of *private* events for social psychology refers to mental events in the individual's own phenomenological experiences that are not observed by others, although the individual has the choice to make them public.

Baumeister (1986) went on to discuss the social psychology of self-presentation to self as audience.

> It is a small theoretical step to make the further assertion that the self is an audience for one's own behavior that can be pleased or dissatisfied by performances just as

can an outer audience. . . . Unfortunately, such formulations seem to introduce a homunculus as the ghost in the machine. (p. 10)

However, people engage in rehearsals of their behavior with internalized or imagined reference groups *as if* those groups were present while continuing to distinguish between what is real and what is imagined. Linking phenomenological aspects of consciousness to social behavior has been essential to social psychology in the study of self-esteem and emotion issues, for example.

Heesacker and Bradley (1997) examine emotion and emotion-related processes toward a psychological science of emotion. The relevance of social psychology to emotion as an internalized psychological concept points to a new opportunity for social psychology and counseling to work together. Research on the "self" (Moore, Britt, & Leary, 1997) highlights other subjective areas of research and practice. Interest in the social psychology of self is another example of the field's interest in each individual's subjective interpretation of his or her social world. Increased recognition of cultural variables has further contributed toward a subjective perspective. "Counseling psychologists are recognizing therapy as a culturally contextualized practice whereby the counselors' own beliefs, expectations, values and biases influence professional practice, and this recognition has resulted in the development of training programs geared toward enhancing cultural self knowledge" (Moore, Britt, & Leary, 1997, p. 222). We need to know how culture influences self-awareness and behavior, and, to do that, we need to find applications of social psychology to the internalized dynamics of the self. "Social cognitive theory's explicit concern with the interplay of social and cognitive factors may provide a fulcrum for rapprochement among psychological branches that have historically favored either intrapersonal or interpersonal accounts of human functioning" (Lent & Maddux, 1997, p. 240).

Lent and Maddux (1997) identify six general assumptions about psychosocial functioning related to counseling according to the principles of social cognitive theory:

1. People develop symbols through creating internal models to communicate complex ideas, and these symbols allow for vicarious learning and self-reflection.
2. Behavior is goal directed and intentional, based on people's symbolizing capabilities.
3. People self-regulate their own behavior and environment in the pursuit of personal goals.
4. There is an interaction of inner-personal factors with events and behaviors through what Bandura (1989) calls a "triadic reciprocal causation."
5. Person factors interact with contextual variables so that optimal development depends on the harmony of individual and social forces.
6. Psychotherapy occurs in a social context and is dependent on sociocognitive influences, whether self-directed or other-directed.

The mainstream of contemporary social psychological research has shifted from a focus on interpersonal (between people) to intrapersonal (within the person) processes (Steiner, 1986; Strong, 1995). There is also a recent corresponding emphasis on cognitive strategies in counseling and counselor training. Hirsch and Stone (1983) examine perspectives of cognitive psychology to explain how counselors conceptualize clients and develop strategies for processing information in counseling. Social psychology has focused on information processing, drawing analogies from computer technology and artificial intelligence research.

There is some controversy about whether this intrapersonal emphasis strengthens or weakens the bond between social psychology and counseling psychology. Strong (1995) claims it weakens the bond:

> Social psychologists focus on how individuals process information and conceptualize these processes by drawing analogies from computer technology and other mechanistic models. Although this perspective may be of some interest, it is of little help to practitioners who must rely on interpersonal processes—on what goes on in the space between people—to perform their curative and help-giving work. (p. 687)

Others argue that, through language, thought, symbols, metaphors, and significant others, we bring our society into ourselves just as we launch ourselves into society. At a symbolic level, at least, the difference between the individual and the significant social context in which that individual lives is blurred (McCall & Simmons, 1991). There is a possibility that the social psychological research on interpersonal relations might help us better understand the intrapersonal dynamics of working with a troubled client in counseling.

Most theories of identity do not take into account the importance of social identification in defining the self. Social identity is more inclusive than the typical self-concept. Brewer (1991) introduces a model of optimal distinctiveness in which social identity is viewed as a reconciliation of opposing needs for assimilation and differentiation from others:

> According to this model, individuals avoid self-construals that are either too personalized or too inclusive and instead define themselves in terms of distinctive category memberships. Social identity and group loyalty are hypothesized to be strongest for those self-categorizations that simultaneously provide for a sense of belonging and a sense of distinctiveness. (p. 475)

Brewer reviews the literature on uniqueness theory and other models of individuation that assume individuals define themselves in the context of relevant others. Power issues become important to our study of the social psychology of the self.

Social Influence and Power

One internalized variable in counseling theory based on principles of social psychology is the concept of social power. Social power is a consequence of each person's social dependence on the other, from the perspective of the one exerting influence. Goodyear and Robyak (1981) summarize the five social power bases of the counselor as legitimate power, expert power, referent power, informational power, and ecological power. The client works against these five power sources through client resistance and client opposition. Counseling research has assumed that these social influence processes are unidirectional, with the client being the target of a counselor's influence. Strong et al. (1992) suggest that counseling is a relationship marked by the exchange of resources; the counselor-client relationship is a form of social exchange of influence and interdependence. "Many studies have examined the nature and effects of clients' dependence on counselors, but study of the nature and effects of counselors' dependence on clients has just begun" (p. 151). As therapy is successful and the client gains control of the problem, the need for a therapist's influence is diminished. The therapist's influence is limited to areas in which the client recognizes a need for help and perceives the therapist as having the needed resources. The key to success in therapy is to help clients increase their power for independent control of problems. If the counselor exerts too much or too little power, the client will not be helped.

Corrigan, Dell, Lewis, and Schmidt (1980) point out that Strong et al.'s (1992) theory rests on the assumption that a counselor is influential only because of a client's perception of certain desirable counselor characteristics. Thus, the counselor's actual expertise may differ from or be unrelated to the client's ratings of that counselor's expertness. This possibility raises interesting questions.

> Is the perception of expertness differentially derived as suggested and do these differences affect the subsequent quality or quantity of counselor influence? What is the threshold for displayed inexpertness undermining legitimacy? Does this threshold vary according to client, situation or both? Does the legitimacy of the role persist throughout the course of counseling or is it limited to the initial phase? If the latter is the case, is it necessary that counselor-specific expertness replace legitimacy for the relationship to proceed productively? (p. 433)

Dorn (1986) assumes that attitudes about power precede behavior. Counselors working within the social influence model assume that people come to understand their own basic intentions through an analysis of their behavior and the impact it has on others.

> The client who seeks counseling does so because he or she believes that the counselor possesses the knowledge and resources to assist him or her in moving from this static state of behavior to a more active state of behavior. The counselor's task

is to encourage the client to reattribute his or her difficulty to a factor or factors over which he or she has control. (p. 4)

Dixon (1986) points out that social influence has primarily focused on the client's compliance to a counselor's influence. Clients change attitudes in counseling when a counselor's power and the client's need for a counselor's resources are greater than the client's resistance or opposition. The resistance literature is primarily a documentation of the failures of social influence through non-compliance with the counselor's influence. However, client variables are more difficult to study than counselor variables. Dixon identifies four additional independent variable domains that also emerge as important to social power and resistance: client characteristics, problem characteristics, counselor attributes, and counseling interventions. These ideas contribute toward a "systems approach" to counseling. Banghart (1969), Churchman (1968), Kaufman (1968), Ryan (1969), and Thoresen (1969) were among the first to describe a systems approach to counselor education, stressing the need to specify desired outcomes, to identify the various components in the system, and to arrange the components to maximize realization of the desired goals in a balance of power.

One of the ways that social psychology has studied internalized power issues is through the study of attributes.

The perceiver makes attributions about the characteristics of the other and about the causes of the other's behavior on the basis of different kinds of information that he or she has about the other. One important class of information is the other's membership in difference groups, including one's sex, race, and age groups. There are stereotypes concerning what characteristics go with membership in such groups. (Triandis, 1977, p. 135)

Stereotypes have been a popular topic in social psychology, examining how traits are assigned by one's self to others to reduce the complexity of one's experience through categorization. The same process applies to self-attributions connecting inferences with social behavior. The link between intrapersonal processes, power differences, and the counseling relationship is important in the multicultural context.

Social psychology also provided the basis for an emphasis on the practical and applied approach to counseling. Carkhuff (1972) called for a new "technology" of human and community resource development in training for the helping professions that emphasized the need for specific skills to bring about purposive change in counseling. Likewise, Zifferblatt (1972) despaired at the lack of models to provide counselor educators with ongoing and process-based training systems. Ivey (1971) was just then developing a microcounseling training model that uses simulation and role-play process-focused interaction. The conceptual model described in this book is based on an analysis of counseling as a coalition-formation process, applying the literature on coalition formation from social psychology and on self-talk from counseling to suggest a new way of viewing the counseling process.

THE CULTURAL GRID AS A VISUAL EXAMPLE
OF RELATIONSHIPS

The Cultural Grid is an attempt to visualize a personal-cultural orientation to relationships by separating the more overt and evident interpersonal behaviors from the more covert and implicit intrapersonal expectations. Hines and Pedersen (1980) developed the Cultural Grid to help identify and describe the complexity of a cultural context by combining intrapersonal and interpersonal variables in the same visual example. There are two visual examples of the Cultural Grid: The first one depicts relationships within the person, and the second one depicts relationships between people (Pedersen & Ivey, 1993).

The Intrapersonal Cultural Grid matches the social system (cultural) factors with the individual (personal) variables in a personal-cultural orientation to each context (Pedersen & Pedersen, 1985, 1989a, 1989b). The Intrapersonal Cultural Grid provides a means to describe and understand a person's behavior as influenced by "culture teachers" in the social systems of the client's cultural context (Pedersen & Ivey, 1993). The categories of the Intrapersonal Cultural Grid (see Figure 1.1) provide a conceptual framework for demonstrating how multiple cultural and personal factors interact simultaneously in a combined context, linking each behavior to many expectations, each expectation to many values, and each value to many social systems in which that value was learned (Pedersen, 1997a).

Each cultural context is complicated and dynamic, because different social system variables take their turns at salience in an orthogonal interpretation of self. An awareness of one's cultural identity, therefore, requires being able to identify how each specific behavior is the expression of many expectations, how each expectation is the expression of many values, and how each value is the expression of many different culture teachers.

The social system contexts of ethnographic (ethnicity, nationality, language, religion, etc.), demographic (age, gender, place of residence, etc.), status (social, educational, economic, etc.), and affiliation (formal and informal) are combined and overlap to influence the individual's identity and behavior. The Intrapersonal Cultural Grid is intended to show the complex relationship between each overt, explicit, and interpersonal behavior and the many expectations, values, and/or social systems in which the behaviors have been learned.

The Interpersonal Cultural Grid, on the other hand, is an attempt to describe the relationship between people or groups by separating their expectations from their behaviors. The Interpersonal Cultural Grid (see Figure 1.2) includes four quadrants. Each quadrant explains part (large or small) of any relationship between two individuals or groups. There will be some data in all four cells for any relationship, but the salience may change from one cell to the other over

		BEHAVIOR	EXPECTA-TIONS	VALUE
	Ethnographic (nationality, ethnicity, religion, language, etc.)			
	Demographic (age, residence, physical ability, etc.)			
	Status (social, economic, political, educational, etc.)			
	Affiliation (formal like family or informal like a shared idea)			

PERSONAL

SOCIAL SYSTEMS

Figure 1.1. The Intrapersonal Cultural Grid for Describing Within-Group or -Person Variables

BEHAVIORS

Same   Different

Same/Positive

	Same	Different
	1 Shared Positive	2 Cultural Conflict
		loud/quiet
	Expectations	open/closed
	Trust	direct/indirect
	Respect	formal/informal
	Fairness	close/distance
	Efficiency	task/relationship
	Effectiveness	
	Safety	
	3 Personal Conflict	4 War

EXPECTATIONS

Different/
Negative

Figure 1.2. The Interpersonal Cultural Grid for Describing Between-Group or -Person Variables

time as the relationship changes. We see the behavior, but the expectations, values, and social systems in which that behavior was learned may be hidden from us.

In the first quadrant, two individuals display similar behaviors (e.g., smiling) and have similar positive expectations (e.g., for friendship). The relationship is congruent and harmonious. There is a high level of accuracy in both individuals' interpretations of one another's behavior and in the shared positive expectations behind their behavior. The overt, explicit, and interpersonal interaction is congruent with the covert, implicit, and intrapersonal expectations. There is little conflict in this quadrant, and the relationship can be described as comfortable.

In the second quadrant, two individuals have different behaviors but share the same positive expectations. There is a high level of agreement in that both persons expect trust and friendliness, for example, but there is a potentially low level of accuracy. Each person perceives and incorrectly interprets the other's behavior as different and probably hostile. This quadrant is characteristic of cultural conflict in which each person is applying a self-reference criterion to interpret the other's behavior. The conditions described in the second quadrant are very unstable, and, unless the "hidden message" of their shared positive expectations is quickly identified and made explicit, the salience is likely to change toward the third quadrant. It is important for at least one of the two persons to discover and identify the presence of shared positive expectations for trust, respect, fairness, or whatever other common bonds exist in their shared cultural context despite their different behaviors.

In the third quadrant, the two persons have the same behaviors, but now they have different or negative expectations. The similar behaviors give the "appearance" of harmony and agreement, but the "hidden message" is that the two actually have different or negative expectations that may ultimately destroy the relationship. Although both persons (or groups) are now in disagreement, that disagreement may not be apparent to both persons because one or both are "pretending" harmony. One person—typically the most powerful—may continue to expect trust and friendliness, whereas the other person is now negatively distrustful and unfriendly, even though they are both presenting the same smiling and glad-handing behaviors. If these two people discover the "hidden message" of distrust, they may regain harmony by going back to an earlier time when they both did actually share the same positive expectations, as indicated in the second quadrant. If they do not discover the "hidden message" of actual hostility, then the conflict is likely to escalate and ultimately move to the fourth quadrant.

In the fourth quadrant, the two people have different and/or negative expectations, and they have stopped pretending to be congruent. The two persons are "at war" with each other and may not even want to increase harmony in their relationship any longer. They may just want to hurt each other. Both persons are in disagreement, and that disagreement is now obvious and apparent. This relationship is likely to result in hostile disengagement. It is very difficult to retrieve conflict from the fourth quadrant because one or both parties have stopped trying to find shared positive expectations. Unfortunately, most conflicts between people or groups remain undiscovered until they reach the fourth quadrant, when the conflict is no longer hidden. An appropriate prevention strategy would be to identify the conflict in behaviors—as indicated in the second quadrant—early in the process when those differences in behaviors might be positive, as long as there is a context of shared positive expectations.

The most important quadrant is the second one, in which the overt, explicit, and interpersonal behavior of people toward one another is interpreted in the context of whatever covert, implicit, and intrapersonal shared positive expectations those people have toward one another. An accurate and meaningful understanding of interpersonal behavior depends on an accurate and meaningful understanding of each party's intrapersonal "hidden messages."

Therefore, two people may both share the same positive expectations of "trust," but one may be loud and the other quiet; of "respect," but one may be open and the other closed; or of "fairness," but one may be task oriented and the other relationship oriented. Only when each behavior is assessed and understood in its own cultural context does that behavior become meaningful. Only when positive shared expectations can be identified will two individuals or groups be able to find and build on common ground toward a constructive counseling relationship (Pedersen, 1997a, 1997b).

Kelly's (1955) personal constructs theory suggests that people will act according to personal constructs they have developed through interaction with their environment. These personal constructs are the ways each individual sees similarities with and differences from a group or another person. Kelly's fixed role therapy was an attempt to change constructs toward a new and more functional perspective for the client. By looking at similarities and differences among the 12 significant relationships in the individual's life through a role repertory technique, Kelly was able to identify the sociocultural patterns that taught the values that shaped the expectations that determined the behaviors for the individual. The Cultural Grid is another way of identifying patterns among the social system "culture teachers" who have taught individuals the values that led them to expectations and shaped their behaviors in each cultural context.

Super (1995) describes the same sequence combining multiple selves with the sociocultural environment in a similar pattern in his linking of needs, values, and interests:

> Needs are wants, manifestations of physiological conditions such as hunger, and they are related to survival. They are the result of interaction between the person and the environment, and some thus manifest in the seeking of help from others and, in more refined form, in the need to help others. Values are the result of further refinement through interaction with the environment, both natural and human. The

result of socialization is the establishment of the types of objectives that people seek in order to satisfy their needs. The need for help thus becomes love and the need to help becomes altruism. Interests are the activities within which people expect to attain their values and thus satisfy their needs. Valuing the well being of others (altruism) leads a person to choose a social service occupation such as social work, teaching, some aspects of personnel work, or even a business or industrial enterprise. (pp. 54-55)

The study of needs will help us understand what we do. The study of values will tell us why we do these things. The study of interests will tell us how we behave in reference to significant groups and relationships around us.

By conceptualizing the self as a multicultural group, the reality of many different cultures influencing our behavior simultaneously becomes apparent, even when only a few of those different cultures are salient for a particular behavior at a particular time. The Intrapersonal Cultural Grid (see Figure 1.1) is based on the perspective that culture is "within the person" and not something external to the self. Cognitive variables are linked to values, expectations, and, finally, behaviors, on the one hand, and culture teachers or sources of those culturally learned values on the other hand.

The person's behavior, by itself or out of context, does not communicate a clear message or intention. Only when that behavior is analyzed within the context of the person's salient social system variables does the person's intended expectation become clear. Expectations are those cognitive variables that include behavior-outcome and stimulus-outcome expectancies that guide an individual's choices. If this . . . (behavior), then that . . . (expectation) will happen. After having examined one's own and the other person's most salient social system variables, it should be possible for that person to identify and/or better understand both his or her own and the other person's expectations for anticipated outcomes such as "friendship," "trust," or "harmony." Having first established the common ground of shared positive expectations, it is then possible to work toward the behaviors that are most efficient and/or effective for expressing or achieving those expectations.

Every counseling relationship occurs in a multicultural context when culture is broadly defined. The Cultural Grid serves to (a) classify salient cultural perspectives in the roles of culture teachers from a variety of different backgrounds, (b) differentiate between personal and sociocultural perspectives of an event, (c) link culturally learned behaviors with culturally learned expectations and values behind those behaviors, and (d) link culturally learned behaviors, expectations, and values to the social systems context in which culture teachers taught their cultures.

Behaviors do not easily reveal the learned expectations, consequences, or meanings that are intended by the person displaying a particular behavior. Similar behaviors may have different meanings, and different behaviors may have the same meanings. It is important to interpret behaviors accurately in terms of the intended expectations, consequences, and meanings attached to those behaviors. The Intrapersonal Cultural Grid becomes a useful tool for helping us understand our personal-cultural orientation in our interpersonal relationships.

First, identify and separate a particular behavior in yourself or someone else. The behavior should include a particular action, decision, or thought. Define that behavior narrowly enough so that it becomes specific. For example, analyze the behavior of reading this book.

Second, identify the expectations behind this behavior. If I do this . . ., then *that* will happen. What do you expect to happen as a result of your behavior? When you decided to read this book, you probably had several expectations in mind. You may have expected to learn new ideas, fulfill a requirement, catch up on the literature, or prepare to work in a multicultural setting. There are many different expectations—both explicit and implicit—for each behavior.

Third, identify the values behind each expectation. Some examples of values might include learning, changing, being relevant, being competent, or being responsible, to name just a few of the values that might justify your expectations that led you to the behavior of reading this book.

Fourth, ask yourself from where those values came. Who taught you those values? This may require you to analyze the thousands of culture teachers in your life who have left their lasting impressions from the great variety of different social systems that have been meaningful to you. Your personal-cultural orientation toward the decision to read this book was constructed out of the expectations and values taught to you by your culture teachers from meaningful social systems in your life.

The Intrapersonal Cultural Grid provides a framework for analyzing the way in which individuals construct their internalized cultural perspectives with multiple identities. You can best understand your own behavior by looking inside yourself to put the behavior in a sociocultural context. By conceptualizing the self as a multicultural group, these thousands of culture teachers who shape your behaviors from moment to moment are given the credit they deserve, and you can become more deliberately aware of your own multicultural identity.

The following chapters will look at the ways in which internalized experiences influence external behavior and at the importance of cultural variables to mediate those internalized experiences.

CONCLUSION

The link between social psychology and counseling has been more important for counseling than it has for social psychology, used as a resource to generate, generalize, and test the findings of social psychology to the counseling relationship. This dependence of social psychological research on interpersonal relationships has been acknowledged, especially in recent years, as a source of counseling theory. The applications of social psychology to understanding intrapersonal relationships are just beginning. Social psychology has served to generate hypotheses in the laboratory that can be tested by counselors in practice at both the interpersonal and the intrapersonal levels.

With the increased attention to internalized dynamics and within-the-person variables in cognitive theories in both social psychology and counseling psychology, the relationship between social and counseling psychologies has become more controversial. There are questions about how these internalized dynamics apply to the counseling relationship. The extension of social influence research to counseling through studies about power in social psychology influencing behavior through internalized dynamics provides a promising link between what is going on within the individual and between individuals. In the following chapters, the applications of social psychology to self will continue to explore this link.

2

The "Problem" as a Counseling Metaphor

Metaphors have proven to be valuable for bringing complicated aspects of the real world into the social laboratory, the classroom, and/or the counseling interview. Hermans (1996) argues on the metaphorical level that the computer and narrative analogies demonstrate how inner voice plays an important role in self-organization. The dialogical model for studying the self has been neglected. Metaphors influence our interaction at both the conscious and the unconscious level in the search for meaning among complex relationships. Through metaphors, we can comprehend complex relationships and patterns through more divergent and less linear perspectives. Young and Borders (1998) provide an excellent review of the literature on the impact of metaphors on clinical hypothesis formation in counseling:

> It is believed that metaphors help clients gain new perspectives on their counseling concerns by generating a wide variety of associations among previously unrelated cognitive structures. As a result of creating new relationships between these structures, clients identify new possibilities for behaving and effecting change in a problem area. (pp. 238-239)

Through the conceptualization of the problem as a third party or force in the counseling interview, it becomes possible to introduce the client's sociocultural context into the interview as a real presence rather than as an abstraction. The advantages of conceptualizing the problem as metaphorically real link the interpersonal behaviors of the counselor and client with the intrapersonal dynamics of the client's cultural context, especially as perceived from the client's point of view. By bringing the client's cultural context into the interview through the problem as a conceptual metaphor, the counseling relationship becomes more inclusive, and the client's cultural context becomes more validated. Rather than as a subordinate in the counselor-client relationship, the client, whose support now becomes essential for a successful client-counselor coalition, is empowered in the counseling relationship.

Gelso and Carter (1985) point out that relationship factors have long been recognized as important to successful counseling outcomes. However, it is difficult to assess the therapeutic relationship independent of the client's and/or counselor's perception of that relationship (Derlga, Hendrick, Winstead, & Berg, 1991). Humanists have focused on the relationship assets for effective therapy and relationship deficits for failure. The emphasis in behavioral and cognitive-behavioral therapies is more on the interventions than on the therapy relationship itself. Systems theory and family therapies emphasize that relationships between two people are incomplete without including the larger system of social relationships. Psychoanalysis focuses on the relationship as a working alliance with a quality that is different from neurotic transference.

> The working alliance includes an emotional bond, an agreement about outcome goals and an acceptance of tasks. This working alliance is established early, the strength of the alliance varies during treatment, the effective alliance requires agreement on goals and tasks to attain those goals, and each client or counselor differs in their ability to form alliances. (Gelso & Carter, 1985, p. 164)

The working alliance is, however, mediated by the client's and counselor's internal dialogue.

Most counseling interactions occur in a dyad relationship through a process of constructing favorable conditions for positive change. Counseling is the structuring of that dyadic relationship to facilitate positive change. The social psychological literature provides guidance for structuring dyads or groups to achieve and maintain client cooperation and compliance through therapy. Behavior disorders or clinical problems are seen as the result of developmental, social, or biological processes in which something has gone wrong. Clinical practice is embedded in a sociocultural matrix in which sociocultural norms define deviance, severity, relative importance, and modifiability (Kanfer, 1984).

The internalized counseling relationship is indicated by similarity between the client's intrapsychic disposition and the counselor's interpersonal interaction, so "complementary interactions based on positive affiliation predicted positive client outcomes while complementarity based on negative affiliation predicted little or no progress in counseling" (Quintana & Meara, 1990, p. 125). The client's perceptions are valid and powerful indicators of what is happening in counseling, and interpersonal complementarity, based on intrapsychic complementarity, begins very early in relationships and grows over time. The intrapsychic relationship is conceived as the interpersonal process turned inward. "Once problematic intrapsychic attitudes are identified, a counselor may treat the client with therapeutic interpersonal attitudes; over time clients may begin to replace their perceptions of self with their counselor's perceptions of them" (Quintana & Meara, 1990, p. 130).

The successful working alliance between the counselor and the client depends on factors such as client and therapist involvement and trust. These desirable factors begin to operate early in counseling, when the client, in a lower power position, is dependent on receiving help from the therapist, who is perceived in a higher power position. High-power responses by counselors encourage high-involvement or low-power responses by clients, rather than neutral or low-involvement responses. Differences in the involvement of clients and counselors are influenced by and in turn influence the level of alliance in counseling (Reandeau & Wampold, 1991). Ultimately, these adjustments become automatic. One source of ambiguity in counseling is the environment or problematical context that brings a counselor and counselee together in a relationship. The literature on coalition formation helps us understand how to build a working relationship with clients and better understand the conflicting relationships of counseling.

Measures of strength in the counseling working alliance are positively related to successful counseling outcomes. This therapeutic alliance is influenced by client characteristics prior to therapy, counselor characteristics prior to counseling, and the counselor's technical ability. The working alliance is enhanced when clients take more active responsibility for the content and direction of the interaction over time. More research is needed to chart patterns in the moment-to-moment changes in the working alliance.

Including the client's internalized perspective in the counseling relationship opens new possibilities for applying social psychological research to the counseling process. This chapter will focus on one such implication in which the "problem" is included metaphorically as a third source of influence in the counselor-client relationship coalition. Most of the research on coalitions, particularly as they relate to counseling, was done several decades ago, but it continues to be meaningful today. More recent research has not gone beyond those earlier conclusions (Komorita & Ellis, 1988; Kravitz, 1987; Miller & Komorita, 1986; Stanton & Morris, 1987; Stevenson, Pearce, & Porter, 1985).

Fischer, Jome, and Atkinson (1998) review the literature supporting the therapeutic relationship as one of the most important factors in counseling, particularly in multicultural counseling. "Within the common factors literature, the therapeutic or healing relationship is consistently mentioned by all scholars as a vital element that is present across all psychotherapies and healing in all cultures" (p. 533). Theoretical examples and empirical data are provided to support the importance of a good therapeutic relationship, along with a shared worldview, an understanding of the client's expectations, and accompanying interventions or rituals.

THE COALITION BETWEEN
A COUNSELOR AND A CLIENT

The primary counseling relationship has been described as a one-to-one dyadic interaction between a counselor and a counselee. The counseling dyad is extraordinary, however, in that the client has brought an external element, namely the "problem" as a metaphor, into the dyad as a personalized source of influence on the client. The conceptual system of this three-way relationship introduces the problem as a third member of the counseling relationship. The assumption that a problem can be treated as if it were a third member of the counseling relationship draws from perceptual field theory that people behave according to how things seem to them and internalize parts of their sociocultural context (Pedersen, 1966). The "problem" is introduced as a working metaphor to incorporate the sociocultural context, with all its positive and negative forces, into the interview in an active rather than a passive role. The use of metaphors in helping us understand a phenomenon is not new to science.

> In fairness to the human sciences, it should be noted that all science is at some level metaphorical. The atomic theory does not say that matter is composed of little balls; it says that matter behaves as if it were composed of little balls. Even the forces and fields that litter physics journals are, strictly speaking, metaphors. (Wright, 1986, p. 9)

The client seeking counseling reacts to the problem as a real but unpleasant or inhibiting element in his or her own perceptual field. Through counseling, the client seeks change that will eliminate unpleasant or inhibiting aspects. This relationship is shown in Figure 2.1. The counselor accepts the client's perception of the problem as real in its influence over the client. The problem seeks to weaken the client-counselor coalition. As the client's influence increases, the problem's influence decreases proportionately. The client's continued dependence on the problem is transferred to a temporary dependence on the counselor and ultimately independence from both.

Counseling occurs in a force field in which the counselor, the client, and the problem interact in a constellation of conflicting goals. Counseling is a function of push and pull factors in which the counselor seeks fulfillment in being helpful, the client seeks to reconcile internalized ambiguity, and the problem, viewed as an active rather than a passive entity, seeks its own survival. There is an elusive and complex quality to problems that, in some respects, resembles the configuration of an active, seemingly independent, and somewhat malevolent personality acting in its own interest. The counseling process can thus be described as a dynamic interaction of contrary forces in the mode of social power theory and in the context of an equilibrium between the counselor seeking coalition with the client and resistance by the problem. The distribution

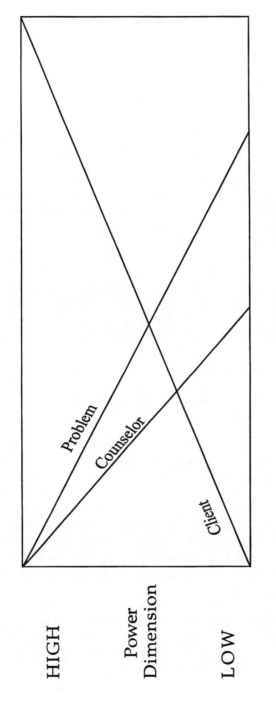

Figure 2.1. A Schematic Description of the Ratio of Power Influence Over Time for Counselor, Client, and Problem

and use of power in counseling properly encourages a temporary, means-oriented alliance between counselor and client as an alternative to the client's continued and indeterminate dependence on the problem. A counselor-client coalition against the problem becomes the vehicle of effective counseling; ineffective counseling results in a client-problem coalition that isolates the counselor. This conceptual model draws heavily from Lewin's field theory, social power literature, and research on the formation of coalitions in triads. Some of the first research and writing on coalition formation in counseling was written 20 to 30 years ago, but it continues to be relevant to the perspective of this book.

Early in this century, George Simmel (cited in Wolff, 1950) described some of the relationships that arise in three-person groups. He focused on the third member as a nonpartisan, representing intellectual noninvolvement and acting as a mediator or arbitrator until a strong, permanent coalition is established, at which time the third member is isolated by the other two. A coalition as thus defined requires identification of action in accord with a common goal. Identification of a common goal increases the probability of coalition formation between two members, but the crux of the definition of *coalition* is "action in accord." The two participants in a coalition deliberately ally themselves with each other and just as deliberately change or reject the third party. Caplow (1956) discusses four basic assumptions that anchor his theories of coalition.

1. Members of a triad may differ in strength. A strong member can control a weaker member and will seek to do so.
2. Each member of the triad seeks control over the others. Control over two others is preferred to control over one other. Control over one other is preferred to control over none.
3. The strength of the coalition is equal to the strength of its two members.
4. The formation of coalitions takes place in an existing triad, so there is a precoalition condition that will provoke the formation of a coalition to oppose the coercion.

To anticipate coalition formation in a triad, we need to know (a) the initial distribution of resources among members, (b) the payoff of reward for each possible coalition in the triad, (c) nonutilitarian strategy preferences existing in the group that would prejudice choice, and (d) the effective decision point. In a coalition, we can expect members to share the reward of their accomplishment according to the size of their contribution to the alliance. Each of the stronger two will seek out the weakest member to receive a larger share later. The middle power member will tend to join with the weaker member to receive a larger share of the ultimate reward. The weakest member thus has considerable influence over the outcome, and the strongest member is often isolated by a coalition between the other two. Strength becomes weakness when the strongest partner is led to overestimate his or her own power and worth and is consequently rejected by the other players.

Initially, the problem controls a proportionately greater share of the power than the client does, causing the client to seek out some external ally through counseling that will assist him or her to regain control. The counselor is ready to assume some responsibility for expertise regarding the problem in general, drawing from his or her experience with similar problems he or she has studied and helped others to solve. Just as the client has called in a counselor for assistance, the counselor must also depend on the client for knowledge about the specific and unique aspects of the problem; this structures a relationship of interdependence between the counselor and client as a necessary and useful precondition to problem solving. The counselor must be able to measure and control the degree of intervention and "power influence" to nurture an alliance between the counselor and client against the problem. The client represents both the person troubled by a problem coming to a counselor for help and a valuable resource person for the counselor on particular aspects of that specific problem. When clients come for counseling, they bring their cultural context in with them. The client is potentially willing to cooperate toward increasing the degree of power influence to the point where he or she is finally independent of *both* problem and counselor.

Coalitions in counseling are temporary alliances for joint action. Pepinsky (1959) contended that counseling is basically a social interaction that follows the same laws and principles of other social interactions. In this way, counseling becomes a two-party transaction in which the contract between counselor and client is analogous to other "seller-buyer" transactions by metaphor. Pepinsky preferred to use the term *coalition* for several reasons:

1. It implies a more personal dimension.
2. It implies the interdependent negotiation of tasks through mutual agreement.
3. It implies the unified action that results from continuous interdependent performance.

Counseling, therefore, has parallels with other transactions in the process of bargaining and negotiation. The objective of counseling is to facilitate changes in the client's behavior according to an agreed-upon strategy between the counselor and the client. The goal of the coalition between the counselor and client is to work toward the point where this alliance is no longer necessary to the client in coping with his or her problem. To accomplish this goal, the relationship must be flexible enough to allow the necessary modifications of strategy during counseling. In counseling, the isolatee, the third party, or the enemy is the problem. The interactions of a changing power balance between the client and counselor in coalition describe the process of counseling, subject to frequent maintenance and modification, as seen in Figure 2.1.

Let us assume that A is the problem, B is the counselor, and C is the client entering counseling, as illustrated in Figure 2.1. The power influence is distributed with the problem being most powerful, but less powerful than the combined strength of counselor and client. The client begins with control over no one. If the client unites with the counselor, the client will control the problem because a BC coalition is stronger than A. The client will be controlled by the counselor, however, within the coalition because B is stronger than C. A client-counselor coalition will increase the number of partners the client controls from none to one. Likewise, if the client forms a coalition with the problem, the client will have control over one member, the counselor, and will be controlled by one member, the problem. Caplow's original prediction was that an AC or a BC coalition was most likely to occur. The counselor would favor a coalition with the client. Through such a coalition, the counselor gains control over both of the members of the triad because B plus C is larger than A, and B is larger than C. A coalition between the counselor and the problem would leave the counselor in control of only one partner, the client. To the problem, a coalition with either the client or the counselor is equally desirable. In both cases, it retains control over the other two members while ensuring that they will not join forces to gain control over the problem.

Caplow (1956, 1959, 1968) predicted either an AC or a BC coalition to be most likely in his Minimum Resource Theory of Coalition Formation in the Triad. Gamson (1961), Kelley and Arrowood (1969), Vinacke (1959), and Vinacke and Arkoff (1957) presented research evidence favoring a BC coalition as the cheapest winning coalition, showing that the two weak members tended to dominate the strong member. Chertkoff (1967) presented a revision of Caplow's coalition theory that likewise favored a BC coalition. The logic of a minimum resource theory is described in three premises:

1. Any participant will expect others to demand from a coalition a share of the payoff proportional to the amount of resources that contribute to a coalition.

2. A person will maximize payoff by maximizing his or her share. Thus, when the total payoff is held constant, each will favor the cheapest winning coalition. The cheapest winning coalition is that winning coalition with the total resources closest to the amount necessary to win.

3. A coalition will form only if there are reciprocal strategy choices between two participants.

A second alternative point of view described by Wahba (1972) as a Coalition Expected Utility (CEU) Model describes coalitions as being formed to maximize their expected utility, so coalitions with the highest expected utility are likely to be formed and coalitions with the lowest expected utility are the least likely to be formed. Other experiments (Chertkoff, 1966; Cole, 1961; Day, 1972; Willis, 1962) provide supporting evidence to demonstrate conditions under which the strong member of a triad was included in coalitions and preferred by others as a coalition partner. It is apparent that under some conditions the most powerful person is the favored partner for coalitions.

A third alternative is game theory, which emphasizes the instability of shifting alliances and the difficulty of forming any stable coalition. Rapoport and Chammah (1965) point out that, although one might assume that a coalition that commands the largest payoff would tend to stabilize, this assumes that the coalition made up of the other participants representing the smallest payoff will also be stable and that they will be satisfied with their smallest share, which is unlikely. Game theory assumes that there is no rational reason to suppose that any particular coalition will be more likely to occur than any other.

DEFINITIONS OF TERMS

Many of the terms from social psychology have been adapted to the counseling situation and require modification and redefinition when applied to counseling.

Problem

The problem refers to some part of the interaction of the client with the environment that has a real or perceived inhibiting effect on the client's effective performance. As the client enters counseling, the problem is part of the client's perceptual field and has the quality of reality for the client. The client seeks counseling help toward the ultimate goal of controlling or eliminating this problem and is seeking a supporting coalition toward that end. The problem represents the enemy to the extent that it is in opposition to the client-counselor coalition. The counselor accepts the client's phenomenological view of the problem as real and regulates his or her action *as if* the problem were a third member in the counseling relationship. Since the problem is part of the client's perceptual field, the only measure of influence the problem exerts in the counseling relationship is as an inverse function of the client's ability to cope with the problem. The counselor gets at the problem through the client.

Although this model may be useful in a global sense for charting the conceptual changes in the power ratio relationships of the overall counseling process, it is necessary to focus on specific aspects of the problem. There are many dimensions in any counseling problem, and the client will be able to cope with each of them with varying degrees of effectiveness. Problems are complex or multifaceted and not simple.

Power Influence

Each counseling relationship has at least three sources of influences: the client, the counselor, and the problem as perceived by the client. Each of these three members of the counseling triad exerts different degrees of influence in the counseling relationship, from very low to very high. The degree of power influence exerted by any one member is characterized by that member's ability to affect the others' behavior and the capacity to control, manage, or influence the other two members of the triad.

The degree of power influence exerted by the problem will be an inverse function of the degree of power influence exerted by the client. If the client has a low capacity to function independent of the other two members, there is a "big" problem. If the client has a high capacity to function independent of the other two members, there is a "small" problem. The counselor adjusts the power influence in such a way as to increase opportunities for the client to exert more influence and to maximize the possibility for a winning coalition to develop.

One way to think of power influence is in terms of a "directive support continuum." When the counselor exerts a high degree of power influence, counseling is providing a *high* degree of "directive support" to the client.

Payoff

It has already been demonstrated that each member will attempt to maximize his or her share in the payoff. In the case of the problem, the payoff would be frustration of counseling and the continued control over the client. In the case of the client, it would be control over the problem as well as less dependence on outside assistance. This might be expressed in being released from the hospital, increased effectiveness, or decreased dependence. In the case of the counselor, it would be satisfaction and increased effectiveness as a helping person, money, increased professional prestige, or any of the characteristics associated with successful counseling. Because the payoffs for the counselor and client are compatible and complementary, they are both able to achieve this goal without conflict, in coalition. The payoff for the problem is incompatible with that of either the client or counselor.

Intervention

As explained in defining power influence, the concept of intervention describes how the client or counselor can effect change in the counseling relationship. Albert Ellis (1955) describes a model for this purpose in the case of the client or counselor. Ellis's counseling theory describes ways in which this intervention or power influence is expressed. Ranging from greatest to least degree of intervention, these are depth interpretation, confrontation, reflection, clarification, and reflection. High power influence describes a situation in which the counselor is able to direct and support the suggestions or interventions of the client. Interventions can have a supporting effect as implemented by the counselor and a liberating effect as implemented by the client.

Ivey (1994) describes an "interpersonal influence continuum" that indicates low, moderate, and high amounts of influence exerted over client talk and the appropriate skill for exerting an appropriate degree of counselor influence.

In rank order from low to high amounts of influence, the following counseling skills are indicated: encouraging and restating; paraphrasing; reflection of feelings; reflection of meaning; open questions; closed questions; focusing; developmental skills; information, instruction, advice, etc.; self-disclosure; feedback; interpretation; logical consequences; directive; and confrontation.

> Quality attending behavior and client observation skills are basic to the flow of the interview and to facilitating client growth. The interviewer must establish contact and note the impact of that contact. These two achievements provide the essential information for determining what skill may be appropriate at what time. Attending behavior can encourage or discourage client talk for the client's benefit; client observation tells you when to change skills and focus. (Ivey, 1994, p. 262)

The counselor exerts the most influence and direction of the interview through influencing skills, whereas listening skills exert the least direct influence and allow the client to determine the direction of the interview, generally speaking. However, Ivey also points out that this framework is an oversimplification, recognizing that any particular counselor intervention, depending on how and when it is used, might exert a great deal of influence or no influence at all. The interpersonal influence continuum provides a starting point for the counselor to appropriately regulate the degree of interpersonal influence for each client in each different interview.

Other possible schema might also be used to describe the implementation of power influence, using the same ratio of relationships. One of these alternatives deals with the developmental aspect of behavior change. The continuum of developmental change from low to high client ability would be identified by four points in the growth of the client's ability in Figure 2.1.

1. Inertia, the first point, is when the client has low ability or desire to cope with the problem and the counselor would react by confronting the client with this low ability or desire but, at the same time, supporting the client through intensive and active probing.

2. Striving, the second point, is when the client's desire to cope with the problem has increased, although the client is not yet in control, and the counselor reacts by encouraging an encounter between the client and the problem, supporting the client as necessary in his or her struggle against the problem.

3. Coping, the third point, is when the client has begun to achieve a qualified control over the problem in an effective manner and the counselor encourages this engagement toward permanent control by the client.

4. Mastery, the fourth point, is when the client has achieved sufficient control over the problem so that the objectives of counseling have been reached and the counselor responds by reflecting the client's victory and ultimately by withdrawing his or her support and thereby dissolving the coalition.

Equalizing Effect

In this model, the counselor would intervene with enough, but just enough, power influence to provide a winning coalition with the client against the problem. The counselor plus client are equal to or greater than the problem (Counselor + Client = Problem). The appropriate power influence from the coalition should be equal to or slightly greater than the power of the problem over the client. If the counselor intervenes with too much power influence, the client is likely to prefer the problem and might revert to a coalition with the problem, rejecting the counselor. If the counselor intervenes with too little power influence, the problem might remain in a position of control, and counseling would not be effective. The client might reject the coalition with the counselor as useless against the problem and, therefore, withdraw from counseling. The counselor-dominating type of coalition might also be unstable over a period of time, and, if it were allowed to continue, it could result in dissolving the coalition. The coalition could probably tolerate the dominating or contending counselor for a short period of time without dissolving, however. By equalizing the balance of power between client and problem through the coalition alliance with the counselor, the client has the opportunity and the security to grow in his or her ability to exert power influence independently.

ASSUMPTIONS OF THE PROBLEM METAPHOR

By this time, the reader will be aware that certain basic assumptions are being made in adapting the idea of coalition to the counseling relationship. It will be important to examine the assumptions to identify and control for the model's own biases.

Assumption 1

The problem can be treated *as if* it were the third member of the counseling relationship. This assumption draws from perceptual field theory, accepting the assumption that people behave according to how things seem to them. The client reacts to the problem as part of his or her own perceptual field, and, as such, the problem has the quality of reality for the client. This is assumed to be true whether the problem is large or small. Although the problem has an externalized inhibiting effect on the client, it rightly belongs within the client's private world of phenomenological reality. The client behaves as if the problem were real and true and, to that extent, separated from the client. The ultimate solution or desirable outcome assumes that the client is able to control the problem, to cope with its inhibiting effects, and to lessen its influence on the client's behavior.

Because the client accepts the problem as real, it affects the client's behavior. Anything that influences the client's behavior in counseling must also affect the counselor's behavior. If the counselor is going to participate in a coalition against the problem, he or she is going to have to accept the client's view of the problem as "real" even if only within the client's perceptual field. Accepting the client's assumptions about reality, the counselor recognizes the real effects of the problem on the counseling process through its influence over the client. In this way, the problem can be separated from the client in such a way that both client and counselor can attack the problem without attacking the client.

The client is *not* disassociated from the problem but recognizes the problem as a nonessential and inhibiting element of interaction with the environment. The client is no longer able to use the problem as a scapegoat because, as a member of the counselor-client coalition, the client is no longer dominated by the problem. The client is forced to confront and make decisions about behavior changes. The client's ability to define and distinguish the problem decreases the inhibiting effect of the problem and dissolves the problem-client coalition. In this way, the problem can be separated from the client, and the various aspects of the problem can be separated from one another.

The problem, although part of the client's perceptual field, is not an essential part of the client. Accepting the client involves making a distinction between the counselor's ally (client) and their mutual enemy (problem). Accepting the client therefore includes accepting the problem as real. Assuming the necessity of working through the client toward an acceptable solution, it might be dangerous to ignore the client's perception of reality.

Assumption 2

A second assumption is that the degree of power influence by the problem, the client, and the counselor can be quantitatively estimated and changed. We are able to perceive the client's effectiveness in dealing with the problem directly. By assuming that the size of the problem is an inverse function of the client's effective coping, we are able to measure the effect of the problem indirectly. A person with *little* coping ability in a specific area of concern has a *big* problem. However, our ability to quantitatively measure changes in counseling is not precise and will always be approximate at best.

Having assumed the degree of power influence exerted on the counseling relationship by the members of the triad, the question remains whether these degrees of influence can be changed by one or more members of the triad. An effective counselor will be able to regulate the degree of counselor influence in the counseling relationship. The counselor must be aware of the effect on the client at different points in different ways and be able to regulate the intensity of that effect. This will be especially true in the counselor's ability to modify power influence in counseling over time, allowing the client to magnify his or her own power influence.

The client will also regulate the degree of power influence and responsibility exerted in the counseling relationship. A counselor's active interaction and capacity to control the problem will presumably increase self-confidence and awareness of potential power over the problem. The focus of this model of counseling is to increase the client's ability to exert that kind of control over the problem. As long as the client is not able to effectively cope with the specific problem without help from the counselor, we might expect the client to be bound to and affected by the problem. The client's allegiance to the problem will diminish as the client gains ability to control the problem.

Assumption 3

The coalition relationship is helpful toward the accomplishment of counseling goals. Leona Tyler (1961) speaks of the counselor becoming an important part of the client's life in the counseling relationship. This attitude of cooperating with the client through empathic understanding is supported by Carl Rogers and by many other counseling models. The problem implicit in the counseling relationship is how much influence should the counselor exert in the counseling relationship to enhance its growth-producing effect? When should the counselor intervene with authority? When should the counselor allow the client to intervene and exert more influence? Furthermore, as the client becomes more effective in coping with the problem through counseling, the client may become more effective in coping with problems outside that relationship as well.

The nature of the counseling relationship is to benefit both the client and the counselor. The counselor is a skilled, professional person and in his or her experience has become well acquainted with many people who have struggled with similar problems. But he or she is ignorant of the unique problem with which the client is involved. If counselors are to become more effective helping persons, they need to broaden their experience to include this specific, unique problem of the client's. The client has struggled with the unique problem for some time and, being unable to overcome it, is being controlled by it. The client has an intimate, personal acquaintance with the unique problem but needs to know how other persons with similar problems have overcome them. The client needs the help of the counselor to accomplish this task and cope with the problem effectively. Both parties in the coalition have something to bargain with, and both need each other. The mutual benefit and interdependence of the coalition partners allow them to help each other as they are helping themselves.

Assumption 4

The problem-client-counselor triad follows a predictable pattern in coalition formation, analogous to the pattern of a three-person triad. At this point, this assumption is an untested hypothesis. The present volume is an attempt to clarify that hypothesis in such a way that it can be tested and can be confirmed or refuted.

Pepinsky (1959), in his adaptation of coalition theory to counseling, concentrates on the dyad relationship of client and counselor. The dynamics of coalition formation and the context in which a coalition is formed suggest a third closely related source of influence antagonistic to that coalition. I have attempted to identify that third source as a product of the client's perceptual field: the problem. In its effects on the client's behavior, the problem becomes the third source of influence in counseling. This way of looking at counseling is useful in understanding some of the dynamics of behavior changes in counseling. The balance of power suggests a wider perspective and the opportunity to reexamine some of the sociocultural environmental assumptions of counseling. This metaphorical analogy could stimulate other insights into the counseling relationship that would be helpful and could, in turn, be tested (Pepinsky & DeStefano, 1982).

Assumption 5

The view of counseling as an instance of coalition is adaptable to a variety of other counseling orientations. This way of looking at counseling has been a highly eclectic application from diverse areas of counseling as well as from social psychology and other fields. For example, the early stages of counseling have support from cognitive models and the later stages from reflective models.

Figure 2.2 describes the idealized development over time for a client from low to high capacity and for a problem or counselor from a high to low degree of intervention in the client's life. At any given point along the time dimension, the influence power of the counselor *plus* the influence power of the client is equal to or greater than the influence power of the problem. But the counselor *alone* is always less powerful than the problem. At every point in the counseling process, the power is distributed unequally. Sometimes the counselor, sometimes the client, and sometimes the problem controls what is happening in the counseling interview. As the client becomes more powerful or in control, the counselor will want to become correspondingly less powerful, giving the client room to grow but providing enough power to prevent the problem from taking over. It is important to recognize that the client may be more in control in some areas of his or her life, such as at work, and less in control in other areas, such as the home. For that reason, the client may be at many different points at the same time on the continuum, from low to high power, depending on the topic and the circumstances. Three hypothetical situations are indicated along the time dimension as X_1, X_2, and X_3 to illustrate the changing equilibrium of power in a counseling relationship.

Stage 1 describes the client as having a very low power influence, being dominated by the problem. The counselor adjusts the influence to nearly match

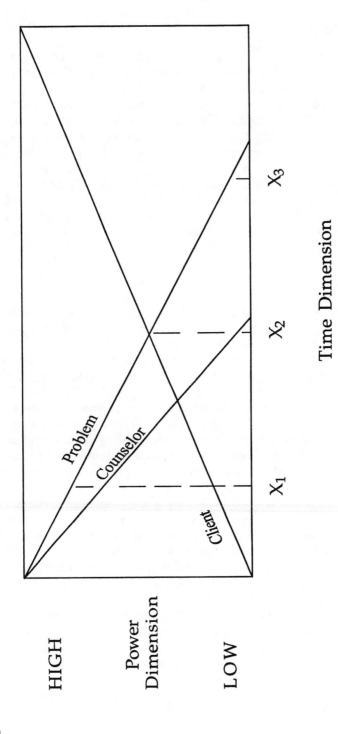

Figure 2.2. A Schematic Description of the Ratio of Power Influence Over Time for Counselor, Client, and Problem With Three (X_1, X_2, X_3) Points in the Counseling Process Indicated

but not exceed that of the problem. If the counselor exerts too little influence, the problem will dominate through a continued coalition with the client. If the counselor exerts too much influence, the client will withdraw in favor of the problem as less threatening or dominating. This situation may describe an earlier phase of the counseling relationship.

Stage 2 shows the client able to exert enough power influence so that the counselor may become the "weaker" member of the triad. The client is still, but to a lesser extent, dependent on the counselor for membership in the coalition against the problem. This situation describes a critical phase in which the power initiative is transferred to the client from the counselor. If the client were to regress down the slope, the counselor would increase the power influence accordingly, while continuing to lead the client toward increased power influence. This situation may describe the middle phase of a counseling relationship.

Stage 3 shows the client able to manage the problem independently without help from the counselor. In the cognitive perspective, the counselor would attempt to encourage a rational awareness of the client's capacity to cope with the problem. The counselor might do this by adopting the role of a teacher, helping the client to think more clearly about solving this problem and develop potential coping abilities. Through interpretation and confrontation, the counselor would demonstrate supporting concern and personal investment in the client. As a teacher, the counselor would help the client develop skills of problem solving applied to the immediate problem. At the same time, the counselor might take a highly rational approach, helping the client structure potential solutions. This will help the client define the nonrational aspects of the problem and make decisions regarding the problem to establish a priority of important goals in counseling. The objective of this stage is that the individual be oriented to reality regarding a balance of power between the problem and alternative solutions.

The interaction to the right of the intersecting lines can be characterized by the more reflective approach of Carl Rogers. The counselor allows the client full expression, having demonstrated an ability to accept such responsibility, and the counselor tends to follow the client's lead in their coalition alliance against the problem. In a sense, their roles are now reversed. The client is beginning to provide depth interpretation and is able to confront insights regarding the problem, which the counselor might well limit to responses of clarification and reflection. The client's perception is now increasing in accuracy and becoming less distorted, while the threatening aspects of the problem are diminishing. This is especially true after the client has passed the second crisis point. The client is testing the cognitive rationale developed earlier concerning his or her nonrational, subjective emotional implications for a lasting solution. The focus is more on the *specific* phenomenological problem and less on this *general* type of problem. Assuming that the client has the greater insight into many aspects of the problem, the counselor turns over leadership to the client and supports the client through reflection or clarification, allowing maximum freedom and responsibility.

APPLICATION OF THE PROBLEM AS METAPHOR

Aspects of the behavioral counseling model are also evident in the use of reward and punishment to encourage client development up the slope. The counselor is in the position of offering a consistently greater reward than can be offered by the problem through reinforcing side payments from the client-counselor coalition. In the application of ego-supportive psychotherapy, a counselor incorporates the techniques of clarification and interpretation as "uncovering techniques." In the first phase, in which the counselor establishes a therapeutic alliance with the ego, one is profoundly ego-supportive. During counseling, the threshold of anxiety is maintained at a level that will not overwhelm the ego, dealing with the conscious rather than the preconscious or unconscious and with the present rather than the past.

The techniques of "lead," as used by Robinson (1950), might also be applied to describe the counseling task in the coalition. The counselor leads with as much pressure as the client or, in this case, the coalition can tolerate. The counselor varies the degree of lead to match the pace of the client. The counselor at first accepts the responsibility of initiating the lead toward the ultimate goal or outcome. On the other hand, as the client gains in coping ability, the counselor allows the client to lead, as long as that lead is toward their common coalition goal. Many other modifications of counseling theory will be apparent to the reader as part of counseling when viewed as an instance of coalition. The model does not specifically dictate the ways in which power influence will or should be exerted exclusive of other unacceptable ways.

There are a number of problems in predicting coalition-formation strategy that become particularly bothersome when we seek to apply the coalition in three-person laboratory groups to real-life counseling relationships. The first of these problems is that of assuming "rationality" in the decisions of the participants. There has been a tendency to equate rationality with self-interest or maximum utility. We can allow for nonutilitarian strategy influence, but we cannot measure or even estimate the effect of nonrational elements. We can, as the game theorists have done, assume that nonrational behavior is randomly distributed and will cancel itself out, concentrating our analysis on rational elements.

The second problem involves accurate measurement of human behavior. The social sciences are not as easily able to demonstrate causal determination as are the physical sciences. Distorted perceptions, half-conscious motivations, selective memories, and other irrationalities intrude on human behavior in many unpredictable ways, particularly in counseling.

A third difficulty involves the zero-sum condition of research on coalition formation that assumes gains of winners are equal to losses of losers. In discussing bargains and negotiations of counseling in which mutual gain is likely, a non-zero-sum model would probably be more accurate.

A fourth difficulty is the accurate estimation of power or resources among the counselor, client, and problem. Power can be demonstrated through threats, payment, promises, or emotional satisfaction, but available measures lack the precision implied by coalition theory.

A fifth problem is that the coalition is fundamentally and inherently unstable. Each participant may gain or lose bargaining power in relation to the other two, or some other change in the environment may turn one or more members of the coalition against the other.

New models to describe the counseling process are needed that can chart directions of progress or change, can suggest appropriate intervention by the counselor, can incorporate a variety of theoretical orientations as appropriate, and can describe counseling in terms of functional accomplishments. The Triad Training Model applies what we know about coalitions to the relationship between counselors, clients, and problems, toward an understanding of how we might establish a coalition between the counselor and the client. Many of the concepts of small groups can be usefully applied to counseling, just as many of the concepts of counseling relate to coalition-formation processes. In examining the assumptions, problems, and advantages of the problem metaphor as a coalition phenomenon, we have the basis for a systematic description relating counseling to specific functions. The next step will be to research the usefulness of such a metaphorical model to determine whether it provides a basis for prediction of outcomes.

CONCLUSIONS

The working alliance of a counseling relationship is based on the notion of social self and the importance of an individual's sociocultural context to that person's identity. If the relationship between a client and counselor is viewed as a coalition and if that coalition is balanced against the metaphorical problem, then the social psychological literature about coalition formation in three-person groups helps us better understand the counseling relationship. The research literature suggests that a counselor must adjust the amount of power influence in counseling to provide a safe context for the client to grow and to make the client-counselor coalition more attractive than a problem-client coalition.

The inclusion of the sociocultural environment through the identity of a metaphorical problem as the third party in a counseling interview requires the redefinition of social psychological terms to this metaphorical triad. In the same way, the underlying assumptions of this metaphorical triad are made explicit and discussed to clarify how the three-way analysis of a counseling relationship is both similar to and different from conventional thinking.

Figures 2.1 and 2.2 are provided to demonstrate the relationships between a problem, client, and counselor as they change over time. Some of the implications for a counselor's appropriate degree of power influence are discussed, suggesting hypotheses that could be tested later. If the problem is a real presence in counseling—as a metaphor—then the next step is to bring in a third actual person who is culturally similar to the client and ask that third person to "be" the problem as perceived in the client's internal dialogue. Or, better yet, bring in a third person to articulate the negative and a fourth person to articulate the positive messages in the client's internal dialogue to better understand the problem from the viewpoint of culturally different clients. This approach will be explored in the following chapters.

3

The Relational Self

Although Erikson (1968) emphasized the importance of autonomy and initiative development during the childhood years in his classic model of identity, it is also true that his psychosocial concepts defined the individual self in a context of the community's values, norms, and social roles. Erikson's model favors the individualistic worldview and perhaps the more masculine roles, but the notion of a "separated self" is now being replaced with a notion of "being in relationship," in which the sense of self reflects the relationships between people. Bond-Claire, Pilner, and Stoker (1998) introduce a new way of thinking about intrapersonal competence in which the self is the object of "implicit mental models." They also look at how it relates to successful functioning in adulthood and at how individuals function in their own terms free from any particular social norm for success. This makes the cultural context central and avoids arbitrary ways of assessing life functioning.

The individualized self rooted in individualism of the Western world is being overtaken by a more "familial self" typical of the global majority, as best described by Clifford Geertz (1975):

> The Western conception of the person as a bounded, unique, more or less integrated motivational and cognitive universe, a dynamic center of awareness, emotion, judgment and action organized into a distinctive whole and set contrastively both against other such wholes and against a social and natural background is, however incorrigible it may seem to us, a rather peculiar idea within the context of the world's cultures. (p. 48)

This chapter will show how the more corporate notion of a relational self is integrated into the individual's identity through internal dialogue.

The classic Freudian combination of intrapsychic forces, in which behavior is determined by unconscious and sometimes conscious interaction between the id as a source of psychic energy and the ego and superego, emphasizes the importance of balance. *Psychosis* is defined as the condition of disorder or imbalance, resulting in delusions, hallucinations, obsessions, compulsions, and morbid fears, whereas *neurosis* is a functional disorder along the same lines but is less disruptive. The consistent emphasis on internal dynamics with less reference to the sociocultural environment of that individual has no doubt influenced the emphasis on individualism in psychological analysis. This psychodynamic platform has had a strong influence on the study of intrapersonal dynamics.

The internal dynamics of the client are important in understanding all counseling relationships. The idea of "self-talk" (Ellis, 1962) or internal dialogue (Meichenbaum, 1977), in which thinking is described as a discourse the mind carries on with itself by talking to itself, goes back at least as far as Plato. To the extent that thought is conducted in words, thinking may be characterized as talking to one's self, usually in terms of a two-sided or positive versus negative discussion. Cognitive behaviorists use the polarity to conceptualize cognitive features of pathology such as rational versus irrational beliefs, positive versus negative appraisals, positive versus negative self-statements, and desirable versus undesirable life events (Schwartz & Garamoni, 1989).

THE SOCIAL SELF-DIALOGUE

Social identity involves the reconciliation of same and different, belonging to a context while at the same time distinguishing oneself from that same context. "Most of social psychology's theories of the self fail to take into account the significance of social identification in the definition of self. Social identities are self-definitions that are more inclusive than the individuated self-concept of most American psychology" (Brewer, 1991, p. 475). This reconciliation takes place in the form of a dialogue within the individual. McCall and Simmons (1982) combine the "I" and the "me" in what Mead (1934) called an "inner forum" of continuous internal conversation. Herz-Lazarowitz and Miller (1995) described four types of inner speech during problem solving: task-related, self-related, other-related, and task-relevant. McKay (1992) reviews data on four fundamental issues addressed by theories of inner speech:

1. What is the nature of inner speech?
2. What are the perceptual and generative aspects of inner speech and where does it come from?
3. How are internal and overt speech related?
4. What role does internal speech play in cognition such as visualization and memory?

This is not a simple dialogue. The individual is reacting to what is being said or thought as one is saying or thinking it. These internal voices are constant and continuous. By monitoring the internal dialogue constantly and continuously, it is possible to discover different perspectives about the same context. It is this organization of multiple perspectives and contexts for reaction that is the "me" in Mead's terms.

> The me is best thought of not as the antagonist in a dialogue with the I but as an audience, all the people in a multiperson discussion who are temporarily silent while the I holds the floor. But though they are politely silent, they are evaluating and criticizing all the while that the I is talking. Each has a somewhat different reaction, corresponding to his different perspective, and when the I has finished and relinquished the floor, so to speak, every member of this metaphorical audience strives to inform him of his own personal reaction to what was said. (McCall & Simmons, 1982, pp. 53-54)

If taken literally, these ideas would seem delusional, but as metaphors, they become useful and meaningful.

The idea of self as a product of social and psychological interaction between the individual and that individual's cultural context combines the intrapersonal level of communication with social, cognitive, and performance aspects of communication. The interaction of brain and culture produces a different notion of self for each individual. The literal voices that have created the culture are internalized in an "inner speech" through which all external communication is processed by internal dialogue. The intrapersonal dialogue is where our interpersonal communication is rehearsed and our behavior competence is enhanced. The theoretical discussions of inner speech first appear in the psychological writings of George Herbert Mead (1982) and in symbolic interactionalist theory, as well as sociocultural theory articulated by L. S. Vygotsky (1934/1986) and A. R. Luria (1961), who both emphasized the dynamic dialectical nature of self in its sociocultural context (Valsiner & Van der Veer, 1988). Vygotsky (1934/1986) used the term *inner speech* as both self-dialogue and a process of thought being realized in words. This perspective assumes, first, that human cognition is inherently social and, second, that human cognition develops as external social interactions are internalized (Vocate, 1994).

The five-volume recently translated works of Vygotsky (1993) provide valuable ideas on the use of dialogic imagination and dialogic speech from the Russian literature written early in this century. Vygotsky approached intrapsychological dynamics through the internalization of language as a linguist. He describes internal dialogue as part of our developmental process. The child first learns egocentric speech and then, at the preschool or school-age stage, transforms that egocentric speech into inner speech as he or she absorbs social forms of behavior. Inner speech becomes an important part of healthy functioning. Egocentric speech is internal in its mental function and external in its structure as it develops into inner speech. Vygotsky described individual mental functioning as derived from the mastery and internalization of social interaction (Daniels, 1996).

Diaz and Berk (1992) acknowledged that Vygotsky pointed out how language mediates social interaction as well as activity within the individual. This link between social (intermental) and cognitive (intramental) still leaves questions about the origin, significance, and functions of private speech. How, for example, can social and private speech be validly differentiated? What tasks promote the use of private speech? How does private speech contribute to a child's cognitive development? Does private speech serve as a self-regulatory tool across the life span?

Through inner speech, the children apply to themselves the same guidelines that others apply to them and that they apply to others. Vygotsky (1987) developed this idea into a developmental model.

> On the basis of contemporary research, it can be established that the cultural development of higher psychological functions occurs in four basic stages. The first of these is the *natural-primitive stage,* or the most primitive of the forms of cultural behavior, in which the child or savage completes arithmetic operations through direct perception of quantities. The second stage is the so-called *stage of naive psychology,* when a child accumulates certain experience about the means of cultural behavior, but cannot make use of those means. In the third stage of *externally mediated acts* the child already makes proper use of external signs to carry out one or another operation (counting on fingers, and so on). Finally at the fourth stage external signs are replaced by internal ones and the activity is internally mediated (for example, in doing mental calculations). In the anomalous cultural development of the mentally retarded or physically defective child, the child is arrested or constrained at one of the stages of cultural development enumerated here for a longer time than the normal child is. (p. 296)

Vygotsky (1987) contends that his approach provides a more adequate explanation of how egocentric speech develops into inner speech than Piaget's does. Vygotsky describes Piaget's theory as assuming that egocentric speech atrophies as the child gets older, decreasing in occurrence as the child develops. If this were so, then egocentric speech would become less frequent and prominent until it would ultimately disappear. "Among the most important and decisive empirical findings of our research is that the structural characteristics of egocentric speech that differentiate it from social speech—the characteristics that make it incomprehensible to others—increase rather than decrease with age" (p. 260).

Inner speech, as differentiated from external speech, tends to increase with age, although the vocalization of that egocentric speech is diminished. We need to know more about the transformation from external egocentric speech to inner speech in the thinking process as it occurs over time. The development of inner speech is more than a mechanical process or the gradual reduction in speech volume. Thinking and speaking are like two intersecting circles with a limited portion of the speaking and thinking processes coinciding in "verbal thinking," which does not include all thoughts or all forms of speech. The domains of nonverbal thinking and nonintellectual speech are separate from verbal thinking.

> Inner speech develops through a long cumulative series of functional and structural changes. It branches off from the child's external speech with the differentiation of the social and egocentric functions of speech. Finally, the structure of speech that the child masters becomes the basic structure of his thinking. (Vygotsky, 1987, pp. 119-120)

Inner speech, according to Vygotsky, is not intended to communicate to others but with oneself, occurring under different conditions and fulfilling a different function from external speech. We should not be surprised, therefore, when inner speech is incomprehensible but perhaps should be surprised when it actually becomes comprehensible. Words and ideas are given a specially idiomatic, unique individual meaning in inner speech, understandable only to the self, like a password to meaning. A whole range of ideas, emotions, thoughts, and sensations can be connected in a single word through inner speech, which cannot be translated into external speech. Vygotsky's contributions to understanding inner speech are significant in the context of contemporary cognitive psychology.

The self appears in multiple forms as simultaneous interacting modules. There are examples of how our modular selves influence our behavior. Wile (1993) applies this perspective to the book-length analysis of a single night in the life of a married couple as they experience conflict and harmony. Gazzaniga (1985) applies this idea to recent brain research and studies of artificial intelligence. Ornstein (1986) describes this as each mind containing different kinds of "small minds" that are temporarily "wheeled into consciousness" and then returned to their place after use. We do not need to fear fragmenting because we are already fragmented, although not to the point of having a multiple personality disorder. Hofstader (1986) describes the mind as a society or democracy with factions competing for control in a confederation of systems in the social brain.

This internalized dialogue can be overt and external or covert and internal. Operationally, self-talk is a dialogue with the self either through a silent inner speech or an audible external dialogue addressed to the self but possibly heard by others also. It may be intentional or unintentional. In either case, the self is both the speaker and the person being spoken to. Both the silent and the audible inner speech are based on an internalized coding/decoding process as the self elicits a response from itself as it would from others through interpersonal communication.

> The distinctive attributes of self-talk, given this definition, are: (a) self-awareness or what Mead (1934) termed reflective consciousness; (b) its dialogical nature—addressing the self as the object of one's talk whether vocalized or silent;

(c) a stimulus, either sign or symbol originating from the self; and (d) an interpretive, symbolic response or feedback from the self. (Vocate, 1994, p. 7)

Mead (1982) described personality as a microcosmic society in which comprehension is facilitated. This is different from the static components of self such as Freud's id, ego, and superego in that it combines the identities of an "I" and a "me."

> The former is the dynamic, spontaneous, creative action taker with biological origins, whereas the Me is the internalized, organized aggregate of attitudes and perceptions garnered from others. The I does and the Me monitors the doing. Any reaction or response to oneself thus results from a social interaction between the two—the I or actor and the Me or critic. (Vocate, 1994, p. 9)

Self-talk therefore becomes a conversation between the individual and the sociocultural context embodied in internalized "other" identities. Self-talk becomes a dialogue, at a symbolic level, between the individual and society in which either may critique the other in the search for meaning.

Markus and Nurius (1986) hypothesize that these multiple selves provide a context for motivation and evaluation through hoped-for positive selves and feared negative selves. Hermans and Kempen (1993) describe the utility of multiple selves in being both the subject and the object. The individual as a subject knows himself or herself as an object from the particular standpoints of other individual members of the sociocultural referent group. Individuals become objects to themselves through internalizing attitudes of other people toward themselves, making communication possible through significant symbols directed both toward others and toward the individual him- or herself.

Self-talk links the individual with his or her environment and the development of competence linking speech and thought. Inner speech rehearses competency in performance by internalizing both the complex meanings of the sociocultural context and the personal perspective or experience of the self. Inner speech, covert vocalization, or private speech are well-researched and well-established concepts in psychology, linguistics, neurolinguistics, education, speech communication, and other fields as well (Vocate, 1994).

People learn about their own emotions, attitudes, and internal states by observing their own behavior, much like they might evaluate the behavior of others (Montgomery & Haemmerlie, 1987). The need to investigate these internal cognitive processes might provide the key to skill generalization. These schemas of cognitive structures facilitate top-down or conceptually driven processing as opposed to bottom-up or data-driven cognitive processing (Fiske & Taylor, 1991). Each schema comes from multiple sources as we actively construct reality. Some beliefs about the self and environmental factors are more salient than others, leading to behavior that is consistent with the situation but not consistent with other self-concepts. Self-regulation is guided by a striving for accuracy in self-knowledge, self-enhancement, and consistency. People continuously form a new sense of "us" relative to their perception of themselves in relation to each other (Shorter, 1987).

A better understanding about how counselors and clients think during counseling is needed. There is growing research literature on the importance of "self-talk" (private monologues) as it influences an individual's performance in counseling and other tasks. The favorite model is the concept of self as a soliloquy, first expressed by G. H. Mead and later by H. Blumer and M. Kuhn (cited in Lonnie, 1994). An alternative view of the self as a soliloquy describes "us" as a phantom community in the soliloquies. Lonnie (1994) describes 10 principles that govern soliloquizing, such as the nature and form of soliloquies, the creation of emotions, hidden sources of sensitivity, painting self-portraits, the origin or nature of phantom communities, and the display of individuality and conformity. The self as a soliloquy displays continuity and flux while also allowing for conformity and individuality in a chaotic, self-regulating, and nonlinear process (Taylor & Schneider, 1989).

Butz (1997) borrows from chaos theory to explain how the self organizes complex experiences into a coherent thought:

> Coherence, or the integrity of the individual's experience of personality, has been referred to as the self throughout the theoretical literature. So when stability is discussed, along with the sense of an individual's coherence, the emphasis will be on the time-honored notion of the self. Nevertheless, one of the key problems with some of the new theories on consciousness, cognition, and other fields is a denial of the self as even a concept. In many instances these theorists are physical scientists just entering the arena of social sciences and therefore are not aware of or do not appreciate the philosophical lineage upon which this construct is based. (p. 104)

Butz (1997) writes about the "transitory self" that emerges after a chaotic period of our experiences and lasts until its transitory adaptive function becomes obsolete, leading to the development of a more adaptive contemporary self. Transitory selves evolve into more complex and adaptive forms but always with a continuous theme, as people feel more or less "like themselves." "It appears that many of the problems associated with self per se are in the human mechanistic linear orientation to the world. Things tend to be seen in static forms" (p. 112). The self is dynamic and in that way similar to self-organizing, nonlinear steady states in which stability becomes a phase of the system's developmental process.

Psychology—and particularly counseling psychology—has relied on the foundation assumptions of an older theologically derived monological perspective of the self. The revolutionary new dialogical paradigm in psychology—and particularly counseling psychology—has presented a more flexible and context-dependent understanding of self. This new "dialogical self" is constructed and reconstructed from encounters with others and reciprocal influences of a multicultural society.

> The construction of the dialogical self is a corrective to the belief that self and society are discrete conceptions. . . . The validity of the notion of multivoiced selves is immediately apparent when we reflect on the complexities of decision making, especially in the context of moral conflict. (Sarbin, 1993, p. xiv)

Self-narratives reflect each person's involvement in a sociocultural context and communities. The client's self is a story or narrative between the person who tells and an actual or imagined listener. Straus (1958) describes the self in this sociocultural context: "In sensory experience I always experience myself and the world at the same time, not myself directly and the Other by inference, not myself before the Other nor myself without the Other, nor the Other without myself" (p. 148). These interrelated story themes provide coherence for the self in otherwise fragmented experiences scattered across times and places. The client presents a decentralized self functioning more as a multiplicity of voices than as a unitary thought process.

Hermans and Kempen (1993) describe this dialogical presentation of self as a crowd of people:

> Psychosynthesis assumes that in each of us a diversity of subpersonalities is striving to express themselves, and growth can be facilitated by knowing them: the hag, the mystic, the materialist, the idealist, the claw, the pillar of strength, the sensitive listener, the religious fanatic, the doubter, the frightened child, and others. (p. 36)

Sullivan's (1953) notion of personified images of self in the "good me" and "bad me" or the "good other" and "bad other" are also brought together in this dialogical-self system of independent and mutually opposing viewpoints by characters in dialogical relationships.

Harry Stack Sullivan (1953) was one of the first psychologists to emphasize systems approaches to understanding individual behavior. His emphasis on whole systems of interacting relationships was a living system metaphor. The interaction between people became the source of understanding, linking external relationships to the psychodynamic intrapsychic perspective. Behavior was determined by patterns of recurrent interpersonal relationships, including imagery, memory, or fantasy. The suggestion that behavior may reflect relationships with persons not actually present was central to Sullivan's contribution. He described this phenomenon as "personifications." The metaphor of "muzak" has been used to describe the background noise of these intrapersonal relationships.

This polyphonic interpretation of self does not depend on an "overarching I" to organize the constituents of the "me." There is, rather, a decentralized multiplicity of "I" positions functioning like independent authors telling the stories about their respective actors. Each "I" has his or her own story to tell. "As in musical polyphonic composition, a particular idea or theme (e.g., aggression, love, jealousy) has not a fixed self-contained, unchangeable meaning. Instead, by leading the theme through various voices, its many facetedness and potentials can be brought to expression" (Hermans & Kempen, 1993, p. 42).

Barrett (1986) describes the self as a facilitator of one's intrapersonal "good audience," representing all accumulated knowledge, common sense, good ideas, advice, and stored learning. Most of this has come from relationships with thousands of significant persons—real or imagined—in one's life, through personal contact, readings, and the media. This internal audience or social system is the sum total of everything a person has learned and experienced in his or her lifetime. Hinde (1997) refers to this same phenomenon as one's consciousness, speaking metaphorically; it is illustrated in Bolby's Internal Working Model (IWM) of self and others in relationships.

> Bolby supposed that the young child forms a mental representation or model of the world containing as prominent components models of the self and of each of his or her attachment figures and representations of the relationships between them. This IWM is internalized and gradually adjusted to form a guide for social behavior. (p. 31)

The counseling relationship becomes an extension of dialogical relationships and narratives within the client and the counselor individually. Clients internalize dispositions from counseling that they perceive counselors hold toward them. In Quintana and Meara's (1990) Structural Analysis of Social Behavior (SASB), the degree of complementarity between the client and counselor is presented as a vital aspect of interpersonal interaction in counseling: "Interpersonal interactions that satisfy the principle of complementarity tend to be stable and mutually reinforcing. . . . The theoretical extension of complementarity to include interpersonal-intrapsychic complementarity is consistent with psychodynamic descriptions of internalization" (p. 123). Interpersonal behaviors are mediated by intrapersonal dynamics.

Lifton (1993) has invented the term *protean self* after the Greek sea god Proteus, who had many different forms in Homer's *Odyssey,* just as the "shape-shifting" self has in accommodating radical changes in its sociocultural context over time. The protean self is an expression of our confusion and the widespread feeling that we have lost our psychological identity. We are controlled by historical forces and social uncertainties.

> Leaders appear suddenly, recede equally rapidly, and are difficult for us to believe in when they are around. We change ideas and partners frequently, and do the same

with jobs and places of residence. Enduring moral convictions, clear principles of actions and behavior: we believe these must exist, but where? Whether dealing with world problems or child rearing, our behavior tends to be ad hoc, more or less decided upon as we go along. We are beset by a contradiction; schooled in the virtues of constancy and stability—whether as individuals, groups or nations—our world and our lives seem inconstant and utterly unpredictable. We readily come to view ourselves as unsteady, neurotic, or worse. (Lifton, 1993, p. 1)

The self-as-subject is typically internalized, and the self-as-object is externalized. Gordon Allport's (1943) eight categories of self demonstrate the multiplicity of the self. Allport comments on the importance of self to understanding human behavior:

One of the oddest events in the history of modern psychology is the manner in which the ego—or self—became sidetracked and lost from view. I say it is odd because the existence of one's own self is the one fact of which every mortal person—every psychologist included—is perfectly convinced. (p. 71)

Understanding the relational self is essential to understanding the cultural self.

The Cultural Self

Culture becomes the link between the individual self and the social context in which that individual self exists. Brunner (1990), in describing how meaning is generated, describes how culture provides

a set of more or less connected, more or less normative descriptions about how human beings tick, what our own and other minds are like, what one can expect situated actions to be like, what are possible modes of life, how one commits oneself to them, and so on. (p. 35)

Culture provides the connection between the relational self and the sociocultural context in which that self exists.

The sociocultural context guides the definition of self in several ways (Markus & Kitayama, 1991). One way is through an "independent self-construal," in which the self is perceived as a separate identity with internal characteristics that are stable across situations regardless of context. This perspective is typical of more individualistic cultures. An alternative way more typical of collectivist societies connects the notion of self to societal roles and relationships. This "interdependent self-construal" is relationship centered, requiring conformity and seeking harmony over personal goals. This interdependent self depends more on context than on internal attributes. Singelis (1994) suggests four patterns of self-construal across cultures: (a) bicultural, with a well-developed independent and a well-developed interdependent self-construal; (b) Western, with a strong independent self-construal and a weak interdependent self-construal; (c) traditional, with a weak independent self-construal and a strong interdependent self-construal; and (d) culturally alienated, with a poorly developed independent and a poorly developed inter-dependent self-construal. In both Eastern and Western concepts of the self, there is a bipolar quality in which the self is both subjective (nominative) and objective (accusative; Marsella, DeVos, & Hsu, 1985).

Kagitcibasi (1996) characterizes Western psychology as affirming the sepa-rated self as a healthy prototype basic to the prescriptive nature of psychology. When this expresses itself as selfishness, self-centeredness, and a lack of social commitment, psychology becomes more a part of the social problems for non-Western cultures than a part of the solution.

> American (and Western) psychology, both reflecting and reinforcing the individu-alistic Western cultural ethos, has drawn the line narrowly and sharply, constitut-ing a clear boundary between the self and non-self. Other cultural conceptions differ from this construal of the self in varying degrees. However, American psy-chology enjoys a dominant position and is self-contained so the knowledge it cre-ates (based on its own empirical reality) is often assumed to be universal. (p. 55)

The degree of relatedness or separateness of the self has emerged as a basic controversy in psychology, and it provides two sharply contrasting explanations of psychological and/or social functioning. This controversy is reminiscent of the polarization of internal and external locus of control, in which internal control was considered to be better, to the disadvantage of those populations (women, lower-socioeconomic-status groups, traditional societies, and some ethnic minorities) that gave less emphasis to internal control. Self-contained individualism, in which control is inherent in the individual, can be contrasted with "ensembled individualism," in which control is located in the interpersonal field (Sampson, 1988).

Johnson (1985) traces the Western concept of self through three stages. The first, pre-Christian times until about 1850, was based on philosophical, theo-logical, and literary descriptions of self as soul and mind, emphasizing sub-jective consciousness and ontological separateness. The second, from approximately 1850 to 1940, was based on an elaborate social self character-ized by George Herbert Mead's interfactional construction. The third stage, from 1940 to the present, is still being developed in a sociocultural and politi-cal application.

The development of self in non-Western cultures is much more difficult to trace. Japanese, for example, distinguish between the social person, or *tatemae,* and the inner being, *honne,* or self. The Confucian Chinese self is pre-dominantly social, in a configuration of roles and a web of self-other mutual expectations. The emphasis is on how an individual sees both "self" internally and the sociocultural expectations of society externally. In the Indian perspective, the self evolves through listening to the "inner voices."

Gao and Ting-Toomey (1998) describe how, in Chinese culture, the self can attain its completeness only through integration with others and the surrounding context. Hsu (1971) contended that Chinese make little distinction between themselves and others, so relational aspects of the self influence all communication. "Chinese communication is not primarily utilized to affirm self-identity or to achieve individual goals but to preserve harmonious relations with family, others and the surrounding environment" (Gao & Ting-Toomey, 1998, p. 6). In Buddhism, the "small self" is distinguished from the "big self"; the small self is equivalent (more or less) to the individual, and the big self is devoid of individuality. In Taoism, self is part of nature, so self and nature combine in a harmonious relationship. Confucianism suggests that the small self is subordinate to the big self. All the Chinese traditions indicate that self is not an independent entity but is relational.

Ho (1991), in a perspective called "methodological relationism," describes the relational orientation as more than merely other-directedness.

> It implies reciprocity, interdependence and interrelatedness between individuals. Social actions follow not so much from the individual's own inclinations, sentiments or needs as they do from the individual's perception of his or her relationships with other people—largely conditioned by cultural definitions. The social presence of others is always entered into social calculations. (p. 84)

In this way, facts about the individuals in a social phenomenon are inadequate by themselves to account for what happened. The principles guiding a social phenomenon are emergent from the relationships of participating groups or individuals, independent of their individual characteristics. The individual characteristics can be understood only in their sociocultural context. Methodological relationism (Ho, 1998) includes the social presence of others in explanations and interpretations in which the individual is embedded in a social network.

Although self-monitoring is one of the most widely used constructs in social psychological research, little cross-cultural or intercultural research has been done on self-monitoring (Gudykunst, Gao, & Franklyn-Stokes, 1997). In part, this is because of the individualistic bias in the construct as typically measured. In their study, Gudykunst et al. (1997) found that Chinese and English subjects differed in their self-monitoring tendencies and their definition of social appropriateness:

> While the English were more able to modify self presentation, the Chinese paid more attention to social comparison and status characteristics, as could be predicted from the literature on collectivist and individualistic cultures. Members of individualistic cultures appear to focus on how they can change their behavior to

meet generalized expectations of others in a social situation (for instance, how a prototypic person is expected to behave in the situation). Members of collectivistic cultures, in contrast, appear to focus on how they can behave appropriately given the relationship to specific people in the social situations. (pp. 265-266)

Kim and Berry (1993), in studying indigenous psychologies, describe the Asian perspectives of self as interpersonal and intersubjective.

In Asian cultures, the self is not an individualistic self, one that is intensely aware of itself, its uniqueness, its sense of direction, purpose and volition. The boundary between self and nonself is not sharply demarcated: the self is not distinct and separate from others, encapsulated unto itself. Rather, the self is what I would call *relational self,* one that is intensely aware of the social presence of other beings. The appearance of others in the phenomenal world is integral to the emergence of selfhood; that is, self and others are conjointly differentiated from the phenomenal world to form the self-in-relation-with-others. This, in short, is the phenomenological representation of selfhood. (p. 256)

Ogbonnaya (1994) likewise describes the person as an intrapsychic community in an African "communitarian" context. This is a context in which, first, the person is a community in and of itself through a plurality of selves; second, there is an interpsychic interaction of these selves in complex relationships; and, third, the person as community enables individuals to have out-of-body experiences. The collective selves of the community are experienced through each individual self in what might be described as a spiritual process. We experience interpersonal cultural relationships through intrapersonal dialogues.

Intrapersonal relationships across cultures are conducted in at least four ways to resemble interpersonal relationships (Lederman, 1996). First, the intrapersonal communication takes place through talking or words. Second, it includes listening to the talking. Third, it is usually dyadic. Fourth, the intrapersonal "selves" treat one another in ways similar to how people treat one another. This internal process allows us to rehearse our interactions with the outside world. Morin and James (1990) and Morin (1993, 1995) examine the relationship between the complexity of self-concept and the more or less frequent use of self-talk. Self-talk mediates self-awareness and the acquiring of self-information useful to problem solving through focusing attention on the problem, formulating an approach to manage the problem, and evaluating the outcome. Engaging in dialogues with one's self or talking to fictitious persons permits the internalization of the other's perspective and seeing one's self as others see them. In that way, inner speech becomes a uniquely valuable cognitive tool for acquiring and processing information about self and becomes an effective tool for forming self-concept.

CONCLUSION

The nature of self as a personal and also a collective identity is central to the psychological literature. Although psychology has, until recently, emphasized individualistic perspectives, a more collectivist perspective is emerging. The construction of a social self through dialogue, real and imagined, within the individual connects that individual with society and culture. The study of internal dialogue and self-talk has been useful to provide a better understanding of how individual identity and a sense of self happens. The notion of including other identities in one's internal dialogue is well grounded in the psychological literature.

The emphasis on collectivism has largely occurred as a result of the influence on psychological perspectives by other cultures. This increased emphasis on the sociocultural context has strengthened our understanding of identity and self by broadening our framework toward a more comprehensive perspective of influences. The self-in-community is a promising perspective for applying psychological perspectives across cultures. Culture teachers from the various social systems become the source of values and expectations in our internal dialogue, which determine our behaviors in each cultural context. This linking of the social perspective with the individual perspective is essential to arguments that will be presented in subsequent chapters.

4

Hearing the Hidden Messages

Kelly (in press) describes a positive relationship between the emotional thoughts that the client left unsaid in therapy and the client's satisfaction with the therapy experience. Furthermore, the more therapists are aware of their clients' negative thoughts, the more likely that clients will perceive the therapist interventions as helpful. These hidden thoughts, or "secrets," that clients leave unsaid have a profound effect on the therapeutic process.

> This study showed that over forty percent of the clients reported that they were keeping relevant secrets from their therapists. The most frequently listed reason was that they were afraid to express feelings. Other reasons that the clients mentioned were that they felt ashamed and embarrassed, did not want the therapist to see how little progress they had made, thought there was not enough time, would not tell anyone their secrets, or were not motivated to address the secrets. (p. 6)

Hidden messages include culture-specific information, both positive and negative, known to the client and expressed through conscious thoughts that the client is thinking but not saying. Though the anticounselor negative voices always seem more obvious, the voice of a procounselor is also important to capturing cultural information embedded within the client. Often, the clients themselves might be unaware of these hidden messages. Hidden messages are more than self-talk, although self-talk is the most obvious example. Corsini (1987) defines *internalization* as "bringing some aspect of the external world into one's private mental life and having that internal representation of the external world exert an influence over one's thoughts and behavior" (p. 610).

SELF-TALK AND INTERNAL DIALOGUE IN THERAPY

Thompson and Nevile (1999) focus on the intrapersonal manifestations of racism such as "dysconscious racism," when "racism is perpetuated not merely by the absence of consciousness but by an impaired consciousness or distorted way of thinking about race" (p. 184). Also, "autocolonialization" provides an example of "internalizing inferiority beliefs that has not only existed for genera-tions but also influences the socialization of children" (p. 193). A third idea they explore is "false consciousness," holding beliefs that are not in one's personal or group interest. "Those described as having false consciousness justify the sys-tem and, thereby, provide legitimacy and support for existing social arrange-ments even at the expense of personal and group interest" (p. 194).

Even when clients cannot articulate their own negative thoughts, they readily admit to having them. Many of these thoughts are not rational and coherent self-statements, and clients may be less articulate in their emotional associations that include other forms of meaning and semantic structure. The hearing of voices for the ordinary individual is, of course, separate from the auditory hallucinations heard by a schizophrenic (Cohen & Green, 1995), and hearing voices is not necessarily an unhealthy phenomenon. Although men-tally ill persons sometimes hear voices, individuals who are not mentally ill also hear voices, including respected leaders and a great variety of the general public (Liester, 1996).

Self-statements influence behavior in the same way that statements by oth-ers do. Clients in therapy need to monitor their own thinking and interacting both with others and with themselves. This approach is particularly empha-sized in cognitive behavior change, in which clients are encouraged to change the "scripted nature" of their behavior (Meichenbaum, 1986). Rational Emo-tive Behavior Therapy (REBT) and Beck's Cognitive Therapy also assume that a client's disturbing emotions are the product of "wrong" thinking. Ellis (1987) teaches clients to challenge the assumptions, beliefs, and self-talk that lead them to self-defeating behaviors by identifying self-limiting or self-defeating internal dialogue. Some examples of self-defeating beliefs are as follows:

- I must always be loved and have the approval of people I care about.
- I must always be successful, talented, and competent.
- I must always have my own way, and my plans must always work out.
- People who hurt me are evil and must be punished.
- Nothing should go wrong, but if it does, there must be a quick and easy solution.
- Other people are responsible for my pain.
- My past actions and experiences will determine my future.

When these beliefs are violated, the client sees the consequences as a catastro-phe. Ellis helps clients replace these self-defeating "self-talk" beliefs with more adaptive thinking.

There are many similarities between Ellis's REBT and Meichenbaum's self-instructional training. Both emphasize the importance of self-statements and the quality of performance. But whereas Ellis emphasizes the modification of irrational and self-destructive ideas, self-instructional training puts more emphasis on constructing positive thoughts, and whereas REBT emphasizes the importance of rationality, self-instruction emphasizes constructive adaptiveness. REBT emphasizes the elimination of negative thoughts, whereas self-instruction emphasizes how individuals cope with those thoughts. Rational Emotive Behavioral Therapy is more direct and emphasizes confrontation to uncover irrational thinking, whereas Meichenbaum's self-instructional therapy focuses on increasing the clients' awareness of their self-talk so that they can change their own self-instructions through cognitive restructuring.

Self-instruction works best for acquiring practical coping skills for problems of impulsive or aggressive behavior, fear of taking tests, fear of public speaking, chronic pain, sports psychology, and a variety of phobias. Meichenbaum's (1986) self-instruction proceeds through several phases. In the first phase, the clients listen to their own typically negative self-statements and become sensitive to their own thinking. In the second phase, the client creates a new internal dialogue to find opportunities for adaptive functioning and new behavioral alternatives. In the third phase, the client learns new skills and benefits from hearing the new and more positive internal dialogue. Some examples of coping statements from the skill acquisition and rehearsal phase are as follows:

> How can I prepare for a stressor? What do I have to do? Can I develop a plan to deal with the stress? How can I confront and deal with what is stressing me? What are some ways I can handle a stressor? How can I meet this challenge? How can I cope with feeling overwhelmed? What can I do right now? How can I keep my fears in check? How can I make reinforcing self statements? How can I give myself credit? (Corey, 1996, p. 349)

Meichenbaum's work on self-talk began with schizophrenics and impulsive children and resulted in his model for self-instructional training.

> Self-instructional training is a technique in which clients learn to keep track of self-statements (what clients say to themselves) and to substitute more adaptive statements (such as, I know I can do this). They learn to make these adaptive statements through homework assignments and practice in nonstressful situations. (Capuzzi & Gross, 1995, p. 371)

Self-instruction training has been used alone and together with other therapies.

The world is as it is only because we tell ourselves that it is so as we talk with ourselves and maintain our world with our own internal talk. Meichenbaum (1977) described this inner resource in his earlier writings:

> In psychology, the term inner speech usually signifies soundless, mental speech, arising at the instant we think about something, plan or solve problems in our mind, recall books read or conversations heard, read and write silently. In all such instances we think and remember with the aid of words which we articulate to

ourselves. Inner speech is nothing but speech to oneself, or concealed verbalization, which is instrumental to the logical processing of sensory data, in their realization and comprehension within a definite system of concepts and judgments. The elements of inner speech are found in all our conscious perceptions, actions, and emotional experiences, where they manifest themselves as verbal sets, instructions to oneself, or as verbal interpretation of sensations and perceptions. (p. 12)

Aaron Beck (1967, 1996) described a "cognitive triad" made up of one's negative view of self, one's negative view of the world, and one's negative view of the future to describe the dynamics of depression. Beck developed his approach first with Kelly's personal constructs and then changed the label *constructs* to the term *schema* or *schemata* to describe cognitive structures that depressed people use to process information. Depressed people generate thoughts that cause them to be depressed, and then those depressing schemata generate even more depressing thoughts, making it difficult for people in depression to become well. Beck (1976) describes conditional rules formed from our early experiences and revised as we move through different experiences. These rules are often formed in absolute terms. They do not always require our self-awareness of them, but they shape how we screen, sort, integrate, and combine data from the world around us. Beck (1996) identifies three types of conditional rules: (a) negative rules (if I get close to others, they will reject me); (b) compensating rules (if I avoid others, I can avoid rejection); and (c) imperative rules (I must be perfect).

Wills and Sanders (1997) differentiate between rules and assumptions:

Rules generally operate without us being aware of them. We selectively pay attention to the world around us, screening, sorting, and integrating information according to our rules. Core beliefs, or schemata, are often expressed in absolute terms, such as I am a bad person, I'm a failure, I'm vulnerable or I'm worthless. . . . Assumptions, in contrast, are often conditional, if . . . then statements, developed to some extent in order to enable the individual to live with the particular beliefs. (p. 44)

If the person's life is going well, particular assumptions may never be triggered unless a crisis or event happens that gives rise to feelings of failure and the latent negative assumptions about self contributing toward that failure.

Beck's largest contribution to cognitive therapies and perhaps the best illustration of his theory is the depression inventory he designed. Beck's (1967) Depression Inventory is designed as a standard measure of depression based on attitudes of depressed patients. The inventory has 21 categories of symptoms and attitudes, which are as follows: (a) sadness, (b) pessimism, (c) sense of failure, (d) dissatisfaction, (e) guilt, (f) sense of punishment, (g) self-dislike, (h) self-accusations, (i) suicidal ideation, (j) crying spells, (k) irritability, (l) social withdrawal, (m) indecision, (n) distorted body image, (o) work inhibition, (p) sleep disturbance, (q) fatigability, (r) loss of appetite, (s) weight loss, (t) somatic preoccupation, and (u) loss of libido.

Other cognitive therapies (Wills & Sanders, 1997) also demonstrate how faulty reasoning results in cognitive distortions and ultimately disturbed behavior and/or emotions. Some of the criticisms of cognitive therapy have been that it is only useful in prescribed areas such as depression; it downplays or ignores emotion; it ignores real-life events and can be overconfrontational for vulnerable clients; its approaches do not take into account early experience and developmental issues; it downplays the importance of the therapeutic relationship; only the most intelligent patients will benefit from it; it does not look at important past events, such as in childhood; it is not suitable for people with long-term difficulties or disorders; and it tries to get people to accept difficulties simply through the power of positive thinking.

Wills and Sanders (1997) address each of these criticisms and myths about cognitive therapy in turn, demonstrating that they are misleading or false and citing empirical evidence to support cognitive therapies.

> Clients very rarely come into therapy asking for help with their negative thoughts. They come to therapy because they are feeling bad. Despite its focus on thinking, cognitive therapy is actually all about reaching and working with clients' salient feelings. Cognitions are emphasized because they can often provide the most direct and useful path to emotions and the easiest way to access the key and hot emotions connected to the client's difficulties. (p. 9)

Cognitive therapies look at the meaning the client is giving to situations, linking particular types of thoughts to particular emotions and behaviors.

Good cognitive therapy does not reduce the client's thinking to categorized irrational belief systems; rather, it tries to understand why that particular client appraises events in that particular way.

> The aim of cognitive therapy is to understand both the person's personal domain and his idiosyncratic way of appraising events. Whilst, on a simplistic level, a person's thoughts and emotions about an event may appear irrational, given his way of seeing the world, the response may be entirely rational. (Wills & Sanders, 1997, p. 11)

The aim of cognitive therapy techniques is to target and modify a client's belief system through understanding the client's conceptualization and understanding of that belief system, where it came from, and how it works.

Kanfer and Goldstein (1986) review the applications of self-instructional training to direct service in a sizable body of literature on how self-talk and private monologues influence performance on a great variety of tasks. Teaching clients to monitor and change their self-statements in stress-inoculation training and creativity training helped them manage stress more creatively in the future, and they spontaneously applied their training to a variety of personal and academic problems. Some of these self-statements in preparing for a stressor are as follows:

> What is it you have to do? You can develop a plan to deal with it. Just think about what you can do about it. That's better than getting anxious. No negative self-statements; just think rationally. Don't worry; worry won't help anything. Maybe what you think is anxiety is eagerness to confront the stressor. (p. 413)

Self-statements for confronting and handling a stressor might include the following:

> Just psych yourself up—you can meet this challenge. Reason your fear away. One step at a time; you can handle the situation. Don't think about fear; just think about what you have to do. Stay relevant. This anxiety is what the doctor said you would feel. It's a reminder to use your coping exercises. This tenseness can be an ally; a cue to cope. Relax: you're in control. Take a slow deep breath. Ah, good! (Kanfer & Goldstein, 1986, p. 413)

Statements for coping with the feeling of being overwhelmed include "When fear comes, just pause. Keep the focus on the present, what is it you have to do? Label your fear from 0 to 10 and watch it change. You should expect your fear to rise." (Kanfer & Goldstein, 1986, p. 413). Reinforcing self-statements include the following:

> It worked! You did it! Wait until you tell your therapist (or group) about this. It wasn't as bad as you expected. You made more out of your fear than it was worth. Your damn ideas—that's the problem. When you control them, you control your fear. It's getting better each time you use the procedures. You can be pleased with the progress you're making. You did it! (Kanfer & Goldstein, 1986, p. 413)

There is an expanding literature about self-talk as it relates to self-help and personal growth issues of clients. Siegrist (1995) reviews the literature on inner speech as a cognitive process to mediate self-conscious and inhibiting self-deception by mediating self-consciousness. Ickes (1988) has studied attributional styles and covert verbalizations of self-talk by depressed patients, suggesting that they have a tendency to interpret situations as evidence of their inadequacy, even when that response might be inappropriate. By magnifying their failures and minimizing favorable outcomes in their self-appraisals, and by making unfavorable social comparisons, they contribute to feelings of inferiority. Fuqua, Johnson, Anderson, and Newman (1984) point out that human cognition is a complex and elusive target for scientific assessment, but the increased tendency to test the role of cognition in counseling and training shows promise for the future.

Morin (1995) examined the characteristics of an effective internal dialogue for the mediation of self-awareness as a problem-solving task. Self-talk served to focus attention on the task, to foster constant self-evaluation, and to take the perspective of others. Morin (1993) suggests that two social mechanisms leading to self-awareness can be reproduced by self-talk. First, engaging in dialogues with oneself and fictitious persons permits the internalization of others' perspectives, and addressing comments to oneself about oneself as others might do leads to the acquisition of self-information. Second, self-observation is possible only when there is a distance between the individual and any potentially observable self-aspect, as through self-talk, which conveys self-information through words in a continuous communication loop.

Morin (1993) argues that acquiring self-information is a problem-solving task—not much different from any other problem-solving task—facilitated by self-talk. Self-talk develops a formulation of the data, analyzing the patterns and, through evaluation, the conclusions. Information about one's self, or self-awareness, occurs in self-talk by gathering self-information, taking the perspectives of significant others, attending to the content of one's self-talk, and drawing conclusions from these data.

> Many authors agree on the existence of at least four categories of self-verbalizations that help guide the process of problem-solving: (1) self verbalizations allowing the formulation of a precise definition of the problem . . . (2) self-verbalizations promoting an effective approach to the problem . . . (3) self-verbalizations helping the subject to focus the problem . . . (4) evaluative self-statements the subject uses to either pace himself or herself when a good solution is reached . . . or readjust his or her strategy when an error is made. (p. 47)

The same criteria we would use to evaluate the value of conversations with others apply to our conversations within ourselves. Effective self-talk will introduce a rich vocabulary, follow a disciplined structure, teach us something about ourselves that we did not previously know, and provide practical insights that have applications to problem solving. It is possible to either increase self-talk or lessen self-talk with a corresponding effect on one's self-consciousness. Morin (1995) suggests that too much or too little self-talk can lead to painful consequences:

> It appears difficult to find a psychological disorder that is not characterized by a heightened degree of self-focused attention. Depression, test anxiety, social anxiety and generalized anxiety, alcohol abuse and possibly schizophrenia, mania and psychopathy are accompanied by heightened self-consciousness. . . . More precisely, excessive self-consciousness could intensify negative affects, serve as a vulnerability factor by placing individuals at risk for the onset or prolonged maintenance of dysfunctions, or contribute to the constellation of variables that bring about dysfunctions. (p. 53)

A balance of self-attention seems to be required, neither too much nor too little, so that individuals are able to shift their focus outside of themselves when the situation demands or when the content of the self-talk is harmful. Both the quality and the quantity of the self-talk are essential to healthy functioning. By allowing ourselves to take the perspectives of others and seeing ourselves as others see us, self-talk becomes the foundation for a larger pyramid of communication networks.

Interpersonal communication builds on intrapersonal interaction. Group communication builds on both intrapersonal and interpersonal interactions. Organizational communication builds on the previous three, intrapersonal, interpersonal and group interaction. Societal communication . . . builds on intrapersonal, interpersonal, group and organizational interactions. (Kreps & Kunimoto, 1994, p. 13)

HOW SELF-TALK INFLUENCES THERAPY

The ability to control self-talk becomes an important therapeutic goal. The inclusion of negative thoughts increases suffering and limits goal-directed behavior, but guilt can also be caused by an individual's retreating from his or her goals or seeking gratification in fantasy. Elliot (1996) reviews the misconceptions of "anthetic therapy" based on the concept of an internal critic or internal voice that causes negative self-talk and dysfunctional behaviors through oppression by the inner critic. Fromm (1962) wrote of a social unconscious made up of repressed thoughts and messages that are destructive to society.

This perspective has been developed by Firestone (1997a, 1997b) into a therapy model based on the inner voice called *voice* therapy, based on guilt reactions mediated by an internal thought process. This inner voice is overwhelmingly negative, seeking to attack, punish, and destroy as an "antiself," antithetical to the survival of the self. This inner voice influences through being critical, destructive, punitive, and vengeful. These messages function in a "parental" role, incorporating real or imagined negative statements remembered from interactions with one's parents. Positive experiences are reframed in negative terms, and potentially intimate relationships are prevented or destroyed.

Firestone (1997a) describes his approach as separation theory.

I refer to my approach as Separation Theory because it focuses on breaking with parental introjects and moving toward individuation. The theoretical position represents an ultimate challenge to the defense system. It is my contention that psychological defenses are maladaptive because they cut deeply into an individual's life experience, and when they persist into adult life they eventually become the essential psychopathology. (p. 4)

Voice therapy involves separation from the addiction to internalized parental messages, contrasting fantasies of themselves being treated as objects by parents with goal-directed lifestyles. By bringing the internalized negative thoughts to awareness, the individual can confront alien components of his or her own internalized personality. Patients do this by verbalizing their negative thoughts toward themselves in the second person—"you" statements—as though they were talking to themselves rather than about themselves.

Firestone assumes that the negative events in one's life are not as punishing as the negative internal dialogues we generate when talking to ourselves about those events. Our ability to conceptualize or speak to ourselves as an object makes it possible to experience internalized thoughts through emotionally loaded statements. These voices are heard and yet they are fundamentally different from the hallucinated voices of a psychotic patient (Firestone, 1997b). The antiself system is the accumulation of negative thoughts or internalized cynical and hostile voices that have become an overlay of hostile negativity on personality. Voice therapy has been used both in crisis intervention, to reduce immediate threat, and in long-term treatment of suicidal patients, to prevent regression to severe depression.

Zastrow (1988) asserts that emotions and actions are caused by what individuals tell themselves about events through self-talk rather than by what really happens. By changing the self-talk, a person can change feelings and actions. Zastrow suggests that positive change through changing self-talk accounts for the effectiveness of client-centered behavior therapy and psychoanalysis. Phillips (1990) has also studied how "inner voices," as patterns of internal conversation in narrative form, influence self-concept. Ledermann (1996) describes this as *internal muzak,* as it influences intrapersonal relationships. What we say to ourselves affects our behavior.

An individual's perception of another's perception of him or her is a metaperception. The symbolic interactionists have contended that metaperceptions are based on social feedback, going outside the self, whereas social cognitivists say metaperceptions are formed by self-perception, going inward. Dyadic social experience includes a direct view of the self and a view of the other as well as a view of the other's view of the self. We not only look at ourselves but we look at others looking at us. According to Langer and Wurf's (1997) research,

> Results indicated that the feedback and the self are both important interactively: when the verbal element of the message is congruent with self conception non-verbal sensitivity occurs, and metaperceptions are based on both the verbal and non-verbal components; when the verbal element of the message is self-incongruent, the evaluative implications of the non-verbal feedback do not matter. (p. 2)

Research on assessing internal dialogue and self-statements in socially phobic or anxious clients is becoming more important in both clinical and research settings. Glass and Arnkoff (1997) review the literature on more than two dozen questionnaire methods to assess thoughts such as self-statements, automatic thoughts, or internal dialogue, looking at reliability and validity issues. Glass and Arnkoff (1994) review the literature on cognitive assessment techniques regarding social phobia and social anxiety with respect to their psychometric criteria, including the perspectives of content, criterion convergent, and discriminant validity. The findings tend to be critical of existing methods. One of the methods being used is the Positive Automatic Thoughts Questionnaire, designed to assess the frequency of positive self-statements with favorable reliability and validity data (Ingram, Kendall, Siegle, & Guarino, 1995). Another method is the thought-stopping procedure, used to interfere with thoughts running through the minds of clients that prevent them from changing negative behaviors.

> For example, thought stopping can be used with a client who thinks that she is too fat. She continues to imagine this troublesome thought running through her mind, and the counselor or therapist shouts, Stop! . . . The use of positive self-statements can go along with thought stopping. . . . The important point is that what clients tell themselves influences their feelings and behavior. (Capuzzi & Gross, 1995, p. 368)

Nutt-Williams and Hill (1990) demonstrated that self-talk was related to perceptions of therapy, so when therapists thought negatively about themselves, they perceived themselves as less helpful and perceived their clients as reacting more negatively. Self-talk provides a way to actively manipulate the environment, evaluate ourselves, find meaning, and direct our behavior accordingly. Self-evaluation both guides our behavior and provides motivation, but the connection continues to be ambiguous. Therapists do not always accurately perceive their clients' reactions, especially when those reactions are negative. This distortion may occur when clients hide their true reactions from the therapist. Another possibility is that therapists—particularly novice therapists—focus on their own self-talk rather than on their client's reactions. Therapists' self-talk might interfere with the ability to accurately decode a client's reactions or inflate the client's negative reactions. Therapists can use self-talk in therapy as a gauge for what is happening to the client as well as for recognizing and reorganizing their own perceptions and managing their anxiety. "Adequate management of both quantity and quality of self-talk may be crucial in allowing therapists to maintain an appropriate focus on clients" (Nutt-Williams & Hill, 1996, p. 176).

Effective counseling depends on the counselors' developing automatic and internalized facilitative behaviors sensitive to the power of their influence and involvement in counseling. Siegrist (1996), in researching whether self-consciousness affected the internal consistency of several scales, found support for the hypothesis that subjects high in private self-consciousness have an intensive and precise knowledge of themselves. Hiebert, Uhlemann, Marshall, and Lee (1988) examined how self-talk relates to anxiety levels in the performance of counseling in prepracticum settings. Neuman and Schwartz (1998) examined how the self-explanations people give themselves are positively associated with learning measures and found that only certain kinds of self-explanations improved problem solving. Patterson (1988) described automatic behaviors as draining minimal energy from our ability to attend and not interfering with our deliberate attentional thinking. Effortful operations, by contrast, require our full attention and detract from deliberate attentional thinking.

Automaticity has been identified as a condition that allows previously learned mental functioning to occur with minimal drain on our limited capacity attentional mechanism. It has been shown in many fields of endeavor from the physical to the highly theoretical that the more building-block steps that become automatic in the complex process, the more attentional capacity is freed for higher level functioning. (Patterson, 1988, p. 201)

Other therapies also acknowledge the importance of a client's internal dialogue. Gestalt "deluging" has helped clients explore mixed feelings in their thinking and decision making. This approach has worked best in counseling persons with self-defeating behaviors to keep the negative thoughts from controlling them. Clients develop internal monologues or "think out loud" to better understand how they function in stressful situations. In Gestalt therapy, people develop mental images about themselves as the "good me" and the "bad me." The "good me" resembles the positive internal messages of a procounselor. The "bad me" resembles the negative internal messages of an anticounselor. People have learned styles of selective inattention to develop inaccurate perceptions of reality according to these internalized personifications of themselves and others.

Psychodrama has adapted the alter-ego concept to the training of counselors through simulations and role playing. Janis and Mann (cited in Janis, 1982) describe the uses of psychodrama in education and counseling to change undesirable behaviors through "emotional role playing." One way of doing this is through taking on an "as if" role as a victim in a crisis, exploring the negative messages and perspectives that an anticounselor might otherwise make explicit. Another way is called "outcome psychodrama," in which clients project themselves into the future to articulate their worries, hopes, and unverbalized feelings and to better understand the potential consequences of their decisions.

Schwartz (1987) describes the application of multiple selves in family therapy to the notion of an "inner family" of competing and cooperating identities within the individual, drawing from advances in brain research and artificial intelligence. Schwartz hypothesizes our emotional lives as a relationship of "modular selves" with related feelings, expectations, and varieties of experiences.

> For example, have you ever become extremely sad or needy and begun behaving toward your partner in a way that you were sure was going to make things worse, but still felt unable to stop? Or felt as if something or someone had taken control of you? Or found yourself embroiled in an intense inner debate that you couldn't turn off no matter what? (p. 26)

The family metaphor is used constructively to describe our thinking.

> Internal relationships influence and are influenced by external family relation-ships. A parent's criticism to motivate you to work harder will stay with you, and you will use similar strategies to motivate yourself through self-talk. If you have such a critical, achievement-oriented sub-self, it is also likely that it will be critical not only of you but of others as well, your children for example. If this critical self takes over when you relate to your kids, it is likely that an internalized critical self will assume the task of motivating them as well, and, eventually, they will criticize their kids and so on. (Schwartz, 1987, p. 81)

Penn and Frankfurt (1994) apply the ideas of social constructionism to family therapy through monitoring perception and inner conversation. The therapeutic narrative includes the external and internal voices of the family and the thera-pists. They advocate "reframing" by bringing the individual's inner monologue into conversation with a more positive voice through therapy.

> The former monological experience becomes an internal dialogical experi-ence—talking with ourselves—and produces a change in our conversation with others. This we feel is the "stuff" of new narratives. Once this change has occurred, the new self/other perception travels back and forth from client to family member, and again, from family member to client, altering their language as it goes. (p. 218)

Penn and Frankfurt advocate adding writing to conversation in therapy. Writing slows down our thinking as each layer of our thought is added in a process in which the same experience will have many different meanings. Examples of writing letters to parents who have died are used to demonstrate the effective-ness of writing in therapy to capture the client's inner voices.

In the last few years, Michael White has developed a technique for "externalizing the problem" in family therapy (Tomm, 1989). The technique separates the problem from the personal identity of the patient, providing the patient with opportunities to take the initiative to escape from the problem's influence.

> In other words, the process of externalizing the problem is progressive. It is not a static reframe of the problem; it is a continuous process of co-constructing a new

reality in the ongoing therapeutic dissection of the problem, cutting it away from the patient's sense of self as a person. That is, there is a systematic separation of problematic attributes, ideas, assumptions, beliefs, habits, attitudes, and lifestyles from the patient's dominant identity. (p. 56)

Contrary to the conventional medical assumption that the mental disorder is in the person, externalizing the problem resists incorporating the problem into the patient's personal identity. The patient is responsible for recognizing his or her option of continuing to submit to the externalized problem or rejecting the problem's continued control. Elements of externalizing the problem are consistent with behavioral therapy and other approaches, but the focus here is on rebuilding a patient's identity at the same time. The externalizing of the problem in White's therapy resembles the role of the problem in the Triad Training Model discussed earlier.

ASSESSING THE EFFECTS OF INTERNAL DIALOGUE

The subjective nature of internal dialogue has made it difficult to measure in any objective protocol. Most of the measures of internal dialogue have been extrapolations and after-the-fact, self-reported explanations. These thought-listing and "thinking out loud" approaches have attempted to capture internal dialogue, after the fact, through secondary analysis. By that time, the person reporting earlier thoughts is already having second and third thoughts or internal dialogues, complicating the assessment process. The following chapter will report on attempts to measure internal dialogue in a variety of more conventional ways, demonstrating the strengths and weaknesses of these more conventional approaches. The chapter will also explore research on the Triad Training Model, in which the internal dialogue is presented through the continuous and immediate feedback from an anticounselor and/or a procounselor during the actual role-played interview. Although we are not yet able to measure internal dialogue, we are able to measure the effect of internal dialogue under different conditions, as with an emphasis on positive or negative messages. Although indications are that internal dialogue is important, we have not yet identified methods to accurately assess the different and precise ways in which it influences the counseling relationship.

Morran (1986) demonstrated "a positive relationship between higher quality clinical hypothesis formulation and higher levels of facilitative performance during counseling sessions" (p. 395). Traditional models of counselor training that focus on behavioral skills are expanded to accommodate the complex interrelationships between a counselor trainee's cognitive and behavioral processes. The techniques of self-control, self-instruction, and mental imagery are strategies to assess and measure a trainee's self-talk. Morran researched the level of task-facilitative self-talk, the level of task-distractive self-talk, and the quality of clinical hypothesis formation, expecting that self-talk would relate to the level of facilitative performance. Surprisingly, the research found a positive zero-order correlation between task-facilitative and task-distractive measures but a consistent positive relationship between the counselor's hypothesis formulation skills and facilitative performance. "This suggests, as one might expect, that it is not how much one self-talks, but the quality of the self-talk that counts" (p. 394).

Kline (1988) reviewed the literature on counselor trainee anxiety as influenced by self-talk through increasing the counselor's focus on self-evaluative thinking. By increasing the trainee's concentration on client verbalization and self-talk as part of skill acquisition, it was presumed that trainee anxiety would be diminished. Neck, Stewart, Crag, and Manz (1995) also examined the application of cognitive processes in the organizational behavior literature, applying thought self-leadership (TSL) to the performance appraisal process. TSL involves internal dialogue to gain purposive control of one's thoughts through self-talk, mental imagery, expressed beliefs, and assumptions. O'Quinn (1986) has also studied the relationship between counselor internal dialogue and counseling performance, emphasizing the importance of distracting versus facilitative self-talk. The importance of self-talk in relation to training is being discovered from a variety of disciplinary perspectives.

> Covert cognitive activity, or self-talk, has long been recognized as an important aspect of therapist training programs. Although several researchers have investigated therapist self-talk . . . minimal empirical evidence exists in the counseling literature that describes the relationship between therapists' in session cognition and therapy process variables. (Nutt-Williams & Hill, 1990, p. 170)

The early "think aloud" (Fuqua, Newman, Anderson, & Johnson, 1986) approaches to assessing internal dialogue were intrusive and time-consuming. It is clear that self-communication as a training objective is important, even if the way that self-communication operates is unclear. "Although popular cognitive-behavioral training strategies are being developed, their judicious application requires increased understanding. The principal and persisting barrier to understanding appears to be the lack of innovative and creative means for measuring internal dialogue" (Fuqua et al., 1986, pp. 170-171).

Several researchers have used thought-listing procedures to measure therapist self-talk (Nutt-Williams & Hill, 1996). This measuring involves listing the thoughts and having trained judges categorize or code the content of the self-talk. The most common global dimensions of self-talk measured in this way are the "focus," or the direction of the therapist's thoughts to self or other, and "affect," or the negative/positive valence of therapist self-talk. Most research has not correlated therapist self-talk to other process variables. Nutt-Williams and Hill (1996) found that trainee self-talk was related to perceptions of helpfulness and perceptions of client reactions. Strohmer, Moilapen, and Barry (1988) examined how individuals test hypotheses about themselves in counseling, presenting clients with observations contrary to the client's view of self. Individuals process this information through self-talk guided by a more complicated sense of consistency and self-schema, rather than simply personal hypothesis testing. Borders, Fong-Beyette, and Cron (1988) measured cognitive processes, underlying skill acquisition, and performance among counseling students, suggesting that beginning counseling students may have few intentional or self-instructive thoughts during a session and that research on the cognitive process requires a more complete contextual account through open-ended response formats, rather than studying isolated cognitions out of their context.

Kendall, Howard, Dennis, and Hays (1989) studied self-referent speech and psychopathology related to positive and negative thinking. They used a self-statement inventory and discovered that introducing positive items made a significant difference in the self-talk of subjects. Siegrist (1995) also developed a questionnaire to measure the extent of inner speech about self and discovered a correlation between depression and public self-consciousness; measures of depression did not correlate significantly with private self-consciousness, although there was significance between self-deception and depression. Hines, Stockton, and Morran (1995) have studied self-talk among group therapists. Although differences in skill development from novice to experienced counselors are complicated, some of this difference seems to relate to self-talk.

CONCLUSION

Internal dialogue in therapy is not only important for the counselor; it provides access to the clients' thinking about themselves and the reason for their being in counseling in the first place. Self-statements influence behavior in specific ways, demonstrated by Meichenbaum, Ellis, Beck, and other well-known therapists.

A variety of strategies are available for incorporating internal dialogue into the direct-service therapy process. Of these approaches, self-instruction is probably the best known, but others such as structured learning are available as well. The positive effects of including attention to self-talk in the counseling process are clearly documented and are adaptable to a variety of therapy styles.

Examples of using internal dialogue through self-instruction, psychodrama, and other conventional therapy approaches are widely available. Specific ways of incorporating internal dialogue into the therapy process are also well defined as part of counseling. The advantages of including internal dialogue are clearly important. The notion of multiple selves as a kind of "inner family" is useful when applied to family therapy and systems theory. This family metaphor provides a useful research link on how internal dialogue applies to direct service and to training.

PART II

The Triad Training Model

The second section of three chapters explains the Triad Training Model as a means of getting access to the internal dialogue of a culturally different client. The first chapter will look at hearing the hidden messages in counseling—particularly in multicultural counseling—through a procounselor and an anticounselor matched with a coached client. The second chapter will examine the training implications of hidden messages in counseling, again providing examples of how the Triad Training Model was used in training. The third chapter will discuss research on the Triad Training Model as it relates to the three-stage multicultural competency development from *awareness* to *knowledge* to *skill*. The combined effect of these three chapters is to explain the Triad Training Model and describe its potential usefulness in counselor education and training.

5

Positive and Negative Internal Dialogue in Counseling

One characteristic of highly functioning counselors is the ability to take multiple perspectives, organizing a wide range of facts, factors, and interacting variables and then synthesizing these data in an integrated pattern to better understand the complex situation in which counseling occurs. As the counselor collects information about the client, analyzes alternative explanations, formulates viable hypotheses, and then selects appropriate intervention strategies, being able to take multiple perspectives becomes an important cognitive skill. Although most of the counselor training literature emphasizes performance skills such as empathy, the research literature documents cognitive skills as equally if not more important in developing good counselors (Fuqua, Johnson, Anderson, & Newman, 1984). Monitoring multiple perspectives is especially important in multicultural counseling interviews.

Multicultural counselors need to understand (a) the explicit verbal exchange between the counselor and the client, (b) the counselor's own internal dialogue, and (c) the client's internal dialogue. The more culturally different the counselor and client are from each other, the more difficult it will be to understand the client's internal dialogue. The positive and the negative messages will be hidden from the counselor. It is a fair assumption, however, that part of the client's internal dialogue will be negative and part will be positive.

One approach to training multicultural counselors is to match a coached client with two other culturally similar persons—one as a procounselor emphasizing the positive and one as an anticounselor emphasizing the negative side of what the client is thinking but not saying. The culturally different counselor can hear both the positive and the negative sides of the client's internal dialogue in a role-played interview by listening to all three of the other participants.

THE BALANCE OF POSITIVE AND
NEGATIVE THINKING

Little is known about the cognitive process of self-awareness and self-consciousness. We have reviewed the literature on how inner speech mediates information about one's self and the external environment in ways that differ from external speech. Self-verbalization was formerly considered to be non-functional and a sign of immaturity, but with a better understanding of the link between inner speech and self-awareness, it is being given more importance.

> Self-awareness theory views conscious attention as dichotomous: attention is directed either towards the self or to the environment. High self-awareness means that for a relatively great part of the time a person focuses on aspects of the self. Not only the situation, but also personal disposition influences the focus of attention. (Siegrist, 1995, p. 259)

Inner speech mediates self-consciousness, but we are not sure how this is done. It appears that the same language that mediates social interaction in social relationships also mediates cognitive activity within individuals. This inner or private speech is typically expressed as a dialogue with two sides, identities, or interactors participating, one typically in a positive role and the other typically in a negative role. The inner voices are not always evenly or equally balanced in terms of the positive and negative messages.

More recent research on internal dialogue suggests that it is asymmetrical. "Furthermore, this research reveals an asymmetry between positive and negative coping thoughts, whereby negative thoughts have greater functional impact and are more likely to change as a result of therapy" (Schwartz, 1986, p. 591). Research on positive and negative internal dialogue suggests that it is characterized by a 1.7 to 1 ratio of (less) positive to (more) negative self-statements for individuals from functional groups and of a ratio of approximately 1 to 1 for individuals from mildly dysfunctional groups. Highly assertive subjects had more positive than negative thoughts, whereas low assertives had about the same number of positive and negative thoughts (Schwartz, 1986).

Schwartz and Garamoni (1989) discuss what has been called the "golden section proportion," researched extensively by personal construct psychologists. The "golden section" is defined as the ratio that is obtained between positive and negative when the smaller is to the larger as the larger is to the whole in a relationship described as $a/b = b/(a + b)$.

> Specifically, the model proposes that functionally optimal states of mind consist of a precise balance of positive and negative cognitions and/or affects, closely approximating the gold section proportion of .618. Such asymmetrically balanced cognitive/affective structures render negative events and cognitions maximally salient and are therefore optimally suited for coping with stress. (p. 272)

These asymmetrical patterns of positive and negative thinking have been confirmed by research using inventories, thought-listing, talking-aloud, and thought-sampling methods.

> In sum, it appears that negative events and cognitions are more salient and make a greater impact than positive ones—that negative thoughts and feelings, relative to positive, may be more central to adaptation. Perhaps psychology's focus on illness rather than health, or the well-known difficulties of defining health in ways other than the absence of illness, can be better understood in terms of this. (Schwartz, 1986, p. 599)

Our internal dialogue is important to our psychological health. If opposing ideas provide a dialogical basis for thinking, then even optimal thinking will include both positive and negative ideas. The asymmetry of positive and negative thinking also suggests that focusing on negative or nonproductive thoughts by a client may be important and require more than merely building positive perspectives in therapy or training. The elimination of negative thinking by itself is no more likely to succeed than increasing positive thinking. The ideal relationship of positive and negative thinking is in this asymmetrical balance.

> In terms of treatment, it may be more critical to eliminate these negative thoughts than to establish positive ones, at least as the *final end point* of treatment. However, research on the process of therapeutic change over time that assesses both positive and negative cognitions may lead to the finding that a period of positive coping thought in the internal dialogue is necessary to facilitate short-term change until these newly acquired patterns of thinking, feeling and acting are integrated into new self structures. (Schwartz, 1986, p. 602)

Schwartz and Garamoni (1989) discuss the importance of balancing the positive and negative sides of a person's internal dialogue in studying positive and negative states of mind, in research on the golden section hypothesis, in information theory, in intrapersonal communication, and in cybernetic self-regulation. "Considering both positive and negative dimensions simultaneously and framing the polarity idea in terms of the *balance* between the opposing poles represents an integrative step with potential heuristic value" (p. 272).

The polarity of cognitive balance versus imbalance is a measurably appealing goal for counseling. Rather than focus only on increasing positive coping cognition or reducing negative dysfunctional cognitions, counselors can conceptualize counseling as striving toward a healthy balance of positive and negative thoughts, even though that balance is asymmetrical. Negative cognition is both necessary and inevitable, just as excessive positive cognition can be undesirable. The task of counselors is to help clients monitor and modify their own positive and negative thinking to achieve a balance between positive and negative elements in their lives.

In assertiveness problems, for example, clients can conceptualize their problem along a bipolar dimension anchored by the extreme (undesirable) states of submissiveness and aggressiveness, with appropriate assertiveness representing the balanced mean. Similarly, problems of self-esteem can be viewed along a continuum anchored by the extremes of self-hatred and self-inflation, with true self-esteem representing the balanced state. (Schwartz & Garamoni, 1989, p. 292)

Counseling is the process of gradual oscillation between extremes until a balance is established in which clients can reduce dependence on their problem and experiment with alternative ways of thinking, feeling, and behaving.

The predominant training methods discussed in the following chapters will include dyadic cross-cultural interviews with culturally different clients using techniques developed by Kagan (1975). The methods used will be Interpersonal Process Recall and Pedersen's Triad Training Model, with cross-cultural interviews with a coached client-anticounselor-procounselor team from the same culture and simulated debriefing by the project staff.

INTERPERSONAL PROCESS RECALL

Interpersonal Process Recall (IPR) is a technique developed by Norman Kagan (1975) that uses videotaped playback of live interviews to help the trainee recall and describe covert actions (thoughts, wishes, feelings, fears, etc.) as well as the more overt and obvious actions on the television monitor. The technique assumes the following:

1. The best authority on an individual's awareness is the individual himself or herself.
2. An individual can readily describe in detail his or her internal awareness better than any outside expert when given the chance in a secure learning environment conducive to self-disclosure.
3. Finding one's own words to label one's own experience is a critical step toward ownership of oneself.
4. Being present to oneself facilitates being present to others.

Participants videotape themselves interviewing and being interviewed about some real personal concern with a person from another culture. Each participant then reviews the tape and, with the help of an "inquirer," is helped to recall his or her private experiences and verbally describe them. The participant learns (a) to understand what the other person was saying, (b) to recognize and label the effect another person was having on him or her, and (c) to share the understanding developed with those one is communicating with when appropriate.

The inquirer role in debriefing with IPR is based on the Socratic method in which questions are posed to stimulate learning. The inquirer acts as a third party to the counselor and client, asking open-ended questions and helping examine reactions that occur during the videotaped counseling session, particularly related to the internal dialogue of the counselor and client. Initially, IPR was used to train supervisors, mental health workers, teachers, physicians, and others. Later, IPR was used for client growth in therapy. Kagan (cited in Kagan & McQuellon, 1981) makes explicit the assumptions of IPR:

1. We think faster than we talk.
2. As we talk, we think things that are quite different from what we are verbalizing.
3. Sometimes we like what people say, and other times we do not. Sometimes others seem to understand us better than other times.
4. We sometimes want people to think about us differently than they actually do.
5. It is hard for an individual to accurately recall what he or she was thinking in an interview without seeing a videotape of the actual interview. The core of IPR is the immediate replay of a counseling session with the facilitation of a skilled inquirer.

Kagan and Schneider (1975) also developed an Affective Sensitivity Scale in which trainees viewed 14 short situations of role-played encounters between two or more individuals and were then asked to identify what feelings the people had toward themselves and toward the other persons. This Affective Sensitivity Training provides a variation of Kagan's IPR for getting access to the culturally different client's hidden messages in counseling. After viewing each scene, the trainees were given a list of items and were asked how they thought the person in the scene would respond if they were completely open and honest with themselves and could identify their real feelings. The example given to illustrate one such scene was as follows:

Scene AX (18 seconds long)

> *Situation:* Teacher and students in a class discussing vocational planning

Opening Statement:

> *Teacher:* "Is there anyone who knows the answer?"

Closing statement:

> *Teacher:* "You look pretty upset."

Item 1. What do you think the student is really saying to himself at this point?

A. This exploring of my feelings is good. It makes me feel good.
B. I feel very sad and unhappy.
C. I'm groping and confused; I can't bring it all together.
D. Upset. You don't know the half of it!

After viewing the scene, the trainee would read the five statements and decide which one best states what the client and/or interviewer would say about their own feelings after viewing the same scene. The students were given 30 seconds to answer each item before being presented with a new item. Generally, there were two or three items per scene, so the trainee had from 60 to 90 seconds to respond to the items of each scene before moving on to the next one. The training package contains 14 scenes and 65 items, with five choices for each item.

Kagan and McQuellon (1981) describe the "heart of the method" of IPR to be recalling thoughts, feelings, intentions, and images that occur in an interaction through debriefing. Kagan and McQuellon trace their model of self-exploration back to the early experimentalist psychologists who, like Wilhelm Wundt and other introspectionists, observed that, in recalling specific events, many events were hidden from others and even from one's self. With the increased use of technology through tape recording and videotaping, self-confrontation techniques became increasingly more popular.

> The Interpersonal Process Recall method was developed by Kagan et al. (1967) and Kagan and Schauble (1969) following Kagan's observation in 1961 that viewing a videotape playback with the help of a probing, nonevaluative inquirer, who allowed the viewer full responsibility for determining when the tape would be stopped, provided a powerful stimulus for self-examination and change. (p. 444)

IPR was first used in supervisory sessions, but it soon became used by mental health workers, teachers, physicians, and many other professional caregivers. The largest problem has been reliable replication of the IPR model, especially in the inquirer role. This resulted in a standardized packaging of the model in seven basic units: elements of effective communications, affect simulation, interviewer recall, in-depth study of the inquirer role, client's recall, mutual recall session, and a theory discussion. Each of these packages attempts to identify hidden messages.

> As people interact they sense each other on many levels, but they label or acknowledge only a very limited range of what they send or perceive. This is a part of all human interactions and serves to reduce the level of genuine intimacy. (Kagan & McQuellon, 1981, p. 447)

One adaptation of IPR is mutual recall by both the client and the counselor as they review portions of their videotaped interactions.

> In mutual recall both client and counselor tell each other and the inquirer of their covert processes in the recorded session, and behavioral rehearsal of immediate intimate exchange can also occur with client and counselor given practice at talking about their relationship. Both then become more like participant-observers of their own interaction—stepping back from the immediacy of their interaction and replaying the videotape in their head. (Kagan & McQuellon, 1981, p. 449)

The central figure in IPR is the inquirer, whose role is to facilitate stimulated recall and self-analysis. At some points, the counselor or client may act as his or her own inquirer; they pose a question to themselves and then answer that question. The inquirer serves to debrief the videotaped interview between the client and counselor, with the client and/or counselor being the primary authority on the hidden messages in that interview. The hidden messages are frequently censored from one's memory of the interview for a variety of adaptive purposes. The inquirer helps make those hidden messages explicit when that becomes the more adaptive alternative.

IPR has been used effectively for improving human interaction by stimulating the accurate recall of otherwise hidden messages. IPR assumes a conflict between, first, the universal need for interpersonal stimulation and, second, the learned fear of intimate relationships. The resulting dynamic is important to the psychological analysis of human behavior so that participants become more aware of their own hidden messages and the positive and/or negative hidden messages of others.

Kagan and Kagan (1990) describe more recent research and training activities using IPR that further validate this approach for training counselors and others. IPR was developed into a sequential model based on counselor developmental tasks.

> Our initial training theory postulated the following three stages: (a) counselor recalled study of self in interaction with clients, based on the observation that all counselors, regardless of background or culture, (b) possess encyclopedic knowledge of human interaction of which they are only vaguely aware but which can become the counseling process to help counselors understand the unique as well as generalizable client aspirations, satisfactions, frustrations, and learning so that counselors learn about their clients from their clients' recall; and (c) the study of and practice in making explicit the mutual impact of counselor on client, especially the meta-communication between them. (p. 437)

IPR demonstrates the practical utility of internal dialogue to facilitate individual behavior change.

THE TRIAD TRAINING MODEL

Although we cannot know the client's internal dialogue exactly, we can assume that some of these messages are "negative," or *anticounselor,* in their orientation while other messages are positive, or *procounselor,* in their orientation. The Triad Training Model is a training model for simulated cross-cultural interviews between a culturally different counselor and a culturally matched team, which includes a coached client, anticounselor, and procounselor (Pedersen, 1968, 1972a, 1972b, 1972c, 1972d, 1973a, 1973b, 1973c, 1974a, 1974b, 1975, 1976a, 1976b, 1976c, 1977, 1979). The anticounselor seeks to explicate the negative messages a client from that culture might be thinking but not saying, whereas a procounselor seeks to explicate the positive messages in the client's mind. Though either an anticounselor or a procounselor may be used without the other, their combined influence is to "hear" the client's internal dialogue "hidden messages" in both their positive and negative aspects. The procounselor and anticounselor provide *continuous, direct,* and *immediate* feedback on the counseling process to both the client and the counselor. Many of the sources of resistance to counseling across cultures consequently become explicit and articulate, even to a culturally different counselor.

The reader should be able to try the model out based on the instructions in these chapters and determine the model's usefulness in local settings. Local resource persons can be trained as client-anticounselor-procounselor teams to provide training resources without bringing in outside experts to the unit or agency. Additional data on the Triad Training Model are being collected to determine its specific strengths and weaknesses in a variety of settings.

The Triad Training Model simulates a force field of positive and negative factors, from the client's viewpoint, in the polarized roles of the procounselor and anticounselor, who make explicit the client's positive and negative internal dialogue. The Triad Training Model seems to work best when the following conditions apply:

1. There needs to be both positive and negative feedback to the counselor during the interview.
2. The simulated interview needs to reflect actual events in realistic ways.
3. The simulated interview needs to occur under conditions that the counselor considers "safe."
4. Procounselors and anticounselors need to be carefully trained to be effective.
5. The feedback to the counselor and client needs to be immediate and explicit during the actual interview.
6. The resource persons need to be articulate as well as authentic to the client's background.
7. The counselor needs to learn how to focus on the client while listening to the anticounselor and the procounselor at the same time.
8. The interview works best when it is spontaneous and not scripted.
9. The debriefing is much more effective if the interaction is videotaped.
10. The actual simulated interview should be brief (8-10 minutes) to avoid overwhelming the counselor with information during or after the interview.

In describing the Triad Training Model, it is important to understand the roles of the procounselor and the anticounselor. The anticounselor is deliberately subversive in attempting to exaggerate mistakes made by the counselor during the interview. The counselor and anticounselor are pulling in opposite directions, with the client judging which is "more right." There are several potential advantages of including an anticounselor in the simulation:

- The anticounselor forces the counselor to be more aware of the client's perspective.
- The anticounselor articulates the negative, embarrassing, and impolite comments that a client might not otherwise say.
- The anticounselor forces the counselor to examine his or her own defensiveness.
- The anticounselor points out a counselor's inappropriate interventions immediately, while the counselor still has time to recover.
- The anticounselor's attempts to distract the counselor trains the counselor to focus more intently on the client.

There are several things that an anticounselor might do in the interview to articulate the negative aspects of a client's internal dialogue. The anticounselor can build on positive aspects of the problem and the client's ambivalence; distract or sidetrack the counselor, attempting to keep the conversation superficial; attempt to obstruct communication between the counselor and client, physically and psychologically; annoy the counselor, forcing the counselor to deal with defensive reactions; exaggerate differences between the counselor and client to drive them further apart; demand immediate and observable results from counseling; communicate privately with the client; identify scapegoats to encourage the counselor's and client's unrealistic perspectives; and attack the counselor's credibility and request that someone more expert be brought in.

These hidden messages of a client's negative internal dialogue are seldom addressed directly in counselor training. The Triad Training Model encourages the direct examination of these hidden negative messages, which a client, especially a culturally different client, does or might otherwise know. This helps the counselor develop skills for dealing with those negative messages during the actual interview process.

The procounselor, on the other hand, attempts to articulate the hidden positive messages that might also be included in a client's internal dialogue. The culturally similar procounselor helps both the counselor and client articulate the counseling process as a potentially helpful activity. The procounselor functions as a facilitator for the counselor's effective responses. The culturally similar procounselor understands the client better than the culturally different counselor and is thus able to provide relevant background information to the counselor during the interview. The procounselor is not a cotherapist but an intermediate resource person who can guide the counselor by suggesting specific strategies and information that the client might otherwise be reluctant to volunteer. In these ways, the procounselor can reinforce the counselor's more successful strategies both verbally and nonverbally.

There are several advantages contributed by the procounselor in the simulated counseling interview:

- The procounselor is a resource person to consult when the counselor is confused or in need of support.
- The procounselor makes information about the client explicit, which might facilitate the counselor's success.
- The procounselor provides a partner for the counselor to work with, rather than the counselor's having to work on the problem alone.
- The procounselor helps the counselor stay on track and avoid sensitive issues that might increase client resistance.
- The procounselor provides beneficial feedback to the counselor to avoid mistakes and build on successful strategies.

The procounselor is attempting to build on positive and constructive aspects of the counseling interview through encouragement and support to the counselor, who may feel under attack by the anticounselor. There are several ways the procounselor might provide that support. The procounselor can restate or reframe in a positive fashion what either the client or counselor said; relate client or counselor statements to the basic underlying problem, keeping things on track; offer approval or reinforcement to the client or the counselor when he or she is cooperating; reinforce and emphasize important insights that need to be discussed and expanded; reinforce client statements as the client becomes more cooperative in the interview; and suggest alternative strategies to the counselor when necessary.

ADVANTAGES OF THE TRIAD TRAINING MODEL

The Triad Training Model lends itself to training classroom-sized groups. Each three-person resource team is matched with a counselor trainee or a small group of 8 to 10 trainees who share the role of counselor. A 10-minute simulated interview is followed by about 10 minutes of debriefing (out of role) with the counselor trainee and the resource persons. Then the resource team moves to another group, and a different resource team takes over. The culture-centered counseling skill requires the ability to monitor the client's positive and negative internal dialogue at the same time to better hear both the positive and negative hidden messages.

The Triad Training Model offers numerous advantages that complement other training models that, although not supported at this point by research evidence, suggest an accommodation of counseling technique and social psychological theory:

- The role-play interaction provides an opportunity for persons from different ethnic or cultural groups to interact under controlled conditions for the accomplishment of limited training goals, to their mutual advantage.
- The role-play interaction provides an appropriate opportunity for persons from different cultural groups to teach one another about the implications of cultural

values for counseling in a setting that will minimize the dangers of either party becoming overly defensive or threatened.

- The application of social psychology research on triads to the roles of the problem, counselor, and counselee in a balance of power and resistance provides a previously unexplored model for charting the counseling process.

- Introducing the anticounselor and procounselor roles provides an opportunity for counselor trainees to empathize with the problem as more than a diffuse abstraction, resulting in a more articulate understanding of the client's problem in its cultural aspects.

- Introducing the anticounselor and procounselor roles provides an explicit modeling of negative feedback that serves to clarify specific sources of resistance in the verbal and nonverbal responses of the counselee.

- Inappropriate counselor intervention is immediately and obviously apparent in the metaphorical contest between the counselor, procounselor, and anticounselor, particularly when a counselor's mistake damages the counseling relationship.

- Videotaped simulations of the exchange between counselor, client, procounselor, and anticounselor provide material that can be used in counselor education to illustrate specific ways in which cultural differences affect counseling.

- Having been exposed to the effect of cultural differences in role play, counselor trainees should be able to generalize from these experiences to increase their expertise for dealing with similar problems later as counselors.

- A careful analysis of research data and transcripts of the interaction will identify implicit as well as explicit—inadvertent as well as deliberate—cultural bias in both the definition of problems and the identification of specific problems in some cross-cultural situations.

- The separation of individual differences from patterned or cultural differences can be taught as a skill necessary to cross-cultural counseling through analysis of the arguments and conflict in the three-way interaction.

- Counselor trainees will be able to rehearse the use of their most immediately available resource for learning about cross-cultural counseling by directly involving members of their own "target audience," such as potential counselees from other cultures, rather than learning about them indirectly through abstract theories about those populations.

- Cultural differences tend to exaggerate and magnify the likelihood of inappropriate counseling interventions. Providing immediate feedback to trainees regarding cultural differences and hidden messages of inadequacy that might otherwise be unnoticed creates opportunities for counselors to intervene more appropriately.

- The simulation of coalition power relationships in counseling may stimulate experimental modes of viewing the counseling relationship to be inevitably cross-cultural in the separation of culturally defined roles as "counselor" and as "counselee."

- If videotaping the cross-cultural counseling interview proves effective as a mode of counselor training, it would provide a supplementary specialization to more traditional programs of counselor education.

- The resources for rehearsing four-way interaction are readily available in every multicultural setting once the basic skills of the "anticounselor" and "procounselor" are learned through modeling demonstration videotapes and studying the transcripts.

- The model provides for a "mutuality" in which potential clients from other cultures have a chance to educate the counselors who will be working with them in a balanced exchange of services.

- Making explicit the procounselor's positive and the anticounselor's negative hidden messages allows a counselee to move more rapidly toward honest feedback, thereby accelerating the transition in early counseling sessions from "rapport building" to "problem solving."

- An experimental ratio of relationships is provided to suggest how changes in each of the four participant roles affect the other.

- An experimental structure is provided to interpret the client's hidden messages in terms of appropriate interventions by the counselor, coordinated to the changing equilibrium of power in counseling.

- The eclectic application of theoretical approaches is suggested for adjusting power influence to nurture a client-counselor coalition in the immediate context of changing a counseling relationship without being tied to any one theoretical technique.

- The effects of counseling practice toward an ultimate goal are described in a way that enables empirical instrumentation to evaluate the model's effectiveness to specific conditions.

- The active and complex influence of problematic aspects in the environment is more clearly recognized in the ways they affect counseling.

- Counseling goals can be behaviorally defined in terms of liberation or increased autonomy rather than merely accommodation.

- The conceptual model lends itself to simulation as a training technique for cross-cultural counselor education.

- The model incorporates "anticounselor" and "procounselor" roles as a counterbalance of hidden messages in counseling.

- The environmental context is expressed in the interview with all its complex influences, where rewards and punishments administered through the environment tend to reinforce appropriate and/or inappropriate client behaviors.

- The problem is recognized as functioning as the dispenser of reinforcers, much in the same way that the environment would in real-life situations.

CONCLUSION

If we assume that our internal dialogue mediates our understanding or comprehension of the outside world, then the more similar the client and counselor are, the more likely that each will be able to anticipate accurately the other's hidden messages through internal dialogue. And the more sociocultural differences there are, the more difficult it will be to accurately anticipate what the culturally different client is thinking but not saying.

Although we know that part of what the client is thinking is negative and part is positive, there are indications that a greater proportion of our thinking tends to be negative, resulting in an asymmetrical balance. There are several ways to train counselors to hear their culturally different clients. IPR is offered as a popular method in which an inquirer debriefs the client and counselor after a videotaped interview to help them clarify their thoughts to one another. The Triad Training Model is another method in which the immediate and continuous debriefing occurs during the role-played interview itself. Some of the advantages and assumptions of both methods are reviewed.

The primary emphasis of the following chapters will focus on the Triad Training Model as a means of learning to hear what culturally different clients are thinking but not saying. Though the Triad Training Model is used exclusively in training, variations of that model for use in direct service will also be presented.

6

Training Implications of Hidden Messages

Counseling behavior is a function of skill and perception, requiring that training strategies account for increasing the trainee's conceptual development. Trainees early in the training procedure tend to use more directive approaches, whereas those later in training tend to respond to client feelings and convey an awareness of or sensitivity to the client's perspective in terms of core, rather than peripheral, concerns so that the client can explore feelings and attitudes through open-ended questions (Lutwak & Hennessey, 1982). Hutchins and Vaught (1997) apply a TFA (thinking, feeling, acting) framework to help students integrate diverse techniques in counseling. Klein (1996) did his dissertation on the relationship of counselor trainee internal dialogue, self-efficacy, and hypothesis formation to therapeutic performance.

Trainees with more highly developed conceptual skills are better able to respond to complex affect than are trainees with lower-level conceptual skills (Kimberlin & Friesen, 1980). The problem has been the measurement of conceptual skills used for internal dialogue.

> The finding that internal dialogue . . . is strongly related to anxiety and moderately related to certain personality dimensions raises questions regarding the independence of internal dialogue from personality. In fact, it seems possible that individuals develop characteristic internal dialogue patterns as a cognitive mechanism for compensating for personality predispositions. Consequently, it may not be possible, or even desirable to measure internal dialogue independent of predisposing personality factors. (p. 11)

The Triad Training Model seeks to combine complicated situational and personality factors in a comprehensive analysis of otherwise hidden messages.

THE IMPORTANCE OF COGNITION IN
COUNSELOR TRAINING

The use of mental simulations helps to make otherwise ambiguous and abstract cognitive events seem more real. As trainees run through these events in their minds, those thoughts become real.

> Mental simulation is the imitative representation of some event or series of events. It may involve the replay of events that have already happened, such as running back through an argument one had with a colleague to figure out where the conversation went wrong. It may involve the cognitive construction of hypothetical scenarios, such as deciding how to confront a procrastinating graduate student. It can involve fantasies, such as the imagined sexual exploits that often lull people to sleep, and it can involve mixtures of real and hypothetical events, such as replaying an argument and inserting what you should have said into the dialogue. (Taylor, Pham, Rivkin, & Armor, 1998, p. 430)

In training, these mental simulations are useful as problem-solving activities, almost like playing a videotape inside one's head with representations being viewed, replayed, dubbed, and even erased as they describe social settings, roles, and specific people. Mental simulations resemble real-world simulations—with a sequence of interdependent actions—allowing the trainee to develop and rehearse a plan of action.

> A major consequence of mental simulation is the evocation of emotional states and their potential control. Imagining a scenario does not produce a dry cognitive representation but rather evokes emotions, often strong ones. . . . An important, and we would argue vital, function of simulations is that they produce links to action by virtue of the self-regulatory activities they evoke. (Taylor et al., 1998, p. 431)

A number of researchers and theorists in the counselor training and supervision field have recommended more emphasis on cognitive processes in counselor training. "However, a review of the counselor training literature indicates that no models currently exist that focus specifically on methods of facilitating trainee acquisition of cognitive skills" (Morran, Kurpius, Brack, & Brack, 1995, p. 384). Morran et al. (1995) describe a cognitive skills model for counselor training emphasizing attending to and seeking information, forming hypotheses and conceptual models, and promoting intervention planning for self-instruction. In a cognitive skills approach, the counselor learns to purposefully direct thoughts toward gathering information and filling in gaps as an active and creative process. New data about both the counselor and client must relate to the ongoing counseling process as a continuous process, sorting out what is relevant from what is irrelevant. These new data are then matched to what is already known, and new perspectives emerge.

Studies of hypothesizing and conceptualizing skills have focused on hypothesis testing, with less attention on how those hypotheses are formulated.

> The cognitive skills related to hypothesizing and conceptualizing include the self-instructional process of directing oneself to (a) consider the possible causal relationships between observed or reported client behaviors, inferred internal characteristics of the client, and client environmental factors; (b) formulate multiple hypotheses to tentatively explain the relationship of these factors to each other; (c) formulate questions or strategies to test and evaluate each hypothesis; (d) discard or tentatively accept hypotheses on the basis of testing evidence; and (e) integrate viable hypotheses to form comprehensive conceptual models of the client. (Morran et al., 1995, p. 386)

Kurpius, Benjamin, and Morran (1985) examined the effects of teaching counselor trainees a self-instruction process strategy, versus teaching knowledge about clinical hypothesis, to increase the trainees' ability more effectively. Trainees were asked to list all the thoughts that had occurred to them immediately after each interview. Thought-listing results demonstrated an interaction between the type of training condition and the level of the counselor trainee. Self-instruction elicited significantly more criterion-related thoughts, especially when combined with a knowledge base of clinical hypothesis formulation. Research on counselor trainees has demonstrated that internal dialogue enhanced clinical hypothesis formulation skills (Kurpius et al., 1985) and was facilitative of training (Fuqua, Newman, Anderson, & Johnson, 1986), and thought listing improved the functioning of counselor supervisors (Rozecki, 1994). Spice (1982) demonstrated how thought selection, self-suggestion, belief development, affirmation, self-talk, internal dialogue, and possibility thinking clarify how our thoughts about ourselves function at a conscious and/or subconscious level to improve our performance.

Morran et al. (1995) suggest that cognitive skills training involves four phases: to sensitize trainees in their own thinking style, link cognitive to behavioral skills, promote critical self-examination of strategies, and provide systematic practice with new ways of thinking and responding. Some of the specific components of cognitive skills might include assessing necessary tasks in counseling, formulating specific therapy goals, rehearsing intervention plans, promoting self-instruction on plans for action, evaluating interventions, providing positive self-reinforcement, and monitoring all these simultaneous processes.

Richardson and Stone (1981) developed a cognitive instructional approach to teach counselor trainees self-talk related to skills of predicting, planning, and problem solving. Their research compared behavioral and programmed learning approaches and found that facilitative self-talk skills led to higher levels of reflection, confrontation, and empathy. Meichenbaum (1974) and

Mahoney and Arnkoff (1978) were among the first to apply the research about self-talk to counseling and clinical relationships. The research on self-talk grew naturally from research correlating internal dialogue to counseling performance, personality dimensions, and state/trait anxiety (Fuqua et al., 1986). Covert internal dialogue was described as important to counselor training. Counselor trainees were found to engage in internal dialogue, although it was unclear whether the nature of that internal dialogue resulted from training or from personality style.

Larson and Daniels (1998) reviewed the literature on training to increase counseling self-efficacy (CSE) and found that role plays and modeling combined are more effective than a control group for novice counselors. "It may be that modeling may be a lower risk intervention early on in training for increasing CSE; role plays may be a higher risk, yet more potent intervention for increasing CSE" (p. 206). Racism functions through culturally learned scripts that outline how we ought to feel and think and will behave. Role-play training allows us to substitute new messages regarding persons who are culturally different from ourselves, gain greater self-awareness of inequitable distribution of resources or power balances, and learn to accept the cultural heritages of others (Batts, 1983). Role playing and modeling provide access to secret and hidden messages in the counseling interview (Boyd-Franklin, 1993). The hidden secrets of African American families have a historical as well as contemporary context, just as the racial script of majority culture counselors contains its own secrets and hidden messages (Stern, 1987). Effective multicultural training to hear the hidden messages enables the counselor to be more constructively adaptive in multicultural counseling interviews.

RATIONALE FOR CROSS-CULTURAL TRAINING

The sociocultural context influences how we think about counseling. We know that cultural background influences both the way counseling is given and how it is received; hearing about other cultures facilitates learning about ourselves. There is, however, a tendency in counseling to assume that clients and counselors share the same value assumptions despite abundant evidence to the contrary. There is an assumption that we all know the meaning of healthy and normal, when, in fact, we may merely be reflecting our own political, social, or economic values as culturally encapsulated counselors.

Counselor trainees can expect to increase their awareness of their own and others' cultural biases by becoming familiar with research on cross-cultural counseling and by learning specific skills that will help them work more efficiently with culturally different clients. They can learn to better understand how mental health is defined in other cultures; recognize cultural prejudices and biases; learn of environments that contribute to self-esteem and positive interpersonal relationships across cultures; and respect cultural diversity across boundaries of nationality, ethnicity, age, gender, socioeconomic status, and other affiliations. Training materials have been used to train persons working with welfare clients, alcoholics, handicapped individuals, foreign students, prisoners, and other identity groups in which there is likely to be a difference in values between counselors and clients.

There are several reasons why a cross-cultural training program for mental health professionals is needed (Basic Behavioral Science Task Force of the National Advisory Mental Health Council, 1996):

1. Traditional systems of mental health services have a cultural bias favoring dominant social classes, which can be counterproductive to an equitable distribution of services.
2. Various cultural groups have discovered indigenous modes of coping and treatment that work better for them and may be usefully applied to other groups.
3. Community health services are expensive when they fail, and cross-cultural training might prevent some programs from failure.
4. Training methods that include indigenous people as resource persons directly in training counselors tend to reflect the reality of different cultures.
5. The constructs of healthy and normal that guide the delivery of mental health services are not the same for all cultures and might betray the culturally encapsulated counselors to become a tool of a particular political, social, or economic system.
6. Increased interdependence across national, ethnic, and social/cultural boundaries requires direct attention to culture as part of mental health training.
7. Most therapists come from dominant majority cultures, whereas most clients do not.

Although most mental health delivery services are provided by white middle-class males, the vast majority of clients receiving these services are nonwhite and from lower socioeconomic levels, and their socialization and value assumptions differ significantly from the counselors' (Pedersen, 1985). The literature on how cultural values affect mental health services describes vividly the need for increased awareness by mental health professionals of value assumptions being made by culturally different clients and the ways in which culturally biased counseling has resulted in low utilization rates of mental health services now available.

Simulations provide relatively safe ways to learn counseling skills without risk to actual clients. Simulated counseling interviews and role playing have been used by all different theoretical approaches to practice skill building in counselor education. In the safety of a simulation, the counselor trainee may make mistakes and learn recovery skills for getting out of trouble after having said or done the wrong thing. Rehearsing skills through role play helps counselors develop more confidence and develop higher skill levels through practicing those skills and receiving feedback (Pedersen, 1994).

The Triad Training Model is a simulation to make explicit the internal dialogue that a client might be thinking but not saying. This model matches a counselor trainee with three resource persons from the same background in a simulated counseling interview. One resource person is in the role of a coached client, who presents the problem for which he or she is seeking help from counseling. A second resource person is in the role of a coached *anticounselor,* who articulates the negative internal messages that the client might be thinking but not saying. The anticounselor will attempt to sabotage the counseling process by emphasizing and exaggerating these negative messages. The third resource person is in the role of a coached *procounselor,* who articulates the positive internal messages that a client might be thinking but not saying. The procounselor will facilitate the success of the counseling process and the counselor. The resulting four-way conversation between the counselor, client, procounselor, and anticounselor provides the counselor access to the client's internal dialogue during the simulated counseling interview. As the counselor becomes more familiar with the positive and negative messages that a culturally different client might be thinking but not saying, the counselor will be able to incorporate those messages into the explicit counseling interview (Pedersen, 1994). This four-way interaction is typically videotaped, and the videotape is reviewed by participants for debriefing and feedback on how well the counselor attended to both the explicit verbal and the more implicit internal client dialogue.

There are several theories of counseling that attend to a client's internal dialogue as an important counseling resource. Psychoanalytic and object-relations theories use identification and internalization to merge the real external world with the client's private perspective. This internalization may take several forms:

1. Introjection describes an internal presence as an integral part of the client's self. This can be an imaginary playmate or other person who may be either friendly or unfriendly.
2. Identification describes modifying one's self to fit a perspective of some other person or model by imitating that person or model, with positive or negative consequences.
3. Incorporation is a blurring of the distinction between the self and significant others, incorporating the other person into the self.

These internalizations become important for understanding how the client and counselor feel about themselves and others. Triads have been used in family therapy by Satir (1964) and others to illustrate pathogenic coalitions. The therapist then uses mediation and judicious side taking to break up and replace pathogenic relating. The use of co-counselors or counseling families and small groups, in which some may be very positive and others very negative, are additional examples from systems theory of how this force field of positive and negative alternatives is important to the understanding of counseling.

TWO TRIAD TRAINING DESIGNS

The first training design to be described is appropriate for a small group of about 10 or 12 counselors working together for a 1-day intensive training experience. The second training design is appropriate for a larger group of about 30 or 40 counselors working together for a 2-day workshop experience. In either design, there are advantages and disadvantages that will be described. The key element in both designs is the selection and training of coached client-anticounselor-procounselor teams. These teams of resource persons should be as close to one another as possible, such as three persons from the same ethnic group, nationality, socioeconomic group, age level, lifestyle, or sex role. In previous workshops, teams of ex-convicts have been included to train social workers and teams of persons with disabilities have been used to train rehabilitation counselors. These teams of resource persons should be acknowledged as the trainers in the workshop. The coached client-anticounselor-procounselor teams should be carefully selected; paid as professionals; and be trained in their coached roles as clients, procounselors, and/or anticounselors. The training involves showing them the demonstration videotape and rehearsing their roles according to the directions on the accompanying manual prior to either training design. This book will provide additional information about the Triad Model with illustrative examples. Each of the training designs described should be led by a facilitator who is already familiar with the Triad Training Model.

INTENSIVE 1-DAY LAB FOR
SMALL GROUPS OF COUNSELORS

Requirement

Three trained client-anticounselor-procounselor teams from three different cultures; one large meeting room to view videotapes and a small nearby video lab to videotape triads; 10 rolls of videotape, 2 video recording decks, 1 camera, and at least 1 monitor.

Design

Following an introduction and presentation of the video demonstration of the Triad Training Model, the facilitator answers questions while one of the counselors leaves the room with a client-anticounselor-procounselor team to make the first videotape. The counselor and team return to the group after having produced a 10-minute videotape of a simulated counseling interview and a

5- to 10-minute videotape of the three debriefing one another. The 20-minute videotape is shown to the larger group for comments and discussion. While the tape is being viewed, another counselor leaves the room with the second client-anticounselor-procounselor team to produce a second tape. By the time the group has discussed the first tape, the second counselor has returned with a second tape. While the second tape is being viewed, a third counselor will leave with the third client-anticounselor-procounselor team to make a third tape. Each counselor participant will take a turn making a tape with one of the teams in sequence. There are three client-anticounselor-procounselor teams so that, after every three simulations, each team will have a brief rest. After all the counselor participants have had a chance to make, view, and receive feedback on their videotapes, there is a general plenary session to summarize insights from the variety of videotapes and to answer questions.

Advantages

Assembling counselor colleagues interested in cross-cultural training for a day together discussing the special circumstances of cultural differences in the counseling process is in itself a useful experience, resulting in ongoing contacts and professional relationships that are extremely useful later. By allowing each participant to produce a tape and receive feedback from colleagues, the experience becomes intensive and specific to the individual counselor. By including three different teams from three different cultures, the trainees are allowed some flexibility in matching themselves with a particular culture. At the same time, the group is able to compare and contrast how counseling clients from one culture is different from counseling clients from another culture. The videotapes produced during such a workshop can themselves provide a valuable resource, depending on the willingness of participants and the client-anticounselor-procounselor teams to allow the videotapes to be used.

Disadvantages

It is sometimes difficult to secure the facilities to run such a workshop. It requires considerable videotaping equipment, one larger meeting room, and a nearby videotaping studio room. The client-anticounselor-procounselor teams must be paid as professional resource persons. This is particularly true if the workshop organizer is being paid, but, in any case, it establishes the role of the resource persons as central to the instruction function of the workshop. In this particular design, each participant will miss the group feedback on one tape while he or she is producing his or her own videotape. The advantages of making and discussing the videotape while it is still fresh outweigh the disadvantage of the participants' missing one session, however. It is essential to select and train the client-anticounselor-procounselor teams with extreme care. Some teams are able to role-play the "problem" more easily than others, but, in all cases, the training includes viewing models of how the anticounselor and procounselor should function on videotape and then rehearsing their roles until they are comfortable with them. They should have several preselected problems that they would be able to present to the counselor trainee. The anticounselor/procounselor and the client should have selected one another and be able to anticipate what the other team member will do or feel in as many situations as possible. The anticounselor should be verbally articulate, although some anticounselors have used nonverbal approaches very effectively.

INTENSIVE 2-DAY LAB FOR
LARGE GROUPS OF COUNSELOR TRAINEES

Requirements

One trained client-anticounselor-procounselor team from the same culture for every eight counselor trainees; one large meeting room, large enough for everyone to meet together, and adjoining smaller rooms that would allow groups of 10 persons to meet with a minimum of distraction from one another; one videotape play-back deck and monitor are required.

Design

The first session would begin with an introduction of the client-anticounselor-procounselor teams to the participants, a statement of the agenda for the workshop, a clear statement of the workshop goals, and time for questions. Then the video demonstration of the Triad Training Model would be shown to the entire group with time for questions and some discussion. After the discussion, there can be a demonstration by the facilitator and a team of the cross-cultural Triad Training Model in front of the entire group, or the entire group may be instructed to divide themselves into triads so that they may briefly experience the model with the facilitator and coached resource teams circulating among the triads to answer questions. Once the group participants have a clear notion of the model, they will be divided into groups of eight according to prearranged assignments to ensure that each group will be as het-erogeneous as possible in terms of culture, age, sex role, lifestyle, training, socioeconomic status, and other available characteristics. The coached cli-ent-anticounselor-procounselor teams will be assigned to each of the different groups for a period of 45 minutes. During this time, the coached team will elect a volunteer from their group to function as counselor. The team will have pre-pared three or four problems beforehand that they can develop in a cross-cultural simulated counseling interview. They will role-play the interview for 5 or 10 minutes and then go out of role for a 5- or 10-minute debriefing of one another. After the four participants have had a chance to give feedback, they will call on the other group members for additional observations and discussion. The coached team will then elect a second volunteer from the participants and repeat the cycle of a simulated interview, debriefing, and discussion. The team should have time to complete at least two interviews before the 45-minute period. At the end of 45 minutes, the team will rotate to another group in ordered sequence for a second 45-minute period. The rest of the first day will be spent in these small groups with the client-anticounselor-procounselor teams—with lunch and coffee breaks at convenient points. The last 30 minutes of the day will be spent bringing the total group together to share their experiences and insights and ask questions.

The second day will begin with a general session of the total group, with the opportunity to ask questions and suggest insights that might be useful to other participants. The participants will then divide into their same groups of eight participants and continue meeting with the coached client-anticounselor-procounselor teams until each of the teams has met with each of the small groups. By this time, each of the eight participants in each small group should have had a chance to role-play the counselor in the triad.

After the small groups have been completed, the total group will come together for a discussion and the participants will be asked to form their own triads—either with one another or including members of the coached client-anticounselor-procounselor teams, but with the freedom to assume any of the four roles of counselor, client, anticounselor, or procounselor. Participants not wishing to role-play will be encouraged to observe one of the triads in session around the room. Participants will be encouraged to organize their own triads in client, procounselor, or anticounselor roles with problems they have identified out of their own background. This less-structured session will be concluded with the lunch break.

After the lunch break, the client-anticounselor-procounselor teams will be assembled as a panel in front of the total group. Each team member will be given a chance to speak briefly on what he or she observed during the training process. After each team member has had a chance to speak, there will be an opportunity for participants to ask questions and discuss the training process within the larger group. By this time, participants should have numerous questions on the specific ways that culture differences between the coached teams affected the counseling relationship. At the end of the discussion, evaluation forms will be distributed among the participants asking them to complete the evaluation before leaving the workshop.

Advantages

Alternating the small-group and large-group experience allows intensive interaction in which participants can learn from one another's style in some detail and still have the benefit of insights by other participants outside of their immediate small group. By presenting more than one client-anticounselor-procounselor team to each small group, participants can see how different cultures approach the same problems or counselor style in different ways. By going for two days, participants have a chance to assimilate the training data and to think about questions they might want to ask during the last session. Each participant will have a chance to be the counselor in a simulated interview at least once and possibly more often. Participants will also have a chance to experience the roles of client procounselor and anticounselor after the small-group sessions are completed. Participants will be encouraged to present counseling problems they have actually encountered in their own counseling experiences for feedback and suggestions on appropriate intervention.

Disadvantages

Participants will not have a chance to make their own videotapes and see themselves working with clients from other cultures. The logistics of assembling small groups, assigning participants, and rotating the client-anticounselor-procounselor teams can become complicated. The small groups can become so involved in a discussion of issues that they avoid the role-playing tasks and need to be reminded to save their discussion of issues until the last session. The facilitator can circulate among the groups to help them get into role play as much as possible during the small-group sessions. Sometimes participants are not able to attend the workshop the full two days, so the small groups may fluctuate in size. The interaction is extremely intensive, and liberal allowance should be made for coffee breaks between sessions, while keeping as much pressure on the participants as possible. The facilitator should be able to guide discussion during the last session to provide closure to the workshop experience and summarize insights that have occurred during the sessions. The Triad Training Model should serve to stimulate interaction between the coached teams and the participants by directing the participants toward these resource persons as the primary teaching resource for the workshop.

MULTICULTURAL SKILL AREAS

Four skill areas have emerged from working with the Triad Training Model in simulated multicultural interviews. These skill areas are (a) articulating the problem from the client's cultural perspective, (b) recognizing resistance from a culturally different client in specific rather than general terms, (c) being less defensive in a culturally ambiguous relationship, and (d) learning recovery skills for getting out of trouble when making mistakes in counseling culturally different clients. These skill areas are in the process of being tested and validated.

The four areas share some face validity, however. First, we each perceive the world from our own culturally biased viewpoint. If the client does not share the counselor's cultural background, the client's viewpoint is likely to differ from the counselor's. Second, it is important to recognize resistance relating to cultural differences between the counselor and client in specific rather than in general terms before the interview can be expected to proceed. Third, the multicultural interview is frequently ambiguous for the counselor and can easily cause even a skilled counselor to become uncertain or defensive. If the counselor is distracted by becoming defensive, the rapport with a client is likely to diminish. Constant attack by the anticounselor is most likely to bring out a defensive response in the counselor that can be viewed, controlled, and diminished. Fourth, skilled counselors make perhaps as many mistakes as unskilled counselors do. However, skilled counselors are able to get out of trouble and recover from mistakes with increased rather than diminished rapport with the client. The function of training is not only to train counselors how to avoid making mistakes but to help those who make mistakes recover effectively. The Triad Training Model provides opportunities for the counselor to recover from mistakes in a relatively safe environment and to develop recovery skills that fit the counselor's own style and a variety of different situations.

Articulating the Problem

Each of us perceives the world from our own culturally biased point of view. To the extent that a client does not share the counselor's cultural background, the client is less likely to share the same point of view regarding the problem being discussed.

The skill area of "articulating the problem," or perceiving the problem from the client's cultural point of view, contains many microskills. It is useful to consider the following components, many of which are drawn from the literature on counselor skills training, in describing the ability to articulate the problem:

Cognitive rational insight. The counselor develops the ability to define accurately the feelings related to a client's presenting problem.

Paraphrase. The counselor gives back to the client the essence of past verbal statements by selective attention to the content of client verbalizations.

Reflection of feeling. The counselor gives selective attention to key affective or emotional aspects of client behavior.

Summarization. The counselor reflects a client's feelings over a longer period of time and gives several strands of thinking back to the client.

Concreteness. The counselor's statements are less vague or inconclusive and more concrete or specific.

Immediacy. The counselor matches the client's statements by using the same time perspective—whether past, present, or future.

Respect. Enhancing statements by the counselor about self or others are considered to represent respect, whereas negative statements or "put-downs" indicate an absence of this dimension.

Genuineness. There is an absence of mixed verbal and nonverbal messages. In particularly effective communication, verbal and nonverbal message synchrony between client and counselor may be noted.

Positive regard. The counselor gives selective attention to positive aspects of self or others or to the demonstrated belief that people can change and manage their own lives.

Tracking. The counselor is able to follow accurately and even anticipate what the client will say next in the interview.

Recognizing Resistance

It is important to recognize resistance relating to cultural differences between a counselor and a client in specific rather than in general terms. When resistance arises in an interview, it is important to identify and deal with it before proceeding to control the problem dimension of the counseling interview. It is important to watch the interaction between a client and anticounselor partner to determine the nature of resistance in the simulated interview. If the client accepts and validates what the anticounselor says, it is important for the counselor to modify his or her intervention to accommodate what the anticounselor says.

The skill area of "anticipating resistance," or recognizing resistance in specific rather than general terms, recognizes the importance of dealing with negative affect before proceeding with the content in a client's response. The skill area also recognizes the difficulty of identifying negative affect in specific and accurate terms for culturally different clients. It is useful to consider the following microskills, many of which have been validated elsewhere in the literature about counseling skills, as important in identifying resistance in specific rather than in general terms:

Stress-coping insight. The counselor is able to define accurately the client's response pattern to the problem.

Values conflict. The counselor is able to identify ambiguity in the client's basic beliefs.

Questioning. The counselor is able to use either open or closed questions in a culturally appropriate mode.

Directions. The counselor is able to tell the client what to do in a culturally appropriate way.

Confrontation. The counselor is able to clearly note discrepancies within the self or between the self and others.

Interpretation. The counselor is able to rename or relabel the client's behaviors or verbalizations accurately.

Focus on topic. The counselor clearly identifies the subject of the client's special topic or problem.

Focus on group. The counselor is aware of the role of natural support groups for the individual client.

Mirroring. The counselor is able to reflect and adjust voice tone, body position, or other communication style so that it is in synchrony with that of the client.

Self-awareness. The counselor has an explicit awareness of what he or she is doing that might antagonize a client.

Diminishing Counselor Defensiveness

The multicultural counseling interview is frequently ambiguous for the counselor and can easily cause even a skilled counselor to become less sure of himself or herself, leading to defensive counselor behavior. It will be important for the counselor in any interview to avoid the distraction of defensive counselor behavior and to focus on the client's message, which may not be intended as an attack on the counselor personally. If the counselor allows himself or herself to be distracted by becoming defensive, the rapport with a client is likely to diminish. If a counselor is ever going to be defensive, it is more likely to occur in the presence of an anticounselor seeking to sabotage the interview. The Triad Training Model allows counselors to examine their own latent defensiveness and raise their threshold for nondefensive responses.

The skill area of "diminishing defensiveness," or helping the counselor to control the impulse to feel threatened in culturally ambiguous situations, is another widely recognized characteristic of good counseling in all settings. The increased ambiguity of multicultural settings, however, increases the potential for threat. The following microskills, drawn from the counseling literature, provide measures for diminishing defensive reactions in multicultural counseling:

Sense of humor. The counselor is able to facilitate rapport through an appropriate use of humor in the interview.

Self-disclosure. The counselor is able to disclose information about him- or herself in a culturally appropriate way to increase rapport.

Evaluation. The counselor is able to evaluate a client's expression, manner, or tone of response to get at hidden agendas.

Description. The counselor is able to describe the client's response without evaluating it as good or bad.

Spontaneity. The counselor is able to be spontaneous, rather than strategic, in a way that increases rapport.

Receptivity. The counselor is able to accept advice or help from the client in a culturally appropriate way.

Admitting to being defensive. The counselor is able to admit openly to defensive counselor behaviors in a nonapologetic way.

Apologizing. The counselor is able to accept responsibility for a counselor error and apologize in such a way that it strengthens rapport.

Planning. The counselor is able to develop and explicate a plan of action to the client for the period of an interview.

Manipulation. The counselor is able to bring the client to accept what the counselor perceives as being clearly in the client's interest.

Recovery Skills

Skilled counselors make perhaps as many mistakes as unskilled counselors do, but the difference is that skilled counselors are able to get out of trouble and recover from the mistake with increased rather than diminished rapport. The function of training, then, is perhaps not to teach counselors how to avoid making mistakes but, rather, to help counselors who make mistakes recover effectively.

If a counselor is not making mistakes while counseling a client from a culture that is totally unfamiliar to the counselor, then the counselor may not be taking enough personal risk. Counselor training should not merely prevent the counselor from making mistakes but should help the counselor recover from mistakes once they have been made. The Triad Training Model provides opportunities for the counselor to make mistakes and experiment with various recovery strategies. The counselor who feels confident that he or she can recover from any mistakes made in counseling is likely to be less apprehensive about making the mistakes in the first place.

The skill area of "recovery skills" is not otherwise reported in the literature on counseling skills and is frequently overlooked as a teachable or learnable skill area. However, it is clear in viewing examples of expert counseling that the experts make as many mistakes as—and perhaps more than—the novice. The difference is that the experts, having taken a chance and failed, can recover more expertly than the novice. It is therefore important to examine microskills that might contribute to the counselor's ability to recover in a multicultural counseling interview:

Changing the topic. The counselor can redirect the interview appropriately following a controversial interaction.

Focusing. The counselor can refocus the counseling interview on the basic problem instead of on the controversial issue.

Challenging. The counselor confronts the client with his or her own perception of what is really happening.

Silence. The counselor is able to tolerate periods of silence in the interview that contribute to multicultural rapport.

Role reversal. The counselor can solicit consultation from the client as a resource for generating solutions and alternatives.

Referral. The counselor is able to refer the client to another counselor in a culturally appropriate way and at an appropriate time.

Termination. The counselor is able to terminate the interview prematurely in a culturally appropriate way.

Arbitration. The counselor brings in a third person or "culture broker" to mediate the dispute in a culturally appropriate way.

Metaphorical analysis. The counselor identifies the developing metaphors initiated by a client toward the explication of a client's perspective.

Positioning. The counselor identifies an area of unmet need or opportunity not yet recognized by the client and builds on it to the client's advantage.

This training model seems to offer a number of advantages over alternative training approaches. Under controlled conditions, the model provides an opportunity for persons from different cultures to accomplish a training goal they all need and want. As a simulated interview, the model offers participants greater safety to demonstrate strong feelings and provides direct feedback. Separating the roles of client, anticounselor, and procounselor makes the problem less diffuse and abstract to counselor trainees. The anticounselor and procounselor models encourage negative feedback to the counselor to clarify resistance. Inappropriate counselor intervention is immediately apparent in feedback from the anticounselor and procounselor. The model is nontheoretical because it calls attention to good counseling without first requiring a theoretical knowledge of a way a particular approach is good. The members of another culture become resource persons in learning to counsel persons from those same cultures without depending on expert outsiders. If members of the target audience have helped train their own counselors, they have more invested in the success of those counselors working among them. In the balance of power between counselor and anticounselor, the trainees are reminded how the determination for success or failure ultimately lies with the client and not the counselor.

CONCLUSION

The Triad Training Model is described as one approach to monitor the positive and negative internal dialogue of culturally different clients in simulated interviews. Some support from the counseling and social psychological literature is cited to help identify where the Triad Training Model fits in the psychological literature. Some alternative training approaches for capturing and monitoring the client's internal dialogue are also discussed. It is clearly important for counselors to monitor their own and, especially, their client's internal dialogue, but as yet no clear method has been generated for incorporating that skill.

The rationale for training counselors to work in multicultural settings is reviewed, and the importance of simulations for counselor training is discussed. Some of the unique advantages of the Triad Training Model as a training approach that incorporates aspects from Gestalt, psychodrama, systems theory, and a variety of other perspectives are indicated.

Two training designs, one for preservice and one for in-service training, are presented in detail with guidelines for organizing each design in practice. Future chapters will provide more detail on the use of the Triad Training Model and other related alternative models in practice.

7

Developing Multicultural Competencies With the Triad Training Model

The Triad Training Model has been used since 1968 to develop multicultural competence in counselors and other human service providers. Much more emphasis has been given to using the Triad Training Model in training and teaching than has been given to gathering empirical data to evaluate the model. Although the anecdotal reports from persons using the model are positive, the empirical data about the model are still not conclusive.

People who have used the model report that they are better able to articulate the problem from the client's viewpoint after a series of training interviews with the procounselor-client-anticounselor teams. Participants also report that they are better able to identify specific sources of resistance in the counseling interview, based on immediate and continuous feedback from the procounselor and the anticounselor. Participants further report becoming less defensive after training with the anticounselor and less threatened by working with culturally different clients. Finally, participants indicate the importance of developing recovery skills after they have said or done the wrong thing, as pointed out by the anticounselor or procounselor. These anecdotal reports are certainly important, but more empirical research data are needed to test the strengths and weaknesses of the Triad Training Model. This chapter will examine the research that has been done and how it relates to developing multicultural competencies among trainees.

Multicultural awareness is the most basic level of a three-stage developmental competence sequence moving from (a) awareness of culturally learned assumptions, to (b) knowledge of culturally relevant facts and information, to (c) skill for appropriate interventions (Sue et al., 1998). These competencies are stated as aspirational goals that can be operationalized in a variety of ways and are used to encourage new research about the definitions of multicultural competence.

> The first dimension deals with counselor's attitudes and beliefs about race, culture, ethnicity, gender and sexual orientation; the need to check biases and stereotypes; development of a positive orientation toward multiculturalism; and the way counselor's values and biases may hinder effective counseling and therapy. The second dimension recognizes that the culturally skilled helping professional is knowledgeable and understanding of his or her own world view, has specific knowledge of the cultural groups he or she works with, and understands socio-political influences. The last dimension deals with specific skills (intervention techniques and strategies) needed in working with culturally different groups; it includes both individual and institutional competencies. (Sue et al., 1998, pp. 37-38)

The analysis of research on the Triad Training Model will divide research findings into three corresponding categories of awareness, knowledge, and skill.

DEVELOPING MULTICULTURAL AWARENESS COMPETENCIES

The more similarity there is between two persons, the more likely each will accurately communicate (Triandis, 1977). Therefore, the more similarity (ethnographic, demographic, status, and affiliation) there is between the counselor and client, the more likely the counselor will be aware of the client's internal dialogue. The more cultural differences there are between the counselor and client, the less likely the counselor will be aware of the client's internal dialogue. A primary purpose of the Triad Training Model is to develop multicultural awareness among counselors.

Awareness is the ability to understand a cultural context from one's own as well as the other's cultural viewpoint. The truly aware counselor should be able to describe a cultural context in such a way that members of that culture agree with the counselor's perception.

> Such an awareness would require an individual to have: ability to recognize direct and indirect communication styles; sensitivity to nonverbal cues; awareness of cultural and linguistic differences; interest in the culture; sensitivity to the myths and stereotypes of the culture; concern for the welfare of persons from another culture; ability to articulate elements of his or her own culture; appreciation for the importance for multicultural teaching; awareness of the relationships between cultural groups; and accurate criteria for objectively judging goodness and badness in the other culture. (Pedersen, 1994, p. 27)

The Triad Training Model has been used as an in-service training model for counselors working with a variety of different populations, such as training foreign student advisers to work with foreign students; training counselors to work with clients from other ethnic minority groups; training counselors to work with alcoholics and clients who are drug dependent; training counselors to work with clients who are disabled; training counselors to be more sensitive to gender-based attitudes; training military to negotiate differences between rank and service branch; and training prisoners at a federal prison to work with social workers in the cultural context of prison. The range of possible applications extends to any situation in which the culturally learned values, beliefs, or expectations of the counselors are likely to be different from those of their clients. The Triad Training Model allows in-service trainees to make mistakes in the relatively safe context of a simulated interview with clients from the target culture. During the interview itself, the counselor trainees receive immediate, direct, and continuous feedback from members of the very population they are being trained to later serve. One typical example of an in-service training workshop provides an example of anecdotal evaluation data.

Several workshops using the Triad Training Model with the anticounselor but not the procounselor were organized in Hawaii during the spring of 1975. Of the 39 participants in the first workshop for the Department of Social Welfare in Maui, Hawaii, 28 indicated that the training helped them anticipate resistance in clients from other cultures; 25 said training helped them articulate the problem from the client's viewpoint; and 22 wanted additional training with the model. Most saw the anticounselor role as the most powerful and interesting but the client role as the most educating. The most important benefits they reported were becoming more aware of each other's views toward counseling and increasing their awareness of cultural differences. In a second workshop with 34 Hilo mental health workers, 32 indicated that the training helped them anticipate resistance, and 28 wanted more training with the model. They judged the anticounselor role as most powerful and the counselor role as most educative. The primary benefits of training with the model were to make them aware of each other's views toward counseling and more aware of culturally different client needs.

Data were also collected from students at the University of Hawaii to determine whether the Triad Training Model, like microcounseling, resulted in greater counseling effectiveness than did other human relations training. The revised Carkhuff scales (1969) and Gordon's (1972) seven-level scale for communicating affective meaning were used to rate pretraining and posttraining videotapes of a brief cross-cultural counseling interview. A multiple-choice teacher/counselor questionnaire (Shapiro, 1970) and an adjective checklist (Shapiro, 1967) were also used to measure increased awareness.

Students in the spring 1975 class were expected to increase their scores on the Carkhuff and the Gordon scales following training with the Triad Training Model, using a coached client and an anticounselor but not a procounselor. Students were expected to score higher on the multiple-choice test, demonstrate less discrepancy between real and ideal self-description on the adjective checklist, and describe themselves more positively than did the previous class of students in which a human relations training approach was used. Pretest comparisons between the spring and fall classes indicated no significant pretest difference between groups on the written measures. Spring semester students achieved significantly higher scores on the multiple-choice test of counseling knowledge and developed a significantly more positive and congruent self-image on the adjective checklist. In addition, there were also significant increases from pretest to posttest on behavioral ratings for empathy, respect, and congruence (Pedersen, Holwill, & Shapiro, 1978).

Holwill-Bailey (cited in Bailey, 1981) used the Triad Training Model to compare a traditional mode of teaching human relations intercultural skills to counselors with a videotaped dyad design similar to Kagan's Interpersonal Process Recall (IPR) model and a videotaped Triad Training Model design. She used Ivey's Counselor Effectiveness Scale, the Revised Truax Accurate Empathy Scale, the Revised Carkhuff Respect and Genuineness Scale, the Shapiro Adjective Checklist, and the Bender Tolerance of Ambiguity Scale as dependent measures. In a three-way analysis of covariance, all tests between the control group and the treatment group were statistically significant. There was no significance between the measures of students trained with the Triad Training Model and the dyadic IPR training design, however, suggesting that both approaches were equally effective; however, both were superior to the control approaches of traditional counselor education using human relations training. The Triad Training Model has also been used with groups not defined by ethnicity or nationality. Anderson (1978) designed a workshop for using the Triad Training Model for rehabilitation counselors working with clients who were black and deaf.

Sue (1980) field-tested the anticounselor and procounselor versions of the Triad Training Model with students at California State University-Hayward. The anticounselor version was judged more effective in achieving self-awareness, developing cultural sensitivity for contrasting cultural values, and understanding political or social ramifications of counseling. The anticounselor version was also more effective in giving participants an awareness of their cultural values and biases and engendering cultural sensitivity to other ethnically defined groups. The procounselor version was more effective in helping students obtain specific knowledge of the history, experiences, and cultural values of the client's ethnic group. Students were more comfortable with the procounselor version; the anticounselor version was more anxiety provoking. However, when asked to rate the most effective model for learning about multicultural counseling in the shortest period of time, the anticounselor version was seen as superior. The anticounselor brought out issues of racism, bias, and conflicting values through immediate feedback to the counselor trainee, whereas the procounselor tended to facilitate acquisition of skills more gently.

Murgatroyd (1995) described a program using the Triad Training Model to prepare counselors at the University of New Orleans. First, the model helped trainees understand and explore the presenting problem of role-played clients. Second, it made negative thoughts toward counseling and the counselor more explicit. Third, it aided in understanding the "payoffs" a problem offers to the client. Students were divided into two groups. The six students in group one had completed from 9 to 18 credits of graduate study in counseling, while the six students in group two had completed at least 24 credits.

> The model facilitates a faster and deeper exploration of presenting problems for group one counselor trainees. For group two trainees, the model heightens the developmental issue of dependency versus autonomy. They struggle with an authority of positive and negative voices which in turn allows them an opportunity to work through their developmental task and become more mature in their identity. (p. 22)

Murgatroyd described the primary usefulness of the Triad Training Model as helping counselor trainees identify the positive resources of clients through the positive and negative messages of the client's internal dialogue.

> The model unveiled negative thought both about counseling and the counselor. It allowed a student to work with the client's resistance and reframe the client's problem in a positive working direction. It aided in understanding the concept of payoffs, an important part of the problem that influences the patterns of a client's behavior. (p. 17)

Kennington (1999) used the Triad Training Model to train counseling students, teachers, and counselors from Taiwan, Saudi Arabia, Palestine, Ghana, and Armenia, as well as African American and European American groups. The training explored issues that counseling students from diverse cultures and ethnic groups might encounter in becoming aware of hidden messages involving sharing intimate information. "The Triad Model played an important role in permitting the counselor, anti-counselor and client to get into character and reflect at a deeper emotional level than would have been possible had a standard interview or survey format been used" (p. 1).

Most of the supporting research on the Triad Training Model describes its value in giving the counselor trainees increased awareness of their own and their clients' cultural context. The counselor's assumptions are constantly being tested by the anticounselor and procounselor through their immediate and continuous feedback. Biases and stereotypes of the trainee are quickly identified and made more visible during the simulated interview so that the counselor is better able to articulate the problem from the client's cultural perspective. Awareness of the culturally appropriate process or style of counseling as well as the content of the interview is likewise illuminated.

DEVELOPING MULTICULTURAL
KNOWLEDGE COMPETENCIES

The second stage of multicultural development builds on accurate awareness of the counselor's culturally learned assumptions, because in some ways they are similar to and in others different from culturally different clients. The next task is building toward a meaningful understanding of the client's cultural worldview. Meaningful knowledge and information help the counselor better understand the client's cultural context, life experiences, cultural heritage, and historical background. All of the client's behaviors have been learned and are displayed in that cultural context, so understanding the context becomes fundamental to meaningfulness. Meaningful understanding requires both information about the client's context and a framework for analyzing those data. A meaningful relationship with members of the client's cultural community becomes important to understanding the client's cultural context.

If multicultural awareness helps the trainee ask the right questions, then the second stage of multicultural knowledge helps the trainee find the right answers to those questions. Evaluating preconceptions and stereotypes about the client's culture requires knowledge about the myths and perceptions from that culture's cultural viewpoint. Increased knowledge also requires knowing the right way to gather information about the culture in question so that the process as well as the content of gathering information are culturally appropriate. The following questions provide guidelines for gathering multicultural knowledge:

> Does the student have specific knowledge about the culturally defined group member's diverse historical experience, adjustment styles, roles of education, socioeconomic backgrounds, preferred values, typical attitudes, honored behaviors, inherited customs, slang, learning, styles and ways of thinking? Does the student have information about the resources for teaching and learning available to persons in the other culture? Does the student know about his or her own culture in relation to the other culture? Does the student have professional expertise in an area valued by persons in the other culture? Does the student have information about teaching/learning resources regarding the other culture and know where those resources are available? (Pedersen, 1994, p. 28)

Hernandez and Kerr (1985) trained three groups of students using a didactic mode, a didactic plus role play with feedback mode, and a didactic plus Triad Training Model mode with the anticounselor but not a procounselor. On completion of training, the students were videotaped in a counseling session with a coached male Chicano client. The videotaped segments were randomly distributed to six professional colleagues familiar with cross-cultural counseling. The videotapes were rated using the Global Rating Scale (GRS), the Counselor Rating Form–Short, and the Cross-Cultural Counseling Inventory (CCCI). The control group had the lowest average on five of the six measures, and the Triad

Training Model group scored the highest mean scores on four of the six measures. The role-play group earned the highest average on the CCCI, and the control group earned the highest average on the GRS. The more experiential training produced counselors who, from the client's viewpoint, were more culturally sensitive, expert, attractive, and trustworthy. The findings supported experiential training of counselors in general and particularly the use of the Triad Training Model for training.

> These findings support experiential training, and especially the continued use of Pedersen's Triad Model, which is geared towards sensitizing and preparing counselors to work more effectively and efficiently with clients from diverse ethnic backgrounds. (Hernandez & Kerr, 1985, p. 14)

Neimeyer, Fukuyama, Bingham, Hall, and Mussenden (1986) compared the reactions of 20 counseling students using the Triad Training Model with an anticounselor version with students trained using a procounselor version. The two self-report measures used were the Self-Assessment Survey and the Analysis of Values Questionnaire. The Self-Assessment Survey contains five Likert-type items assessing participant feelings of control, competence, confusion, feelings of being understood, and the likelihood of returning for counseling. The Analysis of Values Questionnaire contains 13 seven-point Likert-type items measuring cultural values such as individuality versus group identification, control of nature versus harmony with nature, egalitarian social relationships versus hierarchical social relationships, and future time orientation versus present time orientation. Objective ratings of counselor performance were measured by the Global Rating Scale and the Counselor Rating Form. Results from the Self-Assessment Survey and the Analysis of Values Questionnaire indicated that participants trained in the more confrontational anticounselor version felt more confused and less competent than did participants trained in the procounselor version. No differences were discovered from the scores on the Global Rating Scale and the Counselor Rating Form. The more confrontational anticounselor model, when used alone, was described as better suited to more advanced students who have already developed some confidence in their multicultural understanding, whereas the procounselor model might be better suited for beginning counselors, to provide them with a more supportive multicultural training experience.

> Despite differences in perceived expertness, counselor responses were not rated as differentially effective in the two models. This finding raises questions concerning the relationship between perceived expertness and actual effectiveness. Trainees were not differentially effective in their responses, although they consistently were perceived as more expert in the procounselor condition. Participants in the procounselor model may have been viewed as more expert based on the greater sense of composure (i.e. control and comfort), but they did not provide more

effective counselor responses *per se* than did participants in the anticounselor condition. (p. 12)

Wade and Bernstein (1991) examined cultural sensitivity training using the Triad Training Model with black female clients. Black female clients' perception of the counselors and of counseling was more positive toward counselors who had been trained in the Triad Training Model than toward same-race counselors not trained using the Triad Training Model. Triad Model–trained counselors received higher ratings by 80 low-income black women on expertness, trustworthiness, attractiveness, unconditional positive regard, satisfaction, and empathy; these women also returned for more follow-up sessions with the counselors who had been trained with the Triad Training Model.

> Counselors assigned to the culture sensitivity training condition received 4 hours of training. The training included an overview of the issues and concerns culturally distinct individuals bring to counseling, a group discussion on self-awareness and the minority client, and a skills training component based on Pedersen's Triad Model of cross cultural counseling. (p. 10)

A major finding of this study was that black female clients' perception of the counselors and the counseling process was influenced more by the training than by the race of the counselor.

> Clients assigned to experienced counselors who had received culture sensitivity training rated their counselor higher on credibility and relationship measures, returned for more follow-up sessions, and expressed greater satisfaction with counseling than did clients assigned to experienced counselors who had not received the additional training (control condition). Although same-race counseling dyads resulted in less client attrition, this factor did not influence client perceptions of counselors and the counseling process. (Wade & Bernstein, 1991, p. 9)

Irvin (cited in Irvin & Pedersen, 1995) trained one group in the Triad Training Model using procounselor training first and anticounselor training second and a second group of counselors using the anticounselor training first and the procounselor training second. Twenty graduate counselors in training produced two 10-minute interviews with simultaneous feedback from an anticounselor and a procounselor in the simulated interviews.

Ten trainees experienced the anticounselor before the procounselor, and 10 trainees experienced the procounselor before the anticounselor, to determine the importance of sequencing. Three Kenyan undergraduate students were trained to role-play the coached client-procounselor-anticounselor team. Two self-report measures were used in this study. The Self-Assessment Survey with five Likert-type items was used to assess the participants' feelings of anxiety, competence, perceived clarity of role play, estimates of the client's feelings of being understood, and the likelihood of the client's continuing in counseling.

The Analysis of Values Questionnaire was used to assess the counselor trainee's values and his or her assumptions about the client's values. Results indicated a decrease in the counselor trainee's values and the assumptions about the client's values.

Results indicated a decrease in the counselor trainee's sense of anxiety, apprehension, and defensiveness when the anticounselor was presented first. However, trainees reported a greater sense of control when the procounselor was presented first. Students experiencing the procounselor first were more likely to anticipate future contact with the client, seemed to understand the problem better, and were better able to absorb a confrontation with the anticounselor later. Students who experienced the anticounselor first felt less anxious and more comfortable, demonstrated more self-awareness, and demonstrated a lower level of confusion and less defensiveness. There appeared to be both advantages and disadvantages in experiencing either the anticounselor or the procounselor version of the Triad Training Model first.

The Triad Training Model seems to prepare the counselor trainees to better comprehend the facts and information available to them about the client's cultural context. Merely making those facts available to trainees is not sufficient until and unless they can be made ready to comprehend the meaning of those facts from the client's perspective. Feedback from the anticounselor, procounselor, or both seems to increase the trainee's ability to more accurately process the information in a meaningful way. In conjunction with readings, lectures, and other training approaches, the Triad Training Model helps trainees attend to both the content and the process of gathering information useful to multicultural counseling.

DEVELOPING MULTICULTURAL SKILL COMPETENCIES

The third stage of multicultural development is to develop multicultural skills that build accurately and appropriately on an awareness of culturally learned assumptions and a comprehension of culturally relevant knowledge. Culturally skilled counselors have developed and practice appropriate, relevant, and sensitive intervention strategies for working with clients from different cultural contexts. Skill competencies are directed toward attitudes and beliefs that respect the client's values and cultural practices from the client's cultural perspective. Skill competencies assume knowledge about how counseling can meet the client's needs in the client's cultural context, an awareness of institutional barriers, recognition of cultural bias in tests and techniques introduced from the outside, and a politically astute understanding of the community interests. Skill competencies assume a wide repertoire of helping responses from which the counselor can choose—a willingness to change the system if necessary, credibility with helping resources in the client's culture, language skills when necessary, and the ability to develop a good working relationship with the culturally different client (Sue et al., 1998).

Multicultural skill builds on multicultural awareness and knowledge toward taking right actions at the right time in the right way, and it provides the final test of whether multicultural development has been achieved. Multicultural skills are difficult to evaluate because the same suggested action will not be credible to all persons in the other culture. Skill requires framing the solution in the client's cultural language and framework. Skill requires testing stereotypes against the real and present situation and then modifying the stereotypes accordingly. Skill requires culturally appropriate evaluation criteria so that resulting change will cause an improvement and be constructive. To judge the level of multicultural skill a person has, one might examine several aspects:

> Does the student have appropriate teaching/learning techniques for work in the other culture? Does the student have a teaching/learning style that is appropriate to the other culture? Does the student have the ability to establish empathic rapport with persons from the other culture? Is the student able to receive and accurately analyze feedback from persons of the other culture? Does the student have the creative ability to develop new methods for work in the other culture that go beyond what the student has already learned? (Pedersen, 1994, pp. 28-29)

Chambers (1992) combined the Triad Training Model with Ivey's microskills approach. This variation of the Triad Training Model was found to be effective for increasing the frequency of good verbal counseling responses and decreasing the frequency of poor verbal counseling responses in training and afterward. Chambers used a two-phase five-step process for teaching counseling skills to chemical dependency counselors. The first phase introduced counselors to the Triad Training Model using the anticounselor but not the procounselor version and addressed skills for listening and questioning. The second training phase addressed clarifying and reflecting skills.

> The use of Triad Training was found to be an effective method of (a) increasing the frequency of good verbal counseling responses overall (i.e., from training phase one through follow-up) and (b) decreasing the frequency of poor verbal counseling responses from baseline to training phase one and overall (i.e., from training phase one through follow-up). (p. 2)

The most significant results occurred during training phase one when counselors were introduced to the Triad Training Model. The counselors' verbal responses were reported to change as soon as the Triad Training Model was introduced, and positive effects were sustained throughout the course of the training. Feedback provided by the anticounselor seemed to be corrective and had the greatest effect on reducing poor counselor responses. Anecdotal reports indicated that learning generalized from the role-played situation to counseling sessions and actual interviews later. In discussing these findings, Chambers (1992) indicated that

> the positive results seemed to be directly related to the pairing of the anticounselor's feedback to misapplied skills. The participants have told me that the anticounselor's reaction to skills not used or misapplied was permanently imprinted in their memory, hence it generalized to actual sessions. . . . This is why the anticounselor was more effective with the reduction of poor responses. I believe that the procounselor condition paired with positive applications of basic skills would be helpful, but I must admit I do not think the procounselor condition would increase good responses as significantly as the anticounselor condition reduces poor responses. (p. 1)

Chen, Chen, and Liao (1995) examined the different effects in counselor training using the Triad Training Model compared with a microcounseling model. All the training and testing was done in the Mandarin Chinese language. Participants, 26 students from the Taiwan Teacher's College in the Republic of China, were randomly divided into two groups and provided with 15 hours of basic counseling training over a 6-week period. At that point, each group was trained for 10 hours over a 4-week period, using the two different training models. After training, all students were audiotaped working with culturally similar and dissimilar clients, and the audiotapes were scored using the Counselor Technique Evaluation Scale. All trainees also completed the Counseling Technique Self-Report Inventory. Findings showed that those trained with microcounseling skills were significantly more able than those trained with the Triad Training Model. While counseling culturally similar clients, those trained in the Triad Training Model scored slightly less in counseling skills such as empathy, respect, specification, honesty, probing, and summarizing than did those receiving microskills training, but differences were not statistically significant. However, while counseling clients from a different culture, those trained with the Triad Training Model scored relatively higher in their ability to demonstrate these same counseling skills, but again there was no statistical significance.

The study concluded that students should first be trained in microcounseling skills and that training with the Triad Training Model should come later in the training process. Suggestions for future research were (a) to increase the hours of training in each model, (b) to train students in the procounselor version before training them in the anticounselor version, (c) to select older clients with more life experiences when testing the trainee's skill level, and (d) to measure changes in the trainee's level of self-awareness as a result of training.

Strous, Skuy, and Hickson (1993) used the Triad Training Model in training family counselors in South Africa. Multicultural training of counselors is particularly important in South Africa, where the ethnically diverse majority of 80% has been oppressed by a white minority under apartheid. This research attempted to design a culturally sensitive skill training design using the Triad Training Model. The research involved a role-play presentation of a family counseling session using a procounselor and an anticounselor version, which was sent to family counseling trainers in South Africa. It also included a 17-item evaluation questionnaire to measure supervisors' perception of the potential relative efficacy for training family counselors according to the conventional family counseling supervision, the anticounselor version of the Triad Training Model, or the procounselor version of the Triad Training Model.

> The role plays focused on the plight of a black domestic worker who lives with her husband on her white employer's premises. Their son lives in a segregated black township with his uncle who demands greater financial support from the boy's parents. This brings his parents/spouses into conflict and results in a warning from the mother/wife's employer that she will lose her job if her noisy altercations with her husband persist. (pp. 310-311)

Of the 16 university and 25 clinic-based trainers approached, 12 returned the questionnaire. Results reflected a significant and consistent preference for the procounselor over the anticounselor version and for the anticounselor version over conventional family counseling. These results encouraged the authors to advocate more research using the Triad Training Model in South Africa. Strous et al. (1993) demonstrate how the Triad Training Model takes into account the sociopolitical context of culture and class for training counselors in South Africa. They found the Triad Training Model compatible with systemic family therapy training in which the person and environmental context are seen as a whole. There was a very high degree of consistency in the respondents' perceptions of the procounselor version as most effective (92%) and the anticounselor version as second most effective (83%) when compared with conventional counselor training designs.

Strous et al. (1993) concluded that the theoretical basis of the Triad Training Model need not rely on concepts of client resistance.

> Pedersen's definition of the counseling process recognizes resistance as being an attribute of the problem which is external to the client. This definition identifies the problem rather than the client as dysfunctional and avoids the risk of labeling clients as sick and as requiring the technical imposition of skills by omnipotent-feeling counselors. Future descriptions of the anticounselor design might do well to refer to the external resistance of the problem rather than to the internal resistance of the client. (p. 315)

Explaining why the procounselor version was perceived as more useful than the anticounselor version for cultural and class sensitivity training, Strous et al. (1993) contended that the anticounselor version may not be entirely compatible with the role of the counselor as a context creator. In the procounselor version, the trainee can engage in dialogical construction and coevolvement with the family system. The procounselor version provides relevant cultural and, it is hoped, class-based information to help trainees articulate problems from the client's reference point in a neutral, nonjudgmental way.

Youngs (1996) tested the effectiveness of the Triad Training Model, incorporating the anticounselor and procounselor simultaneously, in training white school counselors to improve service delivery to African American clients. The Triad Training Model was compared with a "contrast" model and a control group using both quantitative and qualitative data from a random sample of African American clients in Grades 8 through 12 in a culturally diverse suburban school district. The results of the quantitative data

> demonstrated that clients rated White school counselors trained in the Triad Model higher in expertness than White counselors trained in the contrast method. Control clients, however, also rated their counselors higher in expertness than did contrast clients. Triad clients did not rate their counselors higher than contrast and control clients in the areas of attractiveness, trustworthiness and empathy. (p. 133)

In addition, triad clients "reported greater satisfaction with the school counseling program than contact clients did. Control group clients, however, also indicated greater satisfaction with the school counseling program than contrast clients did" (Youngs, 1996, p. 133). Even though the quantitative hypotheses were not supported, findings from the quantitative analysis pointed out the effectiveness of the Triad Training Model over the contrast method in the areas of expertness and client satisfaction with school counseling.

Analysis of the qualitative data offered support for the utility of the Triad Training Model. Youngs (1996) showed that the counseling techniques and strategies used by the counselors trained in the Triad Model differed from those trained in the contrast or control techniques, especially in the areas "of phone contacts to families, home visits, use of non-traditional interventions, addressing the issues of culture and race during counseling interviews, and showing sensitivity to the individual needs of clients" (p. 136).

Clients also reported that counselors trained in the Triad Training Model emphasized the personal quality of the relationship more, used the group process more, included more life skills instruction, and demonstrated higher expectations for their clients. Counselors trained in the Triad Training Model did not limit their counseling to educational and career goals but addressed personal and emotional needs such as grief and loss, illness of family members, and relationship difficulties.

Youngs (1996) demonstrated the effectiveness of the Triad Training Model as a multicultural training intervention for school counselors and identified or affirmed specific strategies that have significance for African American schoolchildren. The study showed that the Triad Training Model fosters change in counseling techniques and that high-school-age students can serve effectively as coached clients, procounselors, and anticounselors.

Developing multicultural skill is the most difficult of the three-stage developmental process, based on accurate awareness and comprehensive knowledge. The Triad Training Model forces the counselor trainee to examine his or her preferred style of counseling in terms of how it does or does not fit the needs of culturally different clients. Trainees are given the opportunity to develop credibility based on their responses to the coached client-anticounselor-procounselor team from the host culture. When the trainee has made a mistake, he or she learns recovery skills for getting out of trouble. Training with the Triad Training Model seems to influence the counselor's counseling style and increase the counselor's constructive use of nontraditional techniques or strategies in counseling.

CONCLUSIONS

Although those using the Triad Training Model have been generally supportive of the model's utility when compared with alternative models for cross-cultural training, the results have been nonconclusive. This lack of clear support for or against the Triad Training Model may be because of the difficulty in measuring the effect of the Triad Training Model on the counselor's ability to work across cultures. In part, these difficulties relate to difficulties in defining culture as a complicated and orthogonal construct. In part, this may be because of the lack of long-term evaluation of the skills of those trained in the Triad Training Model. In part, these difficulties may relate to the need for modifying the Triad Training Model itself in some way.

Research demonstrating the importance of internal dialogue for the counselor and client has demonstrated the clear need to incorporate more training in counselor education programs on hearing the client's internal dialogue. So far, most of the research evaluating the Triad Training Model has come from evaluation data by in-service training programs or from dissertation research of graduate students. The research to date gives some support for the value of the Triad Training Model, although the findings have not been conclusive. The data have also been unclear about which version—procounselor, anticounselor, or both—is the best training approach. More research is needed to identify the conditions under which the Triad Training Model works best. The anecdotal evidence by teachers and/or trainers using the model has been the strongest supporting evidence so far, indicating that training with the model has a positive effect in helping counselor trainees increase their awareness of self and others, strengthen their knowledge about clients from other cultures, and sharpen their skills for making appropriate interventions among clients from other cultures. Much more research and evaluation is needed.

PART III

Transcript Applications of the Triad Training Model

The third section of four chapters examines a variety of transcript applications of the Triad Training Model and variations of that model. The first chapter will look at using the Triad Training Model to address problems of sexual harassment, juvenile delinquency, political affiliation, and lesbian lifestyle as cultural issues, broadly defined. The second chapter will present a variety of transcript examples using variations in the Triad Training Model to accommodate the needs of various client populations. The third chapter will present other internal dialogue training models that have been developed from the Triad Training Model and have achieved their own separate identities. The fourth chapter will review the purposes of this book, raise questions for the reader to consider, and highlight the purpose for writing this book in the first place.

8

Sexual Harassment, Juvenile Delinquency, Political Affiliation, and Lesbian Lifestyle as Multicultural Issues and International Applications of the Triad Training Model

According to the broad definition of *culture,* all counseling is multicultural. Any counseling interview can be reframed into cultural categories by focusing on the different sociocultural contexts in which the counselor's and the client's behaviors were learned and are being displayed. The advantages of multicultural reframing are (a) to legitimate the client's cultural viewpoint through increased *awareness* of that viewpoint rather than impose the counselor's self-reference criteria on the client, (b) to value the specialized *knowledge* the client brings into the interview as an important resource, and (c) to *skillfully* define and achieve positive and constructive changes in the client's ability to manage the presenting problems.

The following sample transcripts demonstrate the wide range of demographic groups, status groups, and affiliations that provide significant and potentially salient within-group differences for ethnographic cultural groups. Although these transcripts are not analyzed in depth in this chapter, the reader is given examples of how groups not normally considered to be "cultural groups" can be usefully served by the Triad Training Model.

Cross (cited in Cross & Fhagen-Smith, 1996) introduces the notion of "salience" into the internalization stage of multicultural identity development theory, which moves away from a unimodal understanding of cultural identity. Rather than moving convergently toward a single cultural identity, Cross

(1991, 1995) describes the higher stages of identity development as moving divergently toward a greater awareness of multiple potential identities through "ideological splits." Although Nigrescence theory would predict that a black individual would identify with black culture as most salient at the higher stages of identity development, that need not eliminate the other potentially salient within-group differences of competing identities.

> In the revised model, some persons at Internalization are said to embrace an Afrocentric worldview (categorical salience placed on race and culture); others a bicultural frame of reference (shared or dual saliences) and still others a multi-cultural ideology (multiple reference group orientation). (Cross & Fhagen-Smith, 1996, p. 113)

This salience-based perspective acknowledges the real-world identity conflicts and ideological splits of potentially cooperating and competing cultural identities. Each individual is able to determine for himself or herself which cultural affiliation is most salient at any particular time.

The following four transcripts were developed with Chinese participants role-playing the coached client, procounselor, anticounselor, and counselor. The interview was conducted in Chinese and then translated into English. Although all four role players were Chinese, they were matched so that within-group differences separated the counselor from the other three on each presenting problem. The following transcripts demonstrate how the Triad Training Model can be adapted to a wide variety of problem areas or populations according to the changing cultural salience.

SESSION 1: SEXUAL HARASSMENT
AT THE WORKPLACE

In the first interview, the problem of sexual harassment at the workplace is the salient feature. The procounselor, anticounselor, and client are all female, while the counselor in this interview is male. In this case, gender becomes a salient cultural feature. Recognize also that this interview is taking place in Mandarin Chinese, so the issues of "face," "authority," and "collective responsibility" will be managed differently than in an English-speaking cultural context.

> *Counselor ("Co," hereafter):* How are you doing, Miss Chung? May I ask if there's anything you want to tell me today?
> *Client ("Cl," hereafter):* Um, I have some problems at work, and I don't know how to deal with it.
> *Anticounselor ("Anti," hereafter):* What a shame the counselor is a male!

Co: Can you tell me a little bit more specifically about it? Is it about the pressure from the work or something that has to do with one of your colleagues?

Cl: Um, you might say it's something to do with a colleague. I feel good about the job I'm doing, but I feel so much pressure that I'm even getting afraid of going to the office.

Procounselor ("Pro," hereafter): It seems to me that he's a person of integrity that can be trusted.

Co: Can you be a bit more specific? You mean you feel you are being excluded from the colleague or you are not feeling right about something your colleague did? Or something else? Can you describe a little more specifically?

Cl: Um, you might say it's something about coercion that makes me feel uncomfortable. My job is about. . . I'm a secretary. I'm primarily responsible to my boss. I do whatever he tells me to do. That's it.

Anti: I doubt if I need to continue this with him.

Co: Is [he] giving you too much work to do, or you're not happy about the salary [he] pays you? Or something else?

Cl: The salary? I'm quite happy about the salary [he] gives me. You might say it's quite good, about NT$50,000-60,000 [US$1,500-1,800] a month. I'm quite happy about the pay. I want to do the job. I like this job. I want to continue to do this job. But it's just that it's so unpleasant that I have to see my boss every day I go to the office.

Co: Oh, it's something about you and your boss.

Pro: He got it.

Cl: Yes, you may say that again.

Anti: But I don't know how I can go on telling him any more about it.

Co: So, what you meant to say is you and your boss. . . Well, can you be more detailed? I figure that you are a female secretary, and you're responsible to [him]. Is it that very often the work [he] gives you is beyond what you can handle, or is it something about [his] behavior that makes you feel uncomfortable?

Cl: You know, in fact, [he] treats me quite well, tries not to give me too much work to do. . .

Co: Mm, hmm.

Cl: But, I don't know. . . I don't know if it's because my boss is a male, about 40 years old, and I've just graduated from college without any work experience. I don't know what to do about this. Or if this kind of behavior is considered quite normal in the workplace?

Co: Mm, hmm.

Pro: I think I should tell him some more about it. Maybe he can help me see it from a male's perspective. But I'm afraid he might think I'm just overreacting.

Co: You meant to say the behavior. . . I'd like to know what specific behavior you're referring to which makes you feel so uncomfortable.

Cl: Well, it is . . . for example, you males, the boss, my job in the afternoon . . . my boss wanted me to type a letter. In the middle of typing, he would suddenly give me a call asking me what I'm doing now, then start chatting with me. But he was acting like he was doing something sneaky, afraid of being spotted by other colleagues. I didn't feel there was anything wrong with this at first, but after he did this again and again, I felt something was wrong. Or sometimes he would call me to bring something to his office, then in there he would start, blah, blah, blah, saying something pointless. The moment I stepped out of his office, he called me back, telling me that I should wear shoes with higher heels.

Co: I see.

Cl: I don't know what in the world this is all about. This is an order from him. Should I take it or not? I feel very uncomfortable about this.

Co: I'd like to know if he was joking when he did this.

Cl: Joking?

Co: Yes.

Cl: I-M-P-O-S-S-I-B-L-E! He looked—he's very serious. You know something, there was one time when I was sitting next to him in a conference, and he's there gazing at me all the time. Everyone's there in the meeting, and he's doing this to me. I like my job, the pay is good, and I can dress up—usually I like to wear tight clothes, but I do not feel that there's anything wrong with this. But I don't think he should gaze at me like that in the meeting. What's more, he touched my thigh!

Anti: Will he think I deserve it because he's a male too?

Co: Well, obviously, what he did to you has already offended your right of privacy, which makes you very uncomfortable.

Cl: Exactly. I'm very uncomfortable.

Pro: He's different. He respects what I feel.

Co: Have you ever talked about this with your boss, that what he did makes you feel uncomfortable?

Cl: How can I tell him? Say to him, "Hi boss, you can't keep doing this to me!" I'm very afraid he would fire me, though I want very much to let him know. I don't feel I'm wrong wearing tight shirts or tight skirts, and the skirt is very short—there's nothing wrong with this. I don't feel I should tolerate his harassment.

Pro: I really want to. . . [words not clear]. Maybe he can help me out.

Anti: Maybe this counselor can't understand the conflict in me.

Co: I think you can be sure that your boss is doing this intentionally, not jokingly, not carelessly, since you have such a strong reaction. Well, I think the purpose of why you are here today is to find a solution to get rid of this uncomfortable feeling.

Cl: Yes, exactly. I'm very uncomfortable. I don't know how I can go on like this. I've got a good salary; I don't want to quit my job.

Pro: He really understands me. I'm still in distress and don't know what to do.

Co: Well, I think now that you have such an uncomfortable feeling, you should take a chance and let your boss know how you feel about it. I think it will make you feel better.

Cl: I don't know if we have any agencies in Taiwan like other countries where we can go and report this kind of harassment, and I don't know if I can tell others something like this. There's no way for me to tell my colleagues. They'll say something behind my back instead, something like I deserve it because I wear tight clothes, which might be seen as a misconduct by them.

Pro: It seems to me, he can completely accept me as I am. He has that respectful look on his face.

Anti: I feel I can't get any solution from him in this matter.

Co: Well, has it ever occurred to you that if you changed the way you dress, things would become better for you?

Cl: To change the way I dress?

Co: Yes.

Cl: Do you think what's happened to me has to do with what I wear? Don't you think I have the right to wear as I like?

Anti: What the hell—this counselor's questioning my clothes?

Pro: I can sense he's trying very hard to understand me.

Co: In fact, we can put it this way. If you could not get any protection from the established law or public support, maybe what we can do then is pessimistically prevent this from happening. So that's why I'd like to know if you'd feel that things would be different after you changed the way you dress.

Cl: How can you tell me to change my clothing? I don't know, I really don't know. If I changed, then I couldn't buy any of those clothes, then I don't have to work there because it would be no fun for me to work there anymore because I'd be very unhappy. In fact, I've tried to change, such as tried to wrap on a jacket . . . but the problem is I felt unhappy.

Pro: I think he's trying to understand me.

Anti: I think there's no way he'll understand what I suffered.

Because the counselor was male and the problem was sexual harassment, the anticounselor could easily build on the counselor's pro-male bias and the counselor would have to find common ground with the client that would become more salient than the male-female gender differences. The procounselor tried to do this by reinforcing the counselor's integrity and caring competence. The authority of the boss was also a salient feature for the client, who felt helpless and controlled in her dress and behavior. The organizational culture was still another salient feature, because direct confrontation might result in the withdrawal of support by the boss and other employees in the organization.

SESSION 2: JUVENILE DELINQUENCY

In the second transcript, the presenting problem is juvenile delinquency. The client, procounselor, anticounselor, and counselor are all female, but the counselor is older than the other three, so age becomes a salient feature in this interview. Another salient barrier would be between the more modern or experimental lifestyle of the client and the more traditional or conventional lifestyle of the counselor.

Co: Hi, how are you? Anything you want to tell me today?

Cl: Nothing, I don't want to talk about anything!

Co: Uh, it's because. . .

Cl: I didn't want to come here. I was forced to come. It's not that I wanted to come; I didn't want to come here at all; my parents forced me to come.

Anti: I want to go now.

Cl: Hey, Miss, there's no sense in my staying here, since I don't want to say anything. Can I go now?

Pro: Looks like she cares about me. I should stay and try.

Co: You look pretty bothered. Do you feel like trying to spend some time and tell me why you don't want to talk?

Cl: Um. . .

Anti: What the hell, is there anything I could tell her about what's bothering me?

Pro: Give it a try. Maybe she can help me.

Cl: This is no big deal. It's just that my parents found out I got pregnant, had an abortion. Then here I came, forced by my parents.

Pro: Looks like she's not shocked by my experience.

Co: You don't feel this is serious, but your parents do.

Cl: Of course, I don't feel this is a problem! Some of my friends had abortions already! I just don't feel this is a big deal; I don't know why my parents want to make such a fuss about it.

Anti: This counselor is like my parents. I'm afraid she's going to report something to my parents.

Pro: I feel she respects me very much.

Co: Don't you feel like spending some time talking about the conflict between you and your parents and trying to solve it?

Cl: Solve it?

Co: If not, then what are you going to do? The conflict is still there with them.

Cl: I'll try not to stay home. As long as I don't see them, then nothing's going to happen.

Anti: I feel there's no point in continuing this with her.

Pro: I feel she can help me.

Co: Do you feel you can have the problem solved between you and your parents if you keep going on like this?

Cl: They'll never change!

Co: I know this is difficult for you, isn't it? You want to give it a try and tell me?

Cl: Well, I feel my parents have treated me like a child—no this, no that. They just want me to do everything they told me to do. They want me to study hard. But I don't like studying at all. All I want is to stay with my boyfriend. Studying is so boring. But they just want me to get into a good high school.

Anti: Ai ya, what's the use telling her all this? She's not going to understand anyway.

Pro: She's not like other adults. It seems she respects me very much.

Co: Do you want to tell me what the difference is being with your boyfriend and with your parents, since you want to spend so much time with your boyfriend?

Cl: I'm happy when I'm with my boyfriend. With my parents in sight, headache! It's better not to see them. I stay out very often.

Pro: It feels good that I can say what I feel.

Anti: Do I want to tell her all the details?

Cl: I tell you, I really don't like you adults. I feel you are no different from my parents.

Co: You meant. . .

Cl: Mm. . . Recently, I told this to my teacher and *jeah guan* [personnel dispatched from the military to high schools and colleges who primarily served as disciplinarians before the martial law was lifted in Taiwan]. They looked like they cared about me very much and wanted to help me, but you know what, they then immediately disclosed all my secrets to my parents. That's how they came to know I got pregnant and had an abortion. See what happened to me, here I came, forced!

Co: So, you feel this time is going to be the same result too.

Cl: I think it must be almost the same.

Co: You feel adults are all the same.

Cl: Yes, I hate all of them.

Pro: Hey, she understands me.

Anti: Ai ya, I have gotten used to being cheated anyway. I want to go.

Cl: Miss, can I go or not? There is no point to go on talking like this with you.

Co: Um, what I'm concerned about is you still have this trouble. In fact, I don't have to discuss this with your parents because what I'm concerned about is how you're going to deal with this with your parents.

Pro: It never occurred to me that there's someone here who's so concerned about me. Maybe she can really help me.

Anti: But will it turn out to be the same again as before? She's got that make-believe look like all the others.

Cl: You really will not tell my parents?

Co: I don't think I have to. What I'm concerned about is how you're going to deal with the conflict you have. If my telling your parents would only result in a negative consequence, then there would be really no point to do so, right?

Pro: I feel I can trust her.

Anti: I still have some hesitation.

Cl: Hai (a big sigh). . . . How do you feel I can change my parents? I feel I don't have this ability.

Co: What makes you feel you can't. . .

Cl: For example, they want me to study, be obedient, and then get admitted to a good high school and then they'll feel their face's being saved. But I myself do not feel this has anything to do with me. This is only to make them look good. Anyway, I don't like studying.

Pro: I feel she's able to accept me.

Anti: There's no use discussing anything about my parents.

Co: So you feel your parents want you to study only to save face and not for your own interest.

Cl: That's what I feel. I feel they don't care about how much I hate to study. Besides, no matter how hard I tried, I just couldn't improve a bit. So why should I study?

Co: It's because you've got lots of frustration in school, that's why you don't like to study, correct?

Pro: Hai (big sigh), exactly correct!

Cl: Studying is boring. It's more fun to be with my boyfriend.

Anti: What difference does it make even if she understands me?

Cl: But . . . all my parents want me to do is study. Study, hm. . .

Pro: I feel I can get some support from her. She can understand me, I really need help.

Co: Tell me, how different do you feel about being with your boyfriend and studying?

Cl: You meant. . .?

Co: What are experiences you got from your boyfriend when you were with him?

Cl: When I was with my boyfriend?

Anti: Do I need to tell her about what happened when I was with my boyfriend?

Pro: She seems to be able to even accept what has happened between me and my boyfriend.

Cl: I just felt very happy when I was with my boyfriend. That's all.

Co: What did you do that made you feel very happy?

Anti: Ai ya, how can I ever tell her this?

Cl: What did we do when we're together? Don't you know? We're just simply very happy. . .

Co: You feel embarrassed to tell me, don't you?

Cl: Yeah, a little bit.

Pro: She seems to accept me without making any judgment on me.

Anti: No, I can't tell her, or else I will get the same result as before.

Co: Are you embarrassed to tell me or worried about how I'm going to look at you?

Cl: Mmm . . . I just don't feel like talking about this.

Co: So you don't even want to let me know why you don't want to talk about it.

Pro: Maybe I can tell her; maybe she's the only one I can trust.

Anti: Could it be that she's trying to trap me into talking more with her?

Cl: Hai (sigh), let's not discuss this anymore. It's going to make no difference anyway. I just feel happy with my boyfriend, that's all. And I get bored when I have to study. I get sleepy whenever I have to study.

Co: What do you have to say to your parents when they stop you from seeing your boyfriend?

Cl: I just ignored them, and I left home directly. I then go stay with my boyfriend until they get me back.

Pro: This is stressful to me. I really need help.

Anti: I don't know how long I have to talk to her.

Age becomes salient to the problem of understanding why the client would rather be with her boyfriend than study. The client associates all adults with her parents, as trying to force her to do things she does not want to do. This is reinforced by her previous experiences. The procounselor tries to build a bridge of respect and concern that will become more salient than age differences, but it is a difficult task.

SESSION 3: POLITICAL ISSUES

The salience of political affiliation in Taiwan reflects many aspects unique to that particular context and requires an understanding of historical background between the parties. Understanding the serious consequences for each alternative political action is also necessary before the counselor can begin to provide meaningful counseling. The counselor identifies herself as Taiwanese, whereas the client's family came from Mainland China, putting them on opposite sides of the political controversy.

Co: Hi, how are you doing? Is there anything that you want to talk about today?

Cl: Well, in fact, it's nothing serious. You know, not long ago we had an election in Taiwan. It seems to me it has gone a little messy.

Co: Mm hm.

Cl: I thought it was kind of a normal phenomenon during the time of elections. But later on, I found that some people I met in public areas would try to speak Taiwanese to me, and that made me feel like an outsider when I wasn't able to reply in fluent Taiwanese. I don't know how to describe that kind of feeling.

Pro: It looks to me like this counselor is really concentrating and serious about what I said.

Anti: I doubt if she can understand my problem.

Co: So, you had this feeling of being excluded by this whole environment because you're unable to speak Taiwanese?

Cl: In fact, it's not that serious yet. Because, you know, my father is from Fu Jien [a province located in southeastern Mainland China] and my mother is from Yi Lan [a county located in northeastern Taiwan]. So, in fact, I can understand Taiwanese. It's just that I have been brought up in Taipei and received my education there since I was little. The language we have been using in our daily life is Mandarin [Chinese], so my Taiwanese is not that fluent. Previously, we were not treated differently according to our provincial origins. I wonder if provincial discrimination has been stirred up by the media in connection with our political elections. In any case, the discrimination makes me feel uncomfortable.

Pro: I feel she can understand the uneasiness inside me.

Anti: I doubt if she understood the pain I suffered for not being able to speak Taiwanese.

Co: So, this change stirred up by the media made you feel uneasy about the environment where you have been brought up.

Cl: Uh . . . yes. By the way, may I ask if you're Taiwanese or half-Taiwanese, half-mainlander like me? Or are you mainlander [both parents are from Mainland China]?

Co: I was brought up in a Taiwanese family.

Cl: Oh, I see. I wonder if you could understand how we feel about the change.

Co: You doubt if I could understand the situation you're in now?

Cl: Um, more or less, I think.

Pro: It seems to me she can be trusted, because she can get to the point so directly.

Anti: Would she think that I'm overreacting?

Co: I think I might indeed not be able to understand what it's like to be kicked out even in your own country, but I have some friends and have heard something about it. I think if I were you, I would feel sad about it.

Pro: Hai (sigh), she understands me.

Anti: But, even so, will it make any difference?

Cl: You know, although my father came from Mainland, I was born here, brought up here, had my education here, and am working here. All my friends and my relatives are here. But now the situation in our society. . . I'm being left out just because I can't speak Taiwanese. It makes me very unpleasant.

Co: You feel angry?

Cl: Mmmm . . . angry? Of course.

Anti: What's the use in telling her what I feel? Will it be helpful in solving the problem?

Pro: She catches what I feel. Maybe she can help me to see this problem from a Taiwanese point of view.

Co: Sounds like, in fact, you have totally accepted Taiwan.

Cl: Of course.

Co: It seems that people misunderstood you just because your father came from Mainland and you're not good at speaking Taiwanese. But this is your hometown.

Cl: Yes. But, in fact, during the period when I was in school and later on at work, never did I experience this provincial discrimination. I had no problem dealing with my friends, my colleagues, and my classmates. It never bothered me whether they are Taiwanese or mainlander. And I think they've never cared about which province I am from or the language I use. But the society seemed to have this issue stirred up seriously. Here is an example. During the time of elections not long ago, while I was taking a taxi, I never dared to say whom I supported. Or . . . especially when I was asked in Taiwanese and found myself not being able to answer in Taiwanese, I felt very uncomfortable.

Co: How's your reaction to that?

Cl: I . . . maybe just laughed away this matter, then. . .

Co: But the feeling of uneasiness is still there?

Cl: Yes.

Anti: She's Taiwanese. Maybe she can't understand what I feel, that feeling of uneasiness.

Co: It seems you're holding something back that you want to say.

Cl: Yes, in fact. We all live here, I don't feel this is a big problem. Maybe it's the media that stirred this up. Maybe I'm just overreacting a little. I don't know. . .

Pro: It seems to me she can help me. It doesn't matter if she's Taiwanese or mainlander, she will also feel uneasy about this.

Co: It sounds like you're having a certain sense of uneasiness as well as uncertainty. And probably you're also overreacting a little. I feel it has nothing to do with your friends, your work, and your school, but something with the whole environment.

Cl: Yes.

Co: And with those people you don't know of.

Pro: She's trying to help clarify things for me.

Anti: But will this clarification be helpful in changing the whole environment? I wonder even if we continued this consultation if it would lead to nowhere but an emotional venting.

Cl: To be more specific, the reason I feel uneasy is that even though I can't speak fluent Taiwanese, this is still my hometown. In my mind, this is where my hometown is. Maybe someday in the future I will go back to Mainland China to pay a visit to my father's birthplace, but I have no desire to settle down and develop my career there. But now the situation here is also getting to be undesirable and not worth my efforts. However, I can't think of any other places to go because this is where my country is. You know this kind of feeling? That's all.

Co: What you're concerned about is if the situation here is getting worse, then you'll probably have to leave because there is no future for you to stay here.

Cl: Yes, I'd feel as if there's no place for me. I'd lose the sense of root.

Pro: She indeed captured the point.

Anti: This is too big an issue. Can she help me solve the problem?

Co: So, in fact, you're very clear that you've accepted this place as your hometown.

Cl: Certainly.

Co: Except you're unable to use Taiwanese fluently in communication.

Cl: Yes.

Pro: She doesn't deny me at all because I'm a mainlander.

Co: And you feel it's unfair to you, don't you?

Cl: I don't know. To me, language is just a tool of communication.

Co: So, you are here today in the hope that you can work out something, an attitude for you to deal with this situation while you continue to stay here, where you've accepted as your hometown.

Cl: Yeah. Maybe I want to know how to adjust myself so that I can cope with the situation now in society.

Anti: Would it be that the result, after having discussed this with her, is that I have to try very hard to learn Taiwanese so that I'd be able to cope with the life here now?

The seriousness of the political differences between Taiwanese and mainlander are apparent and present, a powerful salient barrier to the counseling interview. The client describes herself as an outsider, wanting to fit in but not being allowed to do so. The client does not oppose the changes in the balance of political power but does not want to become a victim of those changes. The procounselor builds on the counselor's understanding of and concern for the client as potentially salient features of the interview that might eventually overcome the political barrier.

SESSION 4: LESBIAN LIFESTYLE

The last interview matches a lesbian client with a straight counselor in an interview in which all four participants are female. The most obvious salient feature relates to the client's lesbian lifestyle and sense of rebellion against conventional straight rules of society. It is difficult for the counselor to bridge the barrier and be accepted by the client, just as it is difficult for the client to seek help from someone who is so different from herself.

Co: Hi, may I ask what you want to talk about today?

Cl: I have a problem. I'm already 25 years old. My parents wish so much that I could have a boyfriend. They wonder why I still haven't had any boyfriend. But in fact . . . this is very difficult for me to say . . . in fact, I'm more attracted to the female body. I have no interest in men's, so I can't have a boyfriend.

Pro: She's not shocked by what she heard.

Anti: I wonder if she knew what I was talking about.

Co: So you mean that you not only have the pressure from your parents but you have the difficulty to accept the fact that you're a homosexual.

Cl: Um, I feel, in terms of the situation in which I am, I'm already aware that maybe I'm inclined to be a homosexual. I have already been like this for one year. And I can quite accept this fact. But the biggest problem is that I can't tell my parents and my friends about this.

Anti: I wonder if she can understand what it's like to be a homosexual.

Co: It seems you're lonely.

Pro: She can really understand the loneliness I experienced.

Cl: Anyway (sigh) . . . at present, I just can't tell my parents because they're quite conservative. For example, recently they read a news article about homosexuals in the newspaper. They reacted as if those people are sick, how in the world could this happen? So I'm so afraid to just let them know.

Pro: She can understand the fear and uneasiness in me.

Anti: In fact, I think she will judge me just as my parents would if I disclosed this to them.

Cl: Do you have any homosexual friends?

Co: No, I do not have any friends who are homosexual.

Cl: Oh, I see.

Co: Mm, hm.

Cl: I think you can't really understand why I can't tell my parents. Recently, I read an article about a male homosexual in Texas who killed himself after people found out that he's gay. The same thing would happen to me if my parents knew that I'm a lesbian. What else can I do except choose to kill myself? I just couldn't let them know.

Co: That news must be a shock to you.

Cl: That's what I felt.

Anti: Can she understand the pain I suffered?

Co: If I were you, I would also feel the same.

Cl: Right.

Pro: I feel that she can really understand me.

Anti: But what good does it do to continue talking like this?

Co: But I think since you came here, you don't really want to have the same result happen to you as to that man. You must have other expectations that you want to work out some new idea from this consultation that may help you. . . .I wonder what it is?

Cl: Well, I came here . . . because I can't even tell my best friends . . . of course, not my parents either. I have no one that I could go to talk to. I came here in the hope that I can finally find a place where I can let myself talk. . .

Pro: I need her support.

Anti: In fact, I don't hold any expectation in this matter. This is probably what it can be.

Co: How do you feel now that you've let it out?

Cl: I feel much release that I could talk about it. Before, I could never talk about it.

Pro: I feel she can totally accept me.

Co: So, do you wish to tell your parents and friends about it?

Cl: No, I can never let them know.

Anti: Impossible, definitely impossible.

Pro: But I still have this wish that. . .

Cl: I can never tell them. Hai (sigh).

Co: So you came here just to find someone to talk to.

Cl: Yes. Otherwise, I don't know what else I can do.

Anti: Even so, I still feel ironic. Can't I tell anyone else except her, someone I don't even know, that I'm a lesbian for the rest of my life?

Pro: To be able to be accepted by my parents is my final wish.

Co: But do you only wish to come here every week just to find someone, a stranger, to talk about what you feel? Don't you want your parents and friends to accept you as well?

Cl: Of course I wish they could accept me. But I really doubt it. Besides, my parents are very serious Christians. They definitely see homosexuality as wrong.

Co: So you find it impossible to tell them that their daughter is a lesbian.

Anti: I doubt how much this counselor can help.

Co: Well, I'm not here to talk you into doing this or that. All I want is to make clear what your expectation is for coming here so that I may give you some suggestions you need.

Pro: She seems to guide me step by step.

Anti: But I'm still puzzled about how I'm going to continue this with her.

Co: If what you want is only to come here every week and find someone you can talk with, I'll be happy to be that person for you. But what I'm concerned about is once you step out of here, what are you going to do to face the people around you?

Pro: Ah, she really understands my suffering.

Cl: Of course I want to talk about it. But I really don't feel I have the courage.

Co: Maybe we can work out something here to help you talk about it, and you can try to let your parents understand you and accept the fact gradually. Did you ever give it a try?

Anti: This is impossible.

Pro: Hai (sigh), this is what I hoped.

Cl: I . . . Of course I wanted very much to try, but it's just impossible.

Pro: I need help, I need help.

Co: Sounds like you feel so helpless and hopeless about this matter.

Cl: Yes, to me, this is what I feel.

Co: Hm.

Anti: Even though you've said that you can find a way for me, I doubt that you can really help me.

The client does not present her lesbian lifestyle as the problem, although a straight counselor might interpret it as the salient problem. The client identifies as salient the loneliness of having to keep her lifestyle secret and the risk of public embarrassment, ridicule, or even physical harm should her secret become known. The counselor's lack of familiarity with a lesbian/homosexual lifestyle and not having friends from that lifestyle becomes a serious and salient barrier. On the other hand, the counselor—even as an outsider—provides a safe place for the client to discuss and explore her own feelings and attitudes about the choices she will need to make.

CONCLUSION

The interaction of the client, procounselor, anticounselor, and counselor demonstrated four examples of cultural salience based on demographic, status, and affiliation variables more than on ethnographic variables. In all four problem areas, there was a consistent polarization of sides between a modernized, Westernized, and individualized lifestyle on the one hand and the more traditional, collectivistic Chinese lifestyle on the other. In all four situations, the client was caught between these two polarized forces. The importance of relationship and affiliation with significant others was an important means for

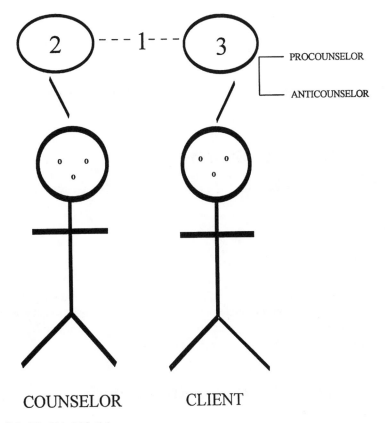

COUNSELOR   CLIENT

Figure 8.1. The Triad Model

the counselor to bridge the salient problem and to identify common ground for counseling.

The procounselor was attempting to promote the counseling relationship as a positive resource and to make that resource salient for the client. The anticounselor was pointing out that even seeking out counseling was in itself an unacceptable behavior for traditional Chinese clients. The potential shame and embarrassment of needing to see a counselor increased the client's vulnerability.

The counselor needed an awareness of the client's background specific to each salient presenting problem and an awareness of how counselor-client differences might influence the counseling relationship. The counselor required special knowledge about the salient presenting problem and the consequences of each alternative choice available to the client. Only when the counselor had accurate awareness and appropriate knowledge could the counselor's skills become relevant as a positive resource for the client.

9

Transcript Examples of the Triad Training Model

There are several variations in the Triad Training Model that have been developed. Each of these variations makes explicit internal dialogues that might otherwise be thought but not articulated out loud. These variations demonstrate possibilities to incorporate internal dialogue in a great variety of training and educational strategies.

THE REHEARSAL DEMONSTRATION MODEL

The Rehearsal Demonstration Model (RDM) is designed to match each spoken and explicit communication with a parallel message, indicating what the person is thinking but not saying, by a coached alter-ego person. Initially, the RDM is fully scripted, and the participants read their scripted role messages. If, for example, the teacher would say, "Wan Lee-ho, why can't you do better work in school?" a student might respond, "I'm sorry." First, the teacher would say, "Why can't you do better work at school?" and the teacher's "unspoken" message might say, "I keep getting after you to do better work, and you never do better work! Why is that? Why is it that you can't work harder?" The student might say, "I'm sorry." The student's "unspoken" message might say, "No matter what I do, it isn't appreciated, so why should I do more work?" If we focus on the verbal explicit message, we only get the messages the teacher or student is saying and not what they are thinking. To work effectively, we need to know not just what is being said but what is being thought from the other culture's perspective. The RDM script might resemble the following:

Educational context

> *Teacher:* Look at me! What happened?

> *Teacher Unspoken:* YOU MUST BE GUILTY OR YOU WOULD
> LOOK ME IN THE EYE. YOUR KIND NEVER LOOK OTHERS
> STRAIGHT IN THE EYE.
> *Student:* I dunno.
> *Student Unspoken:* WHAT'S THE USE? YOU WON'T BELIEVE ME
> ANYWAY. I AM NOT COMFORTABLE LOOKING BACK AT
> YOU!

The interview would then be continued spontaneously, with the individuals assigned to be the "teacher unspoken" and the "student unspoken" making the otherwise implicit thoughts of their partners explicit.

Pedersen and Hernandez (1997) also applied the RDM to interviews in the military situation:

Military context

> *Commander:* Our unit has the best racial climate on the base, and I'm
> sure you'll agree.
> *Commander Unspoken:* THIS SHOULD STOP ANY FURTHER
> QUESTIONS.
> *2nd Lt.:* That depends on how you look at it.
> *2nd Lt. Unspoken:* PERSONALLY, I THINK IT'S THE WORST ON
> BASE.

The RDM was further adapted to a business context in which the role of management and the role of worker were treated as a cultural interaction.

Business context

> *Supervisor:* I talk things over with my people before I act.
> *Supervisor Unspoken:* THESE PEOPLE KNOW NOTHING ABOUT
> MANAGEMENT.
> *Worker:* That's a good procedure to follow.
> *Worker Unspoken:* THEN WHY AM I HERE WITH THE COM-
> PLAINT IN MY HAND?

The RDM training approach offers several advantages:

1. It mobilizes the otherwise implicit educational insights of direct intercultural experiences with persons from other cultures.
2. Each exchange recognizes the multiple levels of spoken and unspoken communication in the intercultural exchange.
3. It helps demonstrate how stereotypes are differentiated from generalizations.
4. It makes explicit specific barriers to intercultural communication.

THIRD PARTY FRIENDLY/HOSTILE

When using the Triad Training Model while consulting with Native American groups in the northwest United States, the leaders indicated that their youth would typically come into counseling with a parent, friend, or relative, who might be friendly or unfriendly to the counseling alternative. They were interested in modifying the Triad Training Model from a role play with an anticounselor and a procounselor to an interaction between a counselor and a "third person friendly" or a "third person hostile." In this variation, the pro- and the antivoice were articulated by the client's actual partner role-playing an actual person.

This variation resembles typical situations in family counseling, as described by Virginia Satir (1964), through conjoint family therapy, in which the positive alliances and negative grievances in the family would be revealed as friendly or hostile messages toward the counselor. Since a procounselor and an anticounselor in the conventional Triad Training Model are not actual people, they are free to be inconsistent, contradictory, and unreasonable. The third person hostile and/or the third person friendly do not have that luxury; rather, they are held accountable to be consistent, reasonable, and appropriate in their expression of hostile or friendly messages. International students who are unfamiliar with counseling have also been encouraged to bring a friend into the counseling interview who was sometimes friendly and sometimes hostile (Pedersen, 1991). Role plays to practice counseling foreign students with a third person hostile or friendly have proven to be productive.

THE INTERPRETER/TRANSLATOR MODEL

A third variation involves a third person in the counseling interview as an "interpreter" or a "translator," who clarifies both the client's messages toward the counselor and the counselor's messages toward the client. Through this function, the interpreter resembles a language interpreter in many ways, even though both the counselor and the client are using the same basic language. Some sample transcripts in which a Caucasian counselor is working with an Indochinese refugee indicate what the interpreter/translator might say or do in the interview.

> *Interpreter ("In," hereafter):* What you are saying also is that you are not very happy that they took the bone out of your back.
>
> *Client ("Cl," hereafter):* Yes, because to me, that is not good. I am not completely myself anymore.
>
> *Counselor ("Co," hereafter):* OK, so what I feel now, or the information you've given me so far, is that you had an operation and it was a little bit more major than what you thought it was going to be. I mean, the doctor did more work on your back than you thought he would do. You're also new to the country, having been here only for

6 months. So you're kind of insecure, kind of lonely? Does that, is that a good word that I can use? Um. . .

Cl: Yes, sir.

Co: Um. . . Have I left anything out?

Cl: No, I think you covered what I had told you. And, in addition to that, I also have some other problem, because after the operation I began to worry about myself and my future life very, very much. I do not know what to do, so I spend days and nights thinking about what am I going to do with myself. And I could not eat, as I said before, I could not sleep, so I kind of stay half-awake all the time. And this leads to a lot of things that I have in my mind. At times, I can see my grandparents, who have died many years ago, or my friend, who has been in the army together with me who has been killed. And they are all there, happy, and they keep calling my name and writing to see me.

In: What he's saying is he's stuck because he worries so much about his life and so forth that, you know . . . in this culture, when you start seeing things . . . especially your members of the family or your close friends who died . . . that means that his life is also going down the drain. That he will die soon. If he were back home, that's what would happen.

There are several salient concerns of a physical, psychological, and spiritual nature for this Hmong Laotian-American client. Physically, the client has suffered abdominal pains and backaches, which led to an unwanted operation. Strange behavior suggests that the client's psychological state has been affected. The most significant problem, however, is the loss of everything familiar in having had to flee to a new country. This has disrupted his spiritual well-being. The client, consequently, attributes all his present problems to the ill doings of spirits. Thus, the counseling dilemma is how to treat this person within the context of his cultural beliefs and expectations when no traditional healer is available.

The interpreter/translator offers what he believes to be an important concern, underemphasized by the client. He tentatively suggests, "What you are saying also is that you are not very happy that they took the bone out of your back." From the client's reaction, it can be assumed that, yes, this was an important concern. It gives the counselor missing information, helping him articulate the problem from the client's perspective. The interpreter's contribution is also crucial in that a Western counselor may have attributed the visions to a very different cause, such as schizophrenia, remaining ignorant of the cultural implications of visions to an Indochinese.

The counselor appears to accept the interpreter's explanation that the visions symbolize fear of a near death for the client. Thus, he receives important implicit cultural information from the interpreter. The counselor, consequently, is able to deal openly with the client's expectation to participate in a ceremony to chase away evil spirits, which could otherwise have remained implicit and disruptive in the counseling process.

The counselor later reported on his experiences:

The culture was different and I'm not sure if I really got a good handle on the presenting problem or if it was presented in its fullest detail. I could relate with someone from another country and their loneliness, but not with the fact of having an operation causing this degree of problem. The client couldn't eat or sleep and the body aches I took to mean some underlying more important physical problem.

The counselor attributes physical symptoms (body aches) to a greater psychological problem, perhaps because of his knowledge that Asian groups tend to somaticize emotional problems. Some Western approaches may infer psychological disturbance from the presence of physical ailments, but there is a danger in overdiagnosing or underdiagnosing physical complaints. The counselor found the presence of a third-person interpreter helpful to explain what visions meant and to clarify counselor communications to the client.

The client found the interpreter to be very helpful in explaining what the client was trying to verbalize and in helping him communicate with this unrelated stranger about his personal life. Since both the interpreter and client came from the same culture, they knew each other's culture, language, and lifestyle.

THE TRIAD TRAINING MODEL WITH A "PROCOUNSELOR"

A fourth variation of the Triad Training Model uses only the procounselor and not the anticounselor. This variation is less stressful and more educative but less threatening. Using the procounselor without the anticounselor has been suggested as better suited for beginning students of counseling.

Cl: I got my midterm grade and I'm not doing well and, uh, I've got to do well. I'm on a stipend, and I'm getting a scholarship, and I don't want to lose it, so, you know, I thought maybe you folks could do something.

Co: Sure, yeah, yeah. So you're really scared that you're going to lose the stipend and you may have to leave school.

Cl: Well, that's a possibility, and, ah, and ah. . .

Procounselor ("Pro," hereafter): It might help if we deal with her expectations in coming in here.

Cl: I mean, ah, I mean I was a pretty good student—straight A—but I don't know what's wrong with the department. It's really all kinda f—ked up. It's really kind of hard when you go into a program and some people tell you one thing, and other people tell you another thing, and ah, you don't know exactly which way, you don't know exactly what to do—so maybe I should send them down here, right?

Co: Right, maybe they need to be here rather than you. Is that what you feel? You are really angry at them, it sounds like. . .

Cl: Well, they're, you know, they're really screwing up and, you know, it is hard to take a program . . . they're not putting out what they want. I don't even know what they want.

Pro: I'm really good at bulls—t. . . Get us off the topic of school. . .

Co: What else is going on? What other kinds of issues are bothering you? Is it mainly school?

Cl: Well, just, you know, I wouldn't say anything is bothering me. . . . I guess everything is bothering me right now because of school. But, ah, you know, if you don't think you can help me, just say so. I don't expect. . .

Pro: Look at how nervous I am and look at how I am shaking.

Co: You're really, really concerned about things. . .

Cl: Wouldn't you be?

Co: Sure, yeah, yeah. And yet you're not sure that I can help you. You won't let me hear. . .

Cl: Why? You haven't helped me yet!

Pro: Maybe it has something to do with you being a man.

Co: Would you rather be working with a woman?

Cl: Ah, yes.

Co: You would. . .?

Pro: Good thinking.

Cl: Yes, because I am a woman, and ah, I think women have kind of an understanding with each other that men and women just don't have. And it's not your fault, you know, I'm not putting you down for being a man, but, ah, you know, but I think that in some circumstances men just, you know, don't have the same kind of background.

Pro: Find out what those concerns are that men cannot relate to.

Cl: And, ah, I guess, you know, I've heard some things too, about, you know, psychiatrists and psychologists and, you know, I think it pays to be careful.

Pro: Maybe you ought to tell him what those are.

Co: What kinds of things are you concerned about?

Cl: Well, just in general, I don't think that male psychiatrists or psychologists can really, ah, you know, I just think they don't have the same point of view, they just aren't going to look at it, ah, they're not going to have the same kind of values and so men might not even hear things the same way.

Co: So, you think, for example, you think my biases might really be different than a woman's or than your biases; my values might be different. . .

Reactions of Participants to the Procounselor

Client Feedback

In this role play of a young graduate student seeking help from the Counseling and Testing Center, I found myself much more apprehensive than I anticipated. My main concern was to present a role that would be stereotypical of a liberated woman so that the male/female subculture could be dealt with. I found the therapist very supporting and after the initial impact of the cameras and lights, I began to enjoy the role. The procounselor seemed to detract from the beginning rapport that was happening despite my protests. The procounselor was intent on getting to the root of my presenting problem as a basis for the development of trust rather than focusing on the empathy that was being conveyed by the counselor. It was amazing to me that, despite my vagueness and distrust, my lack of information-giving to the therapist, and the interruptions of the procounselor, the empathy and concern were conveyed. I felt that this person was helped whether or not she returned to that particular counselor or not.

Counselor Feedback

In this situation, I felt somewhat on the spot and uncomfortable because of the unfamiliar hot lights and videotaping. I was also caught off guard and confused by what I first thought was the procounselor's attempts to get me to proceed in a different fashion (I could have been more honest and confronted that confusion as it was happening). And it took me a while to begin to understand Sarah's [the client's] resistance to me. But all in all, I felt we ended up with a fair amount of empathy having been communicated and with Sarah on her way to getting the help she needed.

Procounselor Feedback

As a procounselor, it was extremely frustrating working with a counselor using a different style than I would use. The counselor did not seem interested in the clues that I gave him and often ignored my suggestions. At times I felt angry with the counselor. Timing of my comments seemed disharmonious, and the session felt disjointed. I was attempting to facilitate problem clarification by focusing on the "here and now" situation by comments on the client's expectation for the sessions. When I realized the direction I was going toward—providing data to the therapist—wasn't working, I switched to supporting the client, e.g., putting my arm around her, suggesting she levels with the therapist, etc. This change of approach felt better than the first direction.

THE TRIAD TRAINING MODEL
WITH AN "ANTICOUNSELOR"

A fifth variation uses only the anticounselor and not the procounselor. This was the format for the original "Triad Model" developed at the University of Minnesota. Only later did I come to believe that the negative messages of the anticounselor needed to be balanced with positive messages of a procounselor to make the interview less stressful and more potentially constructive.

Cl: I'd like to leave my parents' house. I live with them.

Co: Uh huh.

Cl: And, it's just getting . . . it's not very convenient to . . . they live way out. . . . Um, you know. It takes me about 15 minutes to come in from there and from school and to go back and come in and go back.

Co: So you've been thinking about moving out?

CI: Yes.

Co: How is it a problem?

Anticounselor ("Anti," hereafter): See, he doesn't even understand your problem. You just want to move out.

Co: But I'm not sure of whether it's not having another place to stay or how you're going to handle it with your folks.

Cl: Yeah, that's a problem—my folks.

Co: Oh. How do they feel about it?

Cl: They don't like me to move out.

Co: They don't like you to move out, huh? However, I don't know your folks. I don't know your home situation. Who all's home?

Cl: My brother.

Anti: Does that matter whose home and who's not home? It's just that you want to move out. Now, remember, Lynette, your grandmother went through problems also, and she never complained, right? She always says "hang on," you know? You just suffer in silence and things will work out, and she would be through it all. Uh, it will all work out.

Cl: Hmmm.

Anti: She suffered. You're probably feeling inadequate because you're weak, right? Because your grandmother and mother could suffer through everything, you know? You could do it, too.

Co: You have talked to them about it?

Cl: Um, not really talked to them. I mentioned it, and my mother gets very upset and my father sort of yells at me because I'm being ungrateful.

Co: What about your friends? What do they say?

Cl: Well, that's another thing, see, they sort of . . . My Oriental friends feel like, yeah, they understand how my parents feel because it's an insult to move out. But then my Caucasian friends . . . they have this funny way of looking at it, you know. They say, "Oh yeah, you're so dependent; you're 26 years old."

Anti: Why don't you ask him if he thinks you should move out?

Cl: Hm. What do you think I should do? I mean, what's correct? Do you think. . .

Co: Well, I guess if you're going to play by your parents' rules, staying home and suffering, I think is. . .

Anti: You see. He thinks you're suffering at home and that you should move out. Your parents are to blame, you know?

Cl: Do you think I'm suffering at home?

Co: Well, I think something brought you here to talk to me about the dilemma you're in about wanting to move out and being very uncomfortable in having a rough time bringing it up with your folks in such a way that, uh, you can do that.

Anti: Ask him when he moved out . . . when he actually moved out of his house.

Cl: Yeah, when did you move out of your house?

Co: I moved out of my folks' house when I was 16.

Anti: Why did he move out so young, you know? I mean 16 . . . after all that his parents did for him and everything, you know . . . he moved out at 16?

Co: Well, I went away to school. And it was important to live at school. It was another town.

Cl: Didn't your parents get mad that you went to another school?

Co: No. They wanted me to go to school. Education is pretty important. . .

Anti: See. He's implying that your parents don't think education is important!

Reactions of Participants

Client Feedback

I think the counselor's goals were to do an assessment of the nature of the problem and then determine the course of treatment. He also intended to do this within a very supportive relationship. The anticounselor attempted to clue in the counselor about the real nature of the problem by giving him hints about the client but not revealing the total problem.

Counselor Feedback

As a counselor, I saw my job as, first, trying to understand what the client was feeling at a fairly deep and complete level and then help the client as appropriate to her needs and the context. I often find that just feeding back my understanding of the client's feelings, as long as this is done in a truly empathic manner (i.e., accurately and with appropriate affect), is enough to help the client, and sophisticated helping techniques or smart advice is not warranted.

Anticounselor Feedback

I wondered if I was doing a good job as an anticounselor. Maybe I could have been more of a cotherapist—directing my comments to the client, thus indirectly giving the counselor some clues. This was actually my first experience as anticounselor, and the role, as I played it, did not synchronize with the therapeutic setting.

THE TRIAD TRAINING MODEL WITH BOTH A "PROCOUNSELOR" AND AN "ANTICOUNSELOR"

The sixth example models the use of both a procounselor and an anticounselor. This provides a force field of negative and positive influence and seems to best demonstrate the range of client internal dialogue going back and forth from negative to positive and back to negative interpretations.

Co: Well, good afternoon, Bruce. What can I do for you today?

Cl: Well, ah, lately. . . First of all, let me tell you, I am a refugee from Indochina, and I have been here for quite a while. Now, when I was back in my country, I had a good job in the government, and I was a head of household. But, due to the political situation changes, I fled to the United States. When I got here, I was very happy, I was ready to start my life over again. But, very soon after my arrival, I found out that I was not able to do anything that I was thinking about. And, this due to the lack of knowledge of language, and I think that is the main thing. I cannot communicate with other people, so, but I look for job, you know, nobody will hire me. Not only that, but I came here alone, and I left all my, ah, members of my families back in my country, and once in a while I will receive some letters, are very sad, and I very worried about them, and at the same time I am very worried about myself. I really do not know what to do. I don't know where to start.

Pro: You feel helpless and very lonely.

Anti: You feel hopeless now because you are hopeless!

Cl: That's how I feel, yes.

Pro: The counselor can offer you new hope.

Anti: There is no hope for you any more to get reunited with them or for you to have a start over here.

Cl: Well, that's why I come here, to see you today, to see if there would ever be any possible way.

Anti: I don't know if they are really listening to us now. You only start with the two problems and they don't know where we are.

Co: What did you used to do before you came here? What kind of work?

Pro: The counselor can help you find a job.

Cl: Well, I was a public health officer, and I was working in a hospital as an administrator.

Co: I see, you were an administrator? And you've applied for that sort of work?

Cl: I have gone around all the hospitals here, including the Health Department, but nobody would take me because they told me that I cannot understand English, so I cannot work.

Pro: It's very humiliating to beg for work.

Co: What are you living on right now?

Cl: Well, I work as a part-time, as a dishwasher. Yes.

Anti: I'm not sure whether he's asking that question to find out if you have money to pay them. I don't know if they know anything about our situation.

Pro: You're not able to make it on the money you get dishwashing. You need help from the counselor.

Co: So, you want us to go find you the kind of work that you are looking for and to help you so that you can start in the field that you left when you were in Laos?

Cl: Yes, if possible.

Co: OK. We need to find out from you, OK, what your background has been in terms of education, and we have to see if you know the type of work that you have done in Laos, you know, or the kind of education that you have right now is something that we can help you with.

Anti: Hey, Bruce, I don't think that this is a place to look for jobs; they are counselors, they are not job developers. I don't think that they are asking you the right questions or trying to get through the problem yet.

Pro: What is the problem to you? Is it getting a job or something more?

Cl: Yes. I have two main problems. One is to get a job so I can support myself and maybe can help my relatives who are left behind. Secondly is probably the biggest problem, that I want to see my family again.

Co: OK, so now we understand that, first of all, you need to get a job and we'll help you get a job. You obviously communicate very well in spoken English.

Anti: I don't think that they understand our problem; they are still just focusing on the job.

The pro and anti combined model is the standard format of the Triad Training Model. This combination of feedback from both a pro and an anti provides a force field of positive and negative "hidden messages" in the counseling interview.

CONCLUSION

Several examples of the Triad Training Model are offered with transcripts and commentary. The Rehearsal Demonstration Model resembles the use of an alter ego in psychodrama, in which each person has a partner to articulate what the client is thinking but not saying, which is usually negative. This design is useful to demonstrate implicit client messages, but it does not go beyond that identification.

The second example of a third person friendly or hostile again involves feedback during the interview from a third person, but this person is in a real-life role rather than as a positive or negative aspect of the client's unspoken thoughts. In multicultural counseling, clients will frequently bring a partner into the interview, so this training design is good practice for counselors who would typically work with one client at a time.

The third example involves the third person as an interpreter who functions much like a language interpreter to clarify the communication process for both the counselor and the client. Culture-specific information is often unavailable to the counselor in cross-cultural interviews, and this third person helps identify the information essential to competent counseling.

The fourth example is with a procounselor but not an anticounselor. This transcript demonstrates how a procounselor can offer support to both the client and the counselor in an interview. The encouragement by a procounselor is not always explicit enough to change the counselor's intervention in a more appropriate direction, but overt conflict is held to a minimum.

The fifth example is with an anticounselor only, and the attacks on the counselor have a significant impact on the counselor's statements. The anticounselor sometimes traps the counselor into misunderstanding the client, but without alienating the client. The client responds positively to these negative messages.

The sixth example is with an anticounselor and a procounselor to give the full range of positive and negative feedback to the counselor. This transcript illustrates how the counselor is encouraged to see the problem from the client's viewpoint, to recognize resistance in specific rather than general terms, to reduce the counselor's defensiveness, and to recover after having said or done the wrong thing.

10

Other Internal
Dialogue Training Models

The definition of a *good idea* is one that, once generated, takes over and becomes the teacher of those who originally thought up that idea in the first place. The idea of the Triad Training Model has generated a range of adaptations by colleagues who emphasize different aspects of the original Triad Training Model according to the needs of their separate populations. This chapter will discuss four such adaptations, although there may well be additional adaptations that have been developed. In each of these four examples, the author of each adaptation has acknowledged the Triad Training Model as a starting point but has also generated a variety of creative and innovative features that make his or her adaptation significantly different from the Triad Training Model.

THE BICULTURAL CONTEXTUALIZER

The earliest adaptation of the Triad Training Model was done by Dr. Chalsa Loo (1980a, 1980b) and was developed to increase the "cultural sensitivity" of counselors, particularly regarding their understanding of ethnic identity issues. Although there is a third person giving immediate and continuous feedback to the counselor and the client, that third person is neither a procounselor nor an anticounselor but, rather, a "cultural contextualizer." There is very little written about this model, although it is very promising in its design. The function of the cultural contextualizer is, as expected, to put the messages of the counselor and, *especially,* of the client in their appropriate context. Sometimes the cultural contextualizer provides evaluative statements but usually not.

At times, the bicultural contextualizer (BCC) seems like a co-counselor, although the function of the BCC is not to provide counseling but to clarify the ethnic identity issues as they come up in the counseling interview. At other times, the BCC resembles a coclient, although the function of the BCC is not to receive help but to demonstrate areas of special vulnerability that the client might be experiencing. The BCC functions more as a teacher or an observer/participant in the interview, giving both the counselor and the client some clarification of the context in which the counseling is taking place. Typically, the BCC is of the same ethnic group as the client and verbalizes some of the thoughts the client might have either in the interview or later when talking about the interview with other members of that ethnic group.

The following transcript excerpts demonstrate how the cultural contextualizer functions during a simulated interview. The first interview is titled "Understanding Ethnic Identity" (Loo, 1980a) and was done through the Chinatown Research Center and the University of California at Santa Cruz.*

16 *Therapist (T):* As, again, as you're talking it's like your face muscles are, you know, moving like they're feeling like crying, and like, umm, that just starting to talk about it is real upsetting, a flood of feelings or something.

17 *Client (C):* Well, it is.

18 *T:* Can you go on with that, or would it be real hard for you to let yourself cry at this point; are you putting a lot of energy into keeping it down. . .?

19 *C:* I don't feel like crying right now.

20 *T:* Okay. Well, then, can you go ahead and say some more about what the University is doing to you and how that feels?

21 *C:* (sigh) Like I said, it insults my identity. I just get really, just really angry.

22 *Bicultural Contextualizer (BCC):* What kind of identity do you have?

23 *C:* I'm a Chicano.

24 *BCC:* And how is that a problem for you at the university?

25 *C:* (sigh) Well, the University definitely doesn't, uh, the University is sort of there; and it's pretty white, pretty middle-class, sort of bulls—t liberal; and it's just hard to deal with that constantly, you know; that isn't who I am (laugh) or who I want to be.

26 *T:* Like you're getting run through somebody else's mill, huh?

27 *BCC:* Uh, what, are you saying that you, you're responding to the pressure, to, uh, to a pressure of what you said was white, white, white standards or whatever it is? Were you finding yourself responding to that; is that what your unhappiness is about or what is it?

28 *C:* No, I'm just . . . I'm not, you know, it's just very hard to go into classes, and be the only person, like I identify myself as a Chicano, right, and that means something like, that means, I view the world a certain way, and I react to the world a certain way, and having it constantly grate against something like, just classes and people, and their basic (sigh), how do I put it?

29 *BCC:* Tell me about yourself and your Chicano background.

---

*NOTE: Each statement was numbered to identify clearly where it was placed on the original transcript by Chalsa Leo.

30 C: Well. . .

31 BCC: What that means for you. . .

32 C: I'm una asimilata, that means I grew up basically, my early, early background
was when I was very young, I knew Spanish; and I grew up sort of like in a small
community. . .

The bicultural contextualizer goes on to highlight contextual issues such as
the small town where she grew up, her religion, elements of her family life, and
how those contextual factors influenced the interview. The counselor "may"
have discovered these important contextual issues on his or her own, but probably not as quickly, comprehensively, or directly. At other times, the BCC calls
attention to feelings the client has shown in culturally learned behaviors that the
counselor might otherwise have missed: anger toward the majority culture,
which might not otherwise have come up, or shame and embarrassment, which
might have been avoided. At other times in this interview, the BCC describes
positive and negative coping styles typical of a Chicano female in such a
dilemma and clues to feelings of suicide that the client admits but would probably not have disclosed independently. The BCC also confronts the client, who is
trying to avoid sensitive topics, and helps the client make use of the opportunities offered through counseling. The recurring theme of the BCC is identity
issues, as emphasized later during the same interview.

215 BCC: Wait, but, uh wait a minute. Am I hearing you say, that, what you carried
around in your head was a certain set of ideas of what it's like to be Mexican? And
you thought that's what you were?

216 C: Yeah, you know. That, that also was part of it. And, uh. . .

217 BCC: So you were identifying yourself as quote "Mexican." I, I, okay, what I was
thinking was that, I'll share some of my experiences with you, uh personal and otherwise, which is that, when we're growing up, um, we are substituting things as
quote "being Mexican," and because those of us who were raised in this country
were not Mexican, nor are we American.

218 C: Yeah, I realized that after I went to Mexico.

219 BCC: And we're a combination, and to find out that quote "the things you thought
were Mexican" are not is, it's really, uh, difficult, it's really difficult, depending on
how you come to face with that experience, the definition of who you are as Mexican Ameri. . ., I call it Mexican-American, uh, because for me that symbolizes the
two different cultures, and they have different meanings for different individuals,
kind of thing. And that's just, okay, my fantasy was that's what your, what you
could call, I don't know what identification crisis means, because to me that's kind
of a label that tells me nothing about your, your journey in this world.

Approximately one fourth or perhaps one fifth of the time is taken by the
BCC, with three fourths or more of the interview consisting of counselor and

client comments. However, the counselor is able to learn insights from the BCC that might happen much more slowly or not at all without the help of the BCC.

The second interview was titled "Harmful Assumptions" (Loo, 1980b) and was also done at the Chinatown Research Center and the University of California, Santa Cruz. In one instance, for example, the BCC interrupts the interview with an observation:

76 *BCC:* May I, may I interrupt now? I would like to, to also state some of the things I have seen occurring, Helena, and that I, maybe you're not aware of. The reason why I went into the family and, and into some of the family history is because so many, uh, Chicano students that come to the university, uh, feel, uh, guilty for having left their families, uh, in, in a condition whereby they felt maybe, they needed their economic help, they needed you to work sometimes, and this happens very often with, with Chicano students, that as they feel that they should have stayed and so even though the parents might have wanted them to continue with school, they feel that they were needed either in terms of the economic help they could give their parents, many times in terms . . . uh, which I felt you were beginning to get into, in terms like of your relationship in the order of the family, 'cause as you know, being the oldest within a Chicano family is a very, very important position and a very important position of responsibility, and then I would . . . I was wondering and I wanted to go into some of the questions insofar as like your brothers, what are your brothers doing, are your brothers alright? This is one area that I think should be explored, and then the other question is the area that the counselor was going into right now is a very important thing, but you were answering in terms of your alienation from your teachers, professors, and maybe the material even that you're studying. And that would take a great deal longer to explore, uh, one of the things that Chicano students, and other minority students find that in institutions such as this, is that they have, uh, because they have been developed to only meet the needs of, uh certain groups within the society, you know, the building, the food, the content that is taught comes from one perspective, and, uh, uh, and I think many times what has happened with the minority students, bicultural students, only finds a part of himself represented and not another part of himself and this many times causes a conflict and professors many times don't understand that in order to facilitate a process whereby the student doesn't feel that it is threatening and that actually it's threatening their identity.

Usually the bicultural contextualizer's interventions are shorter and more specific in their attempts to contextualize the counseling interaction. An example of more typical BCC interaction later in the same interview demonstrates the more specific intervention by the BCC:

126 *T:* What do you think about when you're alone?
127 *C:* What do I think about? All kinds of stuff, I'm always thinking. . . . Especially right now. I always think when I'm in trouble. That's all I do is think.
128 *T:* Yeah, but, uh, what do you think about, what goes through your mind?

129 C: School, and the teachers, and my friends, and, and my family, my brothers, and money, worrying about that. Oh, everything everybody else thinks about, I think.

130 T: Would you think of yourself as a worrier?

131 C: No, I don't think so.

132 T: But instead of all these things, uh, uh, you don't why don't you think about your schoolwork, about your assignments?

133 C: Because it's hard, you know, it's hard to have to, to have too many things to think about right now, you know, it's I don't feel nobody cares, you know, about giving me help.

134 BCC: Helena, how, how are your brothers doing, where are your brothers, how old are your brothers, what are they doing?

135 C: Um, they're, um all younger than me. One's um, one's living here with me right now.

136 BCC: How old is he?

137 C: Eight . . . eighteen.

138 BCC: Eighteen.

In this interaction, the BCC tries to lead the counselor away from stereotyping the client as a worrier and as someone uninterested in schoolwork to refocus the interview on the client's family context. Instead of blaming the client for failure, the BCC helps the therapist explore the family situation and Helena's role responsibilities in depth as a source of collective support and understanding. As a result of this change in focus, the therapist begins to focus more constructively on Helena's more basic identity issues and her feelings about those issues.

After the interview, the counselor provided some insight into his role in playing the therapist:

> In the counseling interchange, I deliberately enacted the role of an Anglo counselor with whom I worked many years ago. Although apparently sympathetic to minority students, he always thought in terms of we (the established Anglo college community) and they (the Negroes, the ghetto youth, the first generation students, etc.). . . . A causal hypothesis had to be entertained when a minority student was in trouble; a rule-following hypothesis when an Anglo student was in trouble. Implicit (and perhaps unrecognized by the counselor) was a belief that the minority student just did not belong in the Anglo institution. At the same time, the belief was held that we should be kind and sympathetic. In my enactment of this role, I incorporated these beliefs, tried to encourage the client to question the legitimacy of her college-going; at the same time I was genuinely concerned with her depression. (Loo, 1980a, p. 14)

The BCC provides a guide for the counselor in working with bicultural and multicultural clients. A skilled BCC allows the counselor to hear not only the client's thoughts but also thoughts that others in that client's ethnic community might be having that are relevant to the counseling interview. An accurate assessment of the client's cultural context allows the counselor to translate counseling skills appropriately.

THE "ANTICLIENT"/"PROCLIENT"

Martin Strous (1997) has developed an approach for monitoring the counselor's inner dialogue and facilitating a therapeutic alliance in multiracial counseling in the South African context. The Triad Training Model was recognized as the basis for this innovation in its emphasis on the implicit inner dialogue of diverse client groups. However, it did not focus on articulating the equally important area of counselor self-talk or inner dialogue. This innovation is an attempt to increase our knowledge of counselor self-talk in multiracial counseling.

> The anticlient triad design that is proposed is a role personification of antagonistic or unhelpful feelings the counsellor has toward counselling in a culturally or racially diverse client. The proclient triad design that is proposed is a role personification of useful feelings and thoughts the counsellor has toward counselling a culturally or racially diverse client. (p. 6)

The anticlient would articulate feelings that are culturally and racially insensitive and antithetical to the principles of multicultural sensitivity, client empowerment, social advocacy, and human rights. The anticlient reveals feelings and thoughts, social and political attitudes, racist discourses, depreciating client assessment, and denigrative self-evaluation of the counselor's own qualifications to work in a multicultural setting. Strous (1997) lists some of the things an anticlient might say or do: (a) express reasons for the counselor to be distant and defensive; (b) emphasize cultural, racial, and language differences and the futility of communication; (c) point out the counselor's unresolved conflicts and distorted perceptions that contaminate therapy; (d) build on the positive things a problem offers; (e) capitalize on the problem's complexity; (f) coach the counselor to be superficial, obscure, and ineffectual; (g) coach the counselor to overextend and move too rapidly; (h) coach the counselor to antagonize the client; (i) sidetrack the counselor on personal issues; (j) supply misinformation; and (k) capitalize on stereotypes about blacks in South Africa.

The anticlient would allude to stereotypes about multiracial therapy resulting from the apartheid era in South Africa. The following are examples of such stereotypes: Psychotherapy is alien to the thinking of blacks; blacks would rather consult indigenous healers; blacks cannot be trusted; blacks are violent, racist, and/or cognitively inferior; white counselors cannot appreciate black nonverbal cues and customs; blacks have a fundamentally different view of time; blacks are unresponsive to long-term therapy; blacks focus on only short-term goals; blacks are mysterious and unknowable; blacks are unable to use therapy; blacks expect counselors to behave authoritatively; few blacks can afford therapy; and language differences make communication impossible.

The proposed proclient design personifies the useful feelings and thoughts a counselor has in multiracial settings. The proclient emphasizes the counselor's therapy-facilitating thoughts and feelings, explicating the advantages of cultural class and racial sensitivity in therapy and showing allegiance to principles of multicultural psychology, client empowerment, and democratic power sharing to convey appreciation for human rights. Some specific things a proclient might do include the following:

1. The proclient might use the counselor's feelings to understand the client's hopes, values, and predicaments.
2. The proclient might alert the counselor that his or her responses resemble those of other persons in the client's perception.
3. The proclient might inform the counselor of his or her realistic responses to a client's sometimes socially unacceptable responses.
4. The proclient might explicitly verbalize empathic reactions the counselor feels toward the client.
5. The proclient might offer approval to the counselor and provide beneficial feedback.
6. The proclient might help the counselor share the client's worldview.
7. The proclient might express faith in the counselor's ability to work with culturally different clients.
8. The proclient might assist the counselor to overcome his or her own defensiveness.
9. The proclient might help the counselor tackle racially salient issues in a sensitive way.
10. The proclient might supply intuitive and informed feedback about how different levels of racial identity between clients and counselors can improve therapeutic rapport.

The proclient-anticlient model provides data on counselor motivations, intentions, and interactions in cross-racial settings, with a number of advantages that build on the Triad Training Model:

1. Initial multiracial incidents can be role-played or discussed under controlled conditions.
2. Cultural problems and racial identity can be made specific rather than abstract.
3. Externalizing and personifying countertransference issues through the anticlient can ameliorate counselor defensiveness.
4. The counselor becomes more aware of his or her own unspoken self-talk in counseling.
5. Focusing on the counselor's self-talk is consistent with the new emphasis on "dialogical self" in counseling theory.
6. The competing proclient and anticlient self-messages can be reconciled.

7. The positive and negative influences of counselor attitudes and counter-transference can be clarified.

8. The power influence of therapy-hindering and therapy-facilitating inner dialogue as it influences the counseling coalition can be studied.

9. Counselor self-talk can be recorded and transcribed for detailed analysis.

10. It offers an interface with multiple theories, social psychology, community psychology, multicultural counseling, and counseling psychology.

The internal dialogue and feelings of counselors regarding racial issues are seldom made explicit in the interview. This is especially true in South Africa, where therapists have been exposed to the values of apartheid ideology and racism, which denigrate black people, in contrast with valuing all people and discussions about human rights. These competing ideologies result in ambivalent attitudes about racially salient material in the counseling interview by both the counselor and the client. Strous (1997) is investigating how counselors' anticlient internal dialogue reflects racist traditions in South Africa and how proclient internal dialogue reflects racial sensitivity. This ongoing research assumes that

(1) Counselors' therapy-hindering inner dialogues will be rooted in not only self-doubts about their ability to work cross-racially, but also in older racist discourses, conservative social attitudes and denigrative client assessment. (2) Counselors' therapy-facilitating inner dialogue will reveal more radical discourses derived from an ideology of racial sensitivity. (3) When asked to evaluate an exercise requiring them to grapple with the likely resolutions of their proclient and anticlient statements, counselors will express a heightened sensitivity to and a more sophisticated understanding of the influence of racial attitudes in counseling contexts. (p. 12)

Research on the proclient-anticlient model is currently being gathered, and the usefulness of this model is being tested within the South African context.

STEREOTYPE REVERSAL IN COUNSELOR TRAINING

A third adaptation of the Triad Training Model is being developed and researched by Margo Jackson (1998) at Stanford University in California. The goals of the stereotype reversal method of triad training are to help counselor trainees learn (a) to expand counselor trainees' perspective-taking ability with racial or ethnic minority clients' experience with stereotyping; (b) to recognize and challenge their own racially biased assumptions, including power dynamics inherent in their own racial status; and (c) to actively and selectively attend to individuating and stereotype-disconfirming information, including clients' strengths and assets in the social context of coping with pervasive unintentional racism (Jackson, 1996). "The stereotype reversal method is theoretically

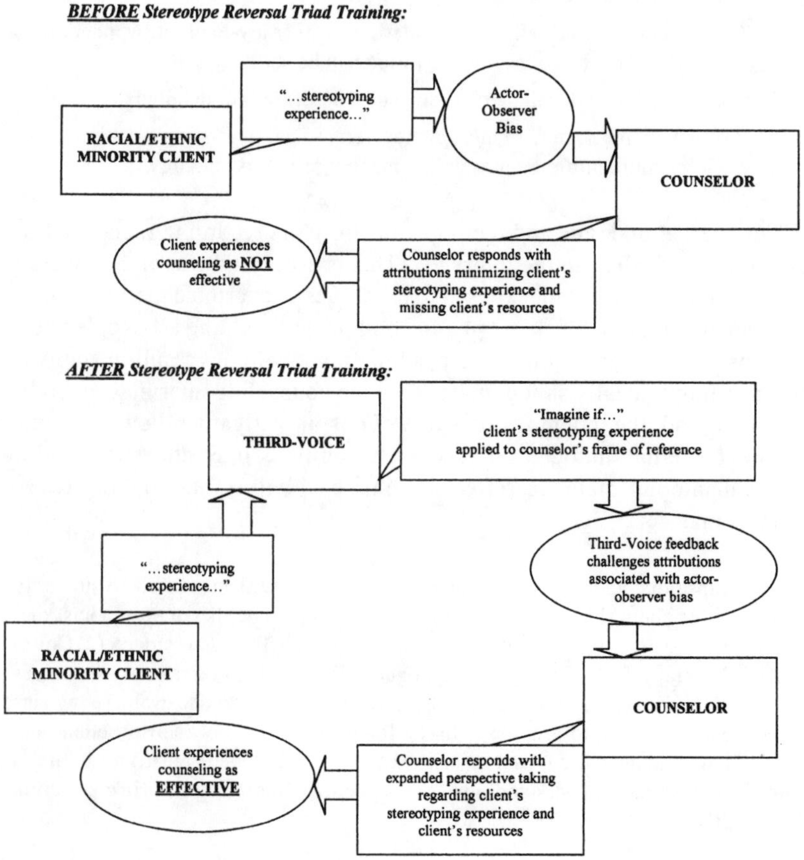

BEFORE *Stereotype Reversal Triad Training:*

AFTER *Stereotype Reversal Triad Training:*

Figure 10.1. Stereotype Reversal Method of Triad Training

grounded in Ridley's et al. (1994) perceptual schema model for developing cultural sensitivity in multicultural counseling and the method focuses on attributional biases . . . and social context factors" (Jackson, 1996, p. 2).

The stereotype reversal method uses the Triad Training Model and incorporates an anticounselor to provide specific feedback to counselor trainees on the client's experience with stereotyping and racial bias. The anticounselor, or "third voice," in the stereotype reversal method cognitively restructures the client's statements as if the social norms were reversed and those same stereotyped assumptions were being applied to the trainee instead of the client. By reversing and cognitively restructuring the client's statements, the counselor trainees are expected to experience stereotyping in their own context in a way that will help them conceptualize stereotyping in the client's context.

Following are some examples of stereotype reversal statements (adapted from McIntosh's 1989 work on increasing awareness of the daily effects of white privilege):

1. Imagine if being white meant that you could not do well in a challenging situation without being called a credit to your race.
2. Imagine if you were asked to speak for all people of your racial group.
3. Imagine if you could not be sure that your children would be given curricular materials that testify to the existence of their race.
4. Imagine if you could not swear, or dress in secondhand clothes, or not answer letters without having people attribute these choices to the bad morals, the poverty, or the illiteracy of your race.

Imagine if when you went home from meetings of organizations to which you belong, rather than feeling somewhat "tied in," you instead usually felt isolated, out of place, outnumbered, unheard, held at a distance, or feared (Jackson, 1996, p. 42).

"Counselors' unintentional racial biases lead to perceptual 'blind spots' and misattributions that limit their multicultural counseling effectiveness" (Jackson, 1998, p. 3). Stereotype reversal training focuses on increasing counselor trainees' awareness of unintentional attributional biases to expand their ability to appropriately consider cultural factors in conceptualizing the presenting problems of racial and ethnic minority clients. In particular, a general effect well documented in social psychology is the "actor-observer bias." That is, from the point of view of observers looking at an individual or group, we tend to stress internal, dispositional causes of behavior. Whereas when we take the perspective of the actors, now facing the circumstances they face, we stress more situational causes. Stereotype reversal training is designed to help counselor trainees reduce their own automatic attributional biases by better developing the ability to perceive presenting problems of racial and ethnic minority clients from the perspective of actors facing their clients' social context circumstances.

A research study on the stereotype reversal method of triad training was conducted in 1997-1998 on six dates at three different campuses, with a 1-day, 6-hour schedule for each (Jackson, 1998). Participants were 40 counselor trainees enrolled in professional psychology doctoral training programs in California. Participants were randomly assigned to one of three triad training conditions—reflective/control, triad/confrontive (anticounselor only), or stereotype reversal—which varied according to the nature of the feedback given by the trainer in the third-voice role during the role plays. All three training conditions consisted of a series of triad role plays in which trainees and a small group of fellow participants were videotaped as they took turns either participating in the counselor role or watching the role play. The role plays were conducted with two trainers who were African American women—one to play the role of the client and one to play the role of the third voice—who gave immediate feedback during the role play to reflect the client's perspective. The problems that the client presented in the role plays were on topics of adjustment, relationships, and academic or career concerns, and all included possible stereotyping concerns. An Interpersonal Process Recall (Kagan & Kagan, 1990) component was incorporated in which, immediately following each role play, participants viewed the videotape and completed questionnaires on their perceptions of the client's problem and the counselor's responses. Then a third trainer facilitated a debriefing group discussion. Results from preliminary analyses of the data suggest that one effect of stereotype reversal training was to increase counselor trainees' exploration of racial concerns and to expand attributions to social context factors that racial and ethnic minority clients face.

Although the stereotype reversal training approach is still in the process of being developed, it offers an innovative adaptation of the Triad Training Model. It incorporates both an interpersonal process recall component and a focus on expanding counselor trainees' awareness of their unintentional attributional biases regarding racial and ethnic minority clients' experiences with stereotyping to help trainees monitor their own internal dialogue from the client's perceptual viewpoint.

COLE'S PROACTIVE APPROACH TO REDUCING PREJUDICE*

The fourth adaptation of the Triad Training Model was developed by Dr. Jim Cole in Washington State, who conducts workshops using his materials and videotapes for a wide range of in-service training of counselors, managers, and other human service providers. The focus of Cole's training is to hear the internal voices of the client by introducing several new roles. The "counselor" becomes the "Concerned Listener." The "client" becomes the "Sharing Person." The "anticounselor" becomes the "Distracter," or the "internal voice." Although there may be many internal voices in the minds of actual clients, the logistics of training is limited to only one voice. Although there is no procounselor or positive internal voice, the Distracter is encouraged to share positive aspects of the interview. The problem orientation is removed from the interview, as is the polarity of "helper" and "helped," bringing participants together with equal power. The trainee is now a Concerned Listener, while those taking the roles of Sharing Person and Distracter provide relevant information. The purpose of training is not to solve problems for disenfranchised persons but to show concern for, learn from, and empathize with those persons.

The focus of Cole's adaptation is to increase the trainee's ability to listen effectively.

---

*For more information, contact James W. Cole, 514 North Pine Street, Ellensburg, WA 98926.

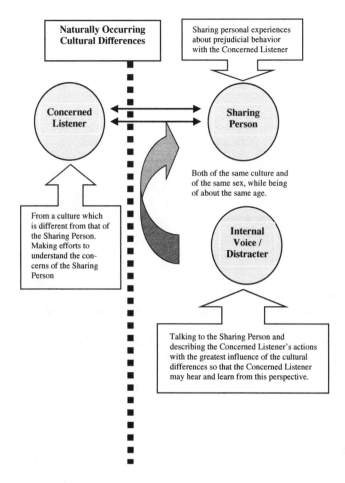

Figure 10.2. The Triad Model for Prejudice Reduction
SOURCE: Adapted from Cole (1996).

Many administrators hear of a problem and immediately start problem solving or defending rather than clarifying, reflecting, and trying to understand the dynamic more completely, or attempting to become empathetic. While this is a problem initially, it also provides an opportunity for teaching some listening skills. Some of these are the typical active listening skills, but others are directly related to cross-cultural communication. (Cole, 1996, p. 2)

Examples of the skills of a Sharing Person, a Distracter, and a Concerned Listener have been videotaped in 18 different examples to provide practice in listening for trainees. In this model, the Sharing Person might follow the theme,

I am genuine in my request to be understood and in my decision on the Concerned Listener's relevance. . . . I will share experiences which are related to the cultural differences and my experiencing the prejudicial behavior of others. I will trust that I will be understood but will not risk too much. (Cole, 1996, p. 3)

The Concerned Listener might follow the theme,

I am relevant and I will try to understand the Sharing Person. . . . I will demonstrate that I understand the situation that the Sharing Person is in and how that situation might feel to the Sharing Person. I can anticipate the Sharing Person's hesitation to share with me, and I can accept that resistance. I can anticipate my own defensive feelings and not act upon those feelings. (Cole, 1996, p. 3)

The Distracter might follow the theme,

The Concerned Listener is not relevant and can't be trusted by us. I am protecting the Sharing Person from the Concerned Listener. . . . I know the Sharing Person's culture and experience and I can use this information to protect the Sharing Person from trusting the Concerned Listener. I will interpret the Concerned Listener's behavior and remarks to show their most prejudiced aspects. (Cole, 1996, p. 3)

Cole (1996, pp. 35-39) provides the following guidelines in his unique training design for the Concerned Listener, the Sharing Person, and the Distracter:

The Concerned Listener

1. The Concerned Listener restates or paraphrases the concerns from the Sharing Person's point of view, using the Sharing Person's perspective. By restating and clarifying the ideas of the Sharing Person, the Concerned Listener shows respect for the cultural context that is part of the concerns being shared.

2. Genuine interest for the Sharing Person is demonstrated as a Concerned Listener restates what is heard in a caring manner.

3. The Concerned Listener makes clear references to the cultural contexts that have been different for the Sharing Person. Differences that have provided different experiences are not ignored but explored.

4. To be sure he or she understands, the Concerned Listener frequently summarizes what the Sharing Person has said. Paying attention to the feelings inferred from what the Sharing Person has said, and stating these clearly and with care, demonstrates understanding.

5. The Concerned Listener makes statements that are tentative as he or she tries to summarize both the information and the feelings that have been shared.

6. The Concerned Listener expects some hesitation or discomfort from the Sharing Person and clearly states an acceptance and understanding of these feelings.

7. As the Concerned Listener hears the Sharing Person's hesitation, he or she shows acceptance for those feelings and gives support and understanding for the apprehension while trying to clarify what is happening for the Sharing Person.

8. The Concerned Listener understands that he or she may feel some need to defend himself or herself and will allow these feelings to pass without acting on them directly.

9. The Concerned Listener avoids a direct defensive statement by showing understanding for the Sharing Person's feelings. The Concerned Listener sometimes admits discomfort, apologizes, shares a feeling, or even laughs at his or her own discomfort. The Concerned Listener might just pause and reflect on the desire to understand.

10. When the Concerned Listener feels that a conflict is developing, he or she will redirect the focus. The Concerned Listener might even want to slow down or just sit in silence for a moment.

The Sharing Person

1. The Sharing Person lets the Concerned Listener hear how it has been to be in his or her situation by sharing with the Concerned Listener personal experiences, how he or she has felt, what impact he or she has had, and the resulting feelings.

2. During the training process, the Sharing Person lets the Concerned Listener hear feelings of anger, frustration, sadness, hurt, or isolation through real-life stories, which illustrate ways he or she has been treated differently because of his or her cultural or group identity. In a sincere manner and without putting a slant on anything said, the Sharing Person responds to the caring of the Concerned Listener and to the comments of the Distracter, and he or she is free to sort out the feelings and listen to the responses or comments from either of them. The Sharing Person should enter into any conversation between the Concerned Listener and the Distracter with the expectation that the Concerned Listener will understand and is interested in the personal experiences and issues presented.

3. The Sharing Person avoids retelling an experience that is too risky or too personal. Certainly, the experiences that are shared are real and hold meaning for the Sharing Person; however, the shared material is not so emotionally loaded that either the Distracter or the Sharing Person forgets that this is a structured exercise. It is important that both individuals care about the issues, but it is also important that the issues do not overshadow the process. Above all, this process is meant to increase understanding and reduce unintentional prejudicial behavior.

4. The Sharing Person can expect to feel pulled between the Concerned Listener and the Distracter at times throughout the structured exercises. Because this pull is a common feeling in this role, when the Sharing Person feels confused, a barrier pause for reflection is often helpful. It is completely acceptable to simply stop for a moment to reflect on the process. The Sharing Person is not responsible for the other members of this process, and their actions can become confusing for the Sharing Person.

5. As much as the Sharing Person might agree with the Distracter at times, it is important that the Sharing Person resist any temptation to join in open criticism of the Concerned Listener. The Sharing Person hears the weight of the remarks of the Distracter and knows that this person understands his or her own cultural experience. At the same time, the Sharing Person needs to be able to feel comfortable ignoring the feedback of the Distracter.

6. The Sharing Person does not try to change the Concerned Listener or the Distracter but simply shares experiences, how these experiences have felt, and how life is different because of his or her cultural or group membership and/or identity. The Sharing Person's role consists of remaining open to the experience taking place.

The Distracter

1. The Distracter needs to have strong feelings of identity with and empathy for the Sharing Person and the Sharing Person's issues.

2. The Distracter is active, not passive, and concrete rather than abstract. In this role, he or she is both positive and negative, complex and dynamic.

3. The Distracter needs to articulate the feedback for the Concerned Listener in a direct and immediate way and to respond to both the verbal and nonverbal behavior of the Concerned Listener. These messages of feedback for the Concerned Listener are directed to the Sharing Person in a way that allows the Concerned Listener to hear them but not in a way that requires a direct response from the Concerned Listener.

4. The Distracter reflects on what has been said by the Concerned Listener, lending the most prejudicial meanings to the Concerned Listener's statements, and, upon the gestures that are made by the Concerned Listener, stating the most prejudicial meaning these gestures might have. This commentary provides an audible "internal dialogue" for both the Concerned Listener and the Sharing Person to hear.

5. Basically, the Distracter questions the motives of the Concerned Listener's statements and actions, offering summaries of statements and actions made by the Concerned Listener and giving them more prejudicial meanings.

6. The Distracter is aware that the Concerned Listener needs to receive both positive and negative feedback during the training session. With this in mind, the Distracter needs to avoid overloading the Concerned Listener with too much negative feedback. On some occasions, the Distracter may even verbally question his or her own earlier statements to soften the impact on a listener who seems to be overwhelmed.

7. In the role of a caring friend, the Distracter speaks directly to the Sharing Person and uses cultural connections with this person. The Distracter uses the words *we, us,* and *our* to make the connections clear. For example, "People like that laugh at us," or "We know better than to trust people like that," or "He does not understand our ways and doesn't really care."

8. The Distracter adds doubt to the most effective things that the Concerned Listener might say by questioning the motives and sincerity of what is said, using references to things that the Sharing Person knows about people like the Concerned Listener and other people from that culture. He or she makes general statements about the Concerned Listener and "people like that," all comments that the Sharing Person can relate to or has heard within their shared culture.

9. Yet the Distracter understands that this is not a fight. The Distracter needs to be heard and realizes that overdoing the role would simply be disruptive. It may be that the most powerful thing the Distracter can do will be to question the Concerned Listener's intentions. A well-placed remark reflecting directly on what has just been said has great power.

10. The Distracter remembers that the Concerned Listener needs to hear some positive things so that he or she does not give up the struggle. The Distracter does not want to overpower the Concerned Listener or flood the conversation, but, at the same time, the Distracter does not want to let the Sharing Person be fooled by the Concerned Listener.

11. The Distracter is aware that the purpose of the structured exercise is to have the Concerned Listener feel the impact of this process and understand the dynamics more clearly, and the Distracter realizes that this cannot happen if the Concerned Listener gives up or retreats and stops trying.

Debriefing

Following the training, there is a debriefing process in which each person in the role play shares what he or she thought, felt, and intended. There are typically several observers watching the role play who will also contribute their insights. At times, they may want to exchange places with one of the role players. When appropriate, the role players are encouraged to stop and reflect on the process briefly before going back into role and continuing. Anecdotal evidence for the usefulness of this training design, gathered through evaluating workshops, is discussed by Cole (1996), as are instructions on how to develop and train the teams, how to recruit disenfranchised participants, and some of the typical problems likely to occur in training.

CONCLUSION

Several variations of the Triad Training Model have been developed and are included to demonstrate alternative means of including immediate and continuous feedback into the counseling interview. The first example is the bicultural contextualizer model, in which the third person, who understands both the client's and the counselor's culture, provides clarification to both of them for a more accurate understanding of the communication process. The issues of cultural identity are highlighted in the transcript, illustrating the BCC model in two different situations. The element of positive or negative evaluation is not part of the BCC, which enhances the harmony of the counseling relationship.

The second example is that of the anticlient/proclient. Whereas the other models incorporating internal dialogue focus on the client's internal dialogue, this alternative focuses on the counselor's internal dialogue. The counselor is confronted with positive and/or negative messages demonstrating racism, or unintentional racism, in how the counseling is being perceived. This gives the counselor an opportunity to reframe his or her own internal dialogue in a more appropriate manner.

The third example involves stereotype reversal and helps the counselor increase his or her empathy level by looking at stereotypes of him- or herself. By identifying parallels between how the client is being victimized and how the counselor would feel under those same conditions, a common bond is developed between the counselor and the client across their cultural differences.

The fourth example involves Jim Cole's Proactive Approach to Reducing Prejudice, in which the counselor becomes the "Concerned Listener," the client becomes the "Sharing Person," and the anticounselor becomes the "Distracter." The problem orientation is removed from the interview, and the distinction between client and counselor is removed. This model has been particularly used outside the field of counseling, with administrators, and has shown itself successful in reducing prejudice.

The Intrapersonal Context of Counseling

This book has developed the position that counseling occurs primarily in the client's and the counselor's intrapersonal contexts and only secondarily as an interpersonal exchange. The interpersonal exchange is mediated and evaluated by the internal dialogues of the counselor and client separately. For the interpersonal exchange to bring about meaningful change, the hidden messages within the client's and the counselor's intrapersonal conversation need to be addressed. Most of the emphasis in this book has been on the client's internal dialogue, under the assumption that a competent counselor can think and talk at the same time, monitoring his or her internal dialogue to generate appropriate counseling responses. However, even competent counselors will have a difficult time hearing the hidden messages of the client, especially when the client is culturally different from the counselor.

The first four chapters of Part I, on psychological research information, examined the implications of establishing a meaningful counseling relationship. The social psychological literature cited in Chapter 1 emphasizes the importance of relationship and rapport variables in counseling, providing a research foundation for the field of counseling that has been widely accepted. The more contemporary emphasis on psychological research about intrapersonal aspects of counseling is a more recent phenomenon. In Chapter 2, applications of the psychological research to the client's presenting "problem" as a metaphorical third party in the counseling relationship provide a visual image of how the counselor might make the client more powerful and the problem less powerful by appropriate intervention. In Chapter 3, applications of previous research to understanding the "relational" self as a multiplicity of potentially salient identities further demonstrate the rich interpersonal activity in a counseling interview. Applications in Chapter 4 of the implications for direct-service delivery of this intrapersonal perspective have been well developed by well-known counseling professionals in a great variety of different contexts. The four chapters in Part I attempt to describe the research foundation for counseling as primarily an intrapersonal phenomenon.

The next three chapters in Part II, on the Triad Training Model, begin with Chapter 5 by describing how counselors can be trained to hear the hidden messages in the counseling interview, with particular attention to Kagan's Interpersonal Process Recall Model and the Triad Training Model as two useful approaches. Chapter 6 examines the Triad Training Model in more detail, particularly as it relates to training counselors to work in multicultural contexts. All counseling interviews are more or less multicultural, depending on the number of potentially salient similarities and differences between the counselor and the client. Chapter 7 examines the multicultural counseling competencies of accurate *awareness,* meaningful *knowledge,* and appropriate *skill* and how this three-stage developmental sequence toward competency fits with research on the Triad Training Model. Although the research on the Triad Training Model is as yet inconclusive, there are many promising indications of its usefulness.

The last three chapters in Part III, on transcript applications of the Triad Training Model, demonstrate the wide variety of training approaches in which the Triad Training Model has been used. Given the broad definition of *culture* to include demographic, status, and formal/informal affiliation as well as ethnographic variables, the Triad Training Model lends itself to training counselors for work with any number of social problems and with clients from a wide range of backgrounds not normally considered as cultures. Interview transcripts using the Triad Training Model are presented in Chapter 8; the salient features were sexual harassment, juvenile delinquency, political affiliation, and lesbian lifestyle. Chapter 9 provides transcript examples of the different variations of the Triad Training Model, discussing the strengths and weaknesses of each variation. Chapter 10 presents a variety of other intrapersonal training models that were originally based on the Triad Training Model but have since developed their own distinct approach.

This concluding chapter attempts to demonstrate the progression of this book toward understanding the importance of intrapersonal dialogue in counseling and the presentation of the Triad Training Model as one attempt to train counselors. There are two assessment forms appended to this book. The first form is a self-assessment for counselors to test their own abilities to decode the hidden messages of culturally different clients, using brief transcripts of counseling interviews. The second form is a workshop evaluation form to help participants identify the strengths and weaknesses of the Triad Training Model as they have experienced it. The competent counselor will need to become more *aware* of culturally learned assumptions, his or her own as well as the client's; more *knowledgeable* about the salient background information describing the client's cultural context; and more *skillful* in identifying the salient features of a client's cultural context and in intervening appropriately to make the client's situation better rather than worse. The culturally competent counselor should be able to answer some, if not all, of the following questions:

1. What are the ways in which cultural differences between a counselor and a counselee affect counseling?
2. How serious is the implicit cultural bias among counselors and counselor training programs?
3. How can counselors evaluate their own implicit cultural bias?
4. How might psychological problems vary with the culture of the clients?
5. Why are some methods better than others in working with persons from other cultures?
6. How can we learn from other cultures in sharpening our own skills as counselors?
7. Can we assume that all counseling is to some extent multicultural?
8. What are the dangers of cultural encapsulation for the counselor?
9. What is meant by the "self-reference criterion"?
10. To what extent is the counselor committed to changing the environment and not merely helping a client adjust to it?
11. Is there evidence that professional counselors are culturally conditioned in their responses?
12. What are some of the barriers to accurate communication across cultures?
13. What is the importance of a client's and counselor's basic assumptions for the counseling process?
14. What are some of the ways that counselor education programs could be modified to make them more sensitive to multicultural value systems?
15. Do the effects of training with an anticounselor and a procounselor generalize to actual counseling interviews?
16. What might be some unique advantages of training counselors to hear the client's hidden messages?
17. What might be some disadvantages of training counselors to hear the client's hidden messages?
18. How well can you ever expect to be trained to accurately hear the culturally different client's hidden messages?
19. How well can you monitor your own positive and negative internal dialogue?
20. Is counseling primarily an intrapersonal process?

Hearing the hidden messages in culture-centered counseling is not easy, but ignoring those hidden messages is inevitably more troublesome than learning to hear them. This process is particularly complicated when the client and the counselor come from different cultural backgrounds. The best one can hope for is to make a more informed "guess" about what culturally different clients are thinking. It is hoped that having experienced the procounselor and anti-counselor in training will help the counselor to internalize those two very different monologues as part of his or her own internal dialogue. By carefully monitoring the verbal and nonverbal cues of culturally different clients, the attentive counselor can generate hypotheses about that client's hidden messages that are more likely to be accurate. By attending to the intrapersonal context of counseling, the counselor can continue to learn from the thousands of "culture teachers" accumulated over a lifetime of experiences who have taught us our values and coached our behaviors. Only when the counselor can hear these voices will that counselor learn to hear the hidden messages in culture-centered counseling.

Appendix A

Self-Assessment in Using the Triad Training Model

CROSS-CULTURAL COUNSELING TEST OF PROCOUNSELOR AND ANTICOUNSELOR

The following brief excerpts from three cross-cultural counseling interviews will include statements by counselors and by clients, followed by a space for you to write in what *you* would say next in the role of the *counselor.*

Part 1

The first set of statements is transcribed from an interview between a white male counselor and a black female client, discussing relationship problems the black female is having at the university.

1.

Client: OK, my problem is that I don't seem to be able to trust the white people here on campus. Being black, I seem to have sort of a problem with this sort of thing, and I don't know what to do about it, and somebody recommended you. Said that you were a good counselor so I decided to come and get some help from you.

Counselor: Do you have any problems relating to the black students on campus, Terry?

Client: No, not really. You know there are people everywhere. Some you don't like, some you do like.

Procounselor says: _____

Anticounselor says: _____

What is the hidden message? _____

Why was the message hidden? _____

How would you respond to the hidden message? _____

2.

Client: One thing about white males, you know, that there is a lot of trouble. Being a black girl myself, a lot of white males get funny ideas about black girls.

Procounselor says: _____
Anticounselor says: _____
What is the hidden message? _____
Why was the message hidden? _____
How would you respond to the hidden message? _____

3.

Client: Well, um . . . they go through life thinkin' that we're somewhat lower than white women because, you know, there is this great big thing about black sexuality.

Procounselor says: _____
Anticounselor says: _____
What is the hidden message? _____
Why was the message hidden? _____
How would you respond to the hidden message? _____

4.

Counselor: How do you feel in terms of our relationship now? You came here, and we have been talking for about 2 to 3 minutes. How do you feel about the way we've been talking?
Client: Well, you haven't helped me for one thing. I mean you just. . .

Procounselor says: _____
Anticounselor says: _____
What is the hidden message? _____
Why was the message hidden? _____
How would you respond to the hidden message? _____

5.

Counselor: Do you feel uncomfortable with me?
Client: Um, not now, not yet.
Counselor: I um . . . I ah . . . (pause) I don't feel any discomfort with you at all.
Client: Oh, well, 'cause I'm a friendly person I suppose. (laugh)

Procounselor says: _____

Anticounselor says: _____

What is the hidden message? _____

Why was the message hidden? _____

How would you respond to the hidden message? _____

6.

Client: Well, there's a whole thing about, you know, sometimes like in theater classes and some kid will say something in an "Aunt Jemima" or a "Stepin Fetchit" voice. . . . And the thing is, they don't expect me to get upset about it, you know, it's all in theater and somehow I end up being the brunt of a joke.

Procounselor says: _____

Anticounselor says: _____

What is the hidden message? _____

Why was the message hidden? _____

How would you respond to the hidden message? _____

7.

Client: Have you?

Counselor: Have I what?

Client: Ever laughed at a black joke or whatever.

Procounselor says: _____

Anticounselor says: _____

What is the hidden message? _____

Why was the message hidden? _____

How would you respond to the hidden message? _____

8.

Client: I have rarely broken a promise to people, people have broken promises to me. They have told me things. Sure I'll do it, and they end up not doing it. Is it just because they don't think I'm serious because I'm a black person? Maybe I'm just a jive person, you know?

Procounselor says: _____

Anticounselor says: _____

What is the hidden message? _____

Why was the message hidden? _____

How would you respond to the hidden message? _____

9.

Client: Um . . . (laugh) well, so that . . . it's not that I can't trust people. . . . It's, I wonder. . . Now I forgot what I'm talking about. Um. . . (pause)

Procounselor says: _____
Anticounselor says: _____
What is the hidden message? _____
Why was the message hidden? _____
How would you respond to the hidden message? _____

10.

Counselor: Are you getting a little uncomfortable, Terry, . . . perhaps because I'm
white, in sharing some of these things with me?

Client: Um . . . not really, and it's like I said, you know, I try to be pretty open-minded
about what I'm talking about. But the thing I want to know is, can you really understand where I'm coming from? What kind of things I'm really dealing with?

Procounselor says: _____
Anticounselor says: _____
What is the hidden message? _____
Why was the message hidden? _____
How would you respond to the hidden message? _____

11.

Client: OK. Like I said, most of my classes have uh . . . you get tired of being the only
black kid in classes. Well, I can't change that because I can't get more sisters and
brothers on campus, right? So the thing is I . . . they can make jokes at me and not expect me to really feel bad when somebody makes a black joke?

Procounselor says: _____
Anticounselor says: _____
What is the hidden message? _____
Why was the message hidden? _____
How would you respond to the hidden message? _____

12.

Client: What exactly . . . what exactly do you think my problem is? (Pause) If you think I
don't understand it.

Counselor: I think you understand your problem really well. I think your problem is
simply ah . . . again, your problem . . . I don't think it's your problem at all. I think it's

the problem that you're experiencing in relating to whites on campus and ah . . . I think ah . . . many blacks experience the same problem.

Procounselor says: _____
Anticounselor says: _____
What is the hidden message? _____
Why was the message hidden? _____
How would you respond to the hidden message? _____

13.

Client: Well, it's like the questions you are asking don't stick in my mind as well as what he [the counselor] is saying to me. It's like he can relate with what I'm, you know, the thing I'm going with and you gave me a lot of stuff about how a lot of black people are approaching the same problem. But the thing is what I want to know is how do I deal with it?

Procounselor says: _____
Anticounselor says: _____
What is the hidden message? _____
Why was the message hidden? _____
How would you respond to the hidden message? _____

Part 2

The second set of statements is transcribed from an interview between a white male counselor and a Latin American female client, discussing relationship problems the Latin American female is having at the university.

1.

Client: Well, I'm having some problems, and I'm having some difficulty studying and really understanding what I'm doing in school and so on. And I know I know enough English to be able to handle it, but it just . . . there are so many things on my mind that are bothering me . . . and they told me to come here to talk to you.

Procounselor says: _____
Anticounselor says: _____
What is the hidden message? _____
Why was the message hidden? _____
How would you respond to the hidden message? _____

2.

Client: The problem that I was having was that I been, you know, that I like to go out to
     meet men. I enjoy their company . . . but it's really scary the way they approach me.

Procounselor says: _____
Anticounselor says: _____
What is the hidden message? _____
Why was the message hidden? _____
How would you respond to the hidden message? _____

3.

Client: Yeah, they treat me like dirt, that's it, you know? And I feel divided inside.
     Like they don't care for me as a whole person.
Counselor: Umm. . . You said divided, what is the division?
Client: The division is that they just want sex. They don't want to see me as a whole
     person.

Procounselor says: _____
Anticounselor says: _____
What is the hidden message? _____
Why was the message hidden? _____
How would you respond to the hidden message? _____

4.

Counselor: Could you tell me what you would rather have from them? How you would
     like a man to treat you when you go out with him?
Client: Well, it's just that, especially the first time . . . for sometime,
Counselor: Um mmmm. . .
Client: I like to get to know the person in a different way.

Procounselor says: _____
Anticounselor says: _____
What is the hidden message? _____
Why was the message hidden? _____
How would you respond to the hidden message? _____

5.

Counselor: So you're really kind of in a bind. You want to meet guys and be friendly
     with them, but you feel like they make you pay for it with your body.
Client: Yeah, and there's this whole stereotype about the hot Latin American. . .

Counselor: Uh huh. . .

Client: And that makes them go even faster. And, of course, I flirt, I'm coquettish, you know? I know that I'm attractive. . .

Procounselor says: _____

Anticounselor says: _____

What is the hidden message? _____

Why was the message hidden? _____

How would you respond to the hidden message? _____

6.

Counselor: Before you came to this country, did you feel at peace with yourself when you were with men?

Client: Yeah.

Procounselor says: _____

Anticounselor says: _____

What is the hidden message? _____

Why was the message hidden? _____

How would you respond to the hidden message? _____

7.

Counselor: So I need to find out first of all what you have been used to and what pleases you and then I can help you learn how to get men to respond to you in that same way here. It is not necessary, you see, that you do respond as they demand. It is perfectly possible, and I guess you have to take this kind of on faith . . . this is, I might say, a problem not just foreign girls have, but American girls have this problem too.

Client: No, you know, they don't have that problem. They seem to enjoy that type of thing, and they don't seem to have a problem with it.

Procounselor says: _____

Anticounselor says: _____

What is the hidden message? _____

Why was the message hidden? _____

How would you respond to the hidden message? _____

8.

Counselor: OK, I better ask you another question then. How comfortable are you with me? Should . . . maybe I'm not the right person to work with you . . . because I'm an American man.

Client: So far you're OK . . . because you are far enough.

Procounselor says: _____
Anticounselor says: _____
What is the hidden message? _____
Why was the message hidden? _____
How would you respond to the hidden message? _____

9.

Counselor: But in this then . . . you are comfortable. I want to make sure of that
    because, if you're not comfortable with me, there is no point in us trying to work
    together.
Client: Well, so far I am. I am comfortable.

Procounselor says: _____
Anticounselor says: _____
What is the hidden message? _____
Why was the message hidden? _____
How would you respond to the hidden message? _____

10.

Client: You just give me the feeling that you're exactly like these other men, too, you
    know? The way you are sitting, you know?

Procounselor says: _____
Anticounselor says: _____
What is the hidden message? _____
Why was the message hidden? _____
How would you respond to the hidden message? _____

11.

Counselor: What should I be doing? To make you feel better.
Client: Well, cross your legs.
Counselor: Cross my legs? For a man to sit with his legs open is a bad. . .?
Client: Well, that means that they want sex.

Procounselor says: _____
Anticounselor says: _____
What is the hidden message? _____
Why was the message hidden? _____
How would you respond to the hidden message? _____

12.

Client: Yeah, you see this thing, these things for me are very intense for me right now because I just came. I've been here for only about a month.

Counselor: Would you feel better if I got back behind the desk, and we sort of had that between us?

Client: No, then you remind me of my father.

Procounselor says: _____

Anticounselor says: _____

What is the hidden message? _____

Why was the message hidden? _____

How would you respond to the hidden message? _____

13.

Client: Then you make me feel like you are rejecting me. You are not rejecting me?

Procounselor says: _____

Anticounselor says: _____

What is the hidden message? _____

Why was the message hidden? _____

How would you respond to the hidden message? _____

14.

Counselor: How do you feel now as opposed to when you came in?

Client: Well, I'm kind of feeling uncomfortable. It was OK for a while and now I feel like, I don't know . . . I feel like I want to go.

Procounselor says: _____

Anticounselor says: _____

What is the hidden message? _____

Why was the message hidden? _____

How would you respond to the hidden message? _____

Part 3

The third set of statements is transcribed from an interview between a white male counselor and a Chinese male client, discussing relationship problems the Chinese male is having at the university.

1.

Counselor: So it seems to me that what you are saying that, even when you do get together, those infrequent times when you get together, even those times don't seem
to be such happy times.

Client: Exactly, you see (pause) what happens at first when we get together ah . . . it is
usually on some kind of vacation. We have 10 days or 12 days, and we have exams
coming up and we are under all kinds of pressure. . .

Procounselor says: _____

Anticounselor says: _____

What is the hidden message? _____

Why was the message hidden? _____

How would you respond to the hidden message? _____

2.

Counselor: Tell me about it, would you please, because I'm really . . . don't know too
much about. . . (pause) What culture are you from, what country are you from?

Client: I come from Hong Kong; maybe I'm Chinese.

Procounselor says: _____

Anticounselor says: _____

What is the hidden message? _____

Why was the message hidden? _____

How would you respond to the hidden message? _____

3.

Client: Ah, well, let me see if I can get it across to you. You see, for us, . . . things like
degree and your grades and so on, they are extremely important.

Counselor: Um mmm. . .

Client: I mean, the society. . . Now our family and so on, they regard it as important,
extremely so. . .

Procounselor says: _____

Anticounselor says: _____

What is the hidden message? _____

Why was the message hidden? _____

How would you respond to the hidden message? _____

4.

Counselor: I am wondering right now if you have made a definite commitment toward marrying this woman. (pause)

Client: More or less, more or less, yeah. You see, for us, an engagement for us is something very serious. I mean, you won't get engaged with a girl unless. . .

Procounselor says: _____

Anticounselor says: _____

What is the hidden message? _____

Why was the message hidden? _____

How would you respond to the hidden message? _____

5.

Counselor: Not yet, I could. (pause) Could you tell me, you see, you're right, I really don't know a great deal about your culture at all, and in order to help you, I really have to have more of an appreciation of it.

Client: You see, the problem is that engagement is important and my family is important, and your degree is important as well.

Counselor: So with so many things coming at the same time that are so important and you feel that you have to make choices between them and leave out some of them?

Procounselor says: _____

Anticounselor says: _____

What is the hidden message? _____

Why was the message hidden? _____

How would you respond to the hidden message? _____

6.

Client: I mean, right now I am not confident that I am going to hack it. (pause) I mean I have one more prelim to go through, and there is this thesis thing . . . and I haven't any idea of what on earth it is going to be. (pause)

Counselor: So that it is really at a point right now where you are saying can I make school. It is a question of breaking, in relation to your fiancée, breaking a strong important value that you have of being . . . of fidelity to her, and it is also a question right now can I make it in school, can I fulfill my obligations to my family and to everyone else who put me here and to myself?

Procounselor says: _____

Anticounselor says: _____

What is the hidden message? _____

Why was the message hidden? _____

How would you respond to the hidden message? _____

7.

Client: Yeah, I guess I could come to you, and we could talk about it, but what good
does that do to me?

Procounselor says: _____
Anticounselor says: _____
What is the hidden message? _____
Why was the message hidden? _____
How would you respond to the hidden message? _____

8.

Counselor: Sung, do you think you can solve some of your problems by working with
other people? Sometimes it is more helpful to work with another person to solve a
problem.

Client: Yeah, sometimes it does . . . provided, I mean . . . provided that person has a
sympathetic understanding of the problem.

Procounselor says: _____
Anticounselor says: _____
What is the hidden message? _____
Why was the message hidden? _____
How would you respond to the hidden message? _____

SCORING GUIDE FOR MULTICULTURAL TES
OF COUNSELOR RESPONSES

The counselor responses will be scored on a 10-point scale with regard to four
skill areas.

1. *Cultural accuracy:* Perceiving the client's message from the client's cultural point of view. When a counselor's statement about the client's viewpoint
includes specific reference to the exact words, concepts, concerns, or implications clearly related to the client's statement or background, it indicates a high
level of cultural accuracy. When the counselor's statement is an extension of the
counselor's cultural viewpoint, unrelated to the client's statement, a low level of
cultural accuracy is presumed.

2. *Resistance identification:* Identifying resistance from the client in specific rather than general terms as it is presented by the client, demonstrated by
clarifying, specifying, or otherwise organizing information from a client's
ambiguously negative statement in a more specific counselor response. When
the counselor's response to a client's ambiguously negative statement is specific
to some source of criticism by the client of the counseling situation, a high level

of skill is presumed. When the counselor's response does not clarify, specify, or focus in on a client's ambiguously negative statement, a low level of skill is presumed.

3. *Deferred defensiveness:* The counselor maintains focus on the client's needs even when receiving criticism and is not distracted by the need to defend his or her credentials. When the counselor maintains continuous focus on the client's needs and purpose for being in counseling even under criticism, a high level of skill is presumed. When the counselor response focuses on the counselor's needs to become more secure in the counseling relationship and ignores the client's needs, a low level of skill is presumed.

4. *Recovery skill:* After having said or done something that aroused the client's anger or suspicion or otherwise distanced the client, the counselor recovers rapport by saying or doing something that is likely to reestablish a client's confidence in the counselor. When the counselor's response maintains both the counselor statement and the client response in furthering the purpose of the interview, a high level of skill is presumed. When the counselor does not focus on the client's viewpoint and is sidetracked or distracted by the client's response to an earlier statement, a low level of skill is presumed.

In scoring the responses, you will indicate either the presence or absence of the designated skill and the degree to which that skill was appropriately used by the counselor. Although each item incorporates more than one skill, the item will be scored for only one of the four skill areas.

Workshop Assessment

PROGRAM EVALUATION OF TRIAD TRAINING

Model Workshops

Name _____ Telephone _____

Address _____

_____

Date of training _____ Number of hours spent in training _____

You role-played the Counselor ( ), Client ( ), Anticounselor ( ),
Procounselor ( ); you watched but did not role-play ( ).

Please respond by circling one of the numbers in each dimension below to indicate *your feelings* about your experience using the multicultural coalition training design. If the adjective at the extreme left describes your feelings, circle the number *1,* and if the adjective at the extreme right describes your feelings, circle the number *7.* If your feelings are somewhere in between these two extremes, circle the appropriate number between *1* and *7.*

PLEASANT	1 2 3 4 5 6 7	UNPLEASANT
FRIENDLY	1 2 3 4 5 6 7	UNFRIENDLY
ACCEPTING	1 2 3 4 5 6 7	REJECTING
ENTHUSIASTIC	1 2 3 4 5 6 7	UNENTHUSIASTIC
LOTS OF FUN	1 2 3 4 5 6 7	SERIOUS
RELAXED	1 2 3 4 5 6 7	TENSE
COOPERATIVE	1 2 3 4 5 6 7	UNCOOPERATIVE
SUPPORTIVE	1 2 3 4 5 6 7	HOSTILE

INTERESTING	1 2 3 4 5 6 7	BORING
HARMONIOUS	1 2 3 4 5 6 7	QUARRELSOME
SELF-ASSURED	1 2 3 4 5 6 7	HESITANT
EFFICIENT	1 2 3 4 5 6 7	INEFFICIENT
OPEN	1 2 3 4 5 6 7	GUARDED

How would you describe the *anticounselor* role?

_____

How would you describe the *procounselor* role?

_____

What are the most serious weaknesses in this training model?

_____
_____
_____

What are the most promising advantages of this training model?

_____
_____
_____

What new insights have you gained as a result of using this model?

_____
_____

Ciient, Counselor, Anticounselor, Procounselor, Interpreter

Which role is the most powerful? _____
Which role is the most interesting? _____
Which role is the most educational _____
Which role is the most threatening? _____

The clients you saw emphasized *cultural differences* between persons:

from different countries	( )
from different ethnic groups	( )
from different sex roles	( )
from different lifestyles	( )
from different age groups	( )

Did the training help you anticipate resistance from clients of other cultures? _____
_____
_____

References

Allport, G. (1943). The ego in contemporary psychology. *Psychological Review, 50,* 451-478.

Allport, G. W. (1961). *Pattern and growth in personality.* New York: Holt, Rinehart & Winston.

Anderson, G. B. (1978). *The effects of the Triad Model of cross-cultural counselor training on rehabilitation counselor interpersonal functioning with black deaf clients.* Unpublished report, New York University Rehabilitation Counseling.

Bailey, F. M. (1981). *Cross cultural counselor education: The impact of microcounseling paradigms and traditional classroom methods on counselor trainee effectiveness.* Unpublished doctoral dissertation, University of Hawaii, Honolulu.

Bandura, A. (1989). Human agency in social cognitive theory. *American Psychologist, 44,* 1175-1184.

Banghart, F. (1969). *Educational systems analysis.* New York: Macmillan.

Barrett, H. (1986). *Maintaining the self in communication.* Novato, CA: Alpha & Omega.

Basic Behavioral Science Task Force of the National Advisory Mental Health Council. (1996). Basic behavioral science research for mental health: Sociocultural and environmental processes. *American Psychologist, 51,* 722-731.

Batts, V. A. (1983). Knowing and changing the cultural script component of racism. *Transactional Analysis Journal, 13,* 255-257.

Baumeister, R. (Ed.). (1986). *Public self and private self.* New York: Springer-Verlag.

Beck, A. T. (1967). *Depression: Clinical, experimental, and theoretical aspects.* New York: Harper & Row.

Beck, A. T. (1976). *Cognitive therapy and the emotional disorders.* New York: International Universities Press.

Beck, A. T. (1996). Beyond belief: A theory of modes, personality, and psychopathology. In P. M. Salkovskis (Ed.), *Frontiers of cognitive therapy* (pp. 1-25). New York: Guilford.

Blachowicz, J. (1997). The dialogue of the soul with itself. *Journal of Consciousness Studies, 4*(5-6), 485-508.

Bond-Claire, J., Pilner, P., & Stoker, S. C. (1998). An expert-novice approach to assessing implicit models of the self. In A. Colby & J. B. James (Eds.), *Competence and character through life* (pp. 113-137). Chicago: University of Chicago.

Borders, L. D., Fong-Beyette, M. L., & Cron, E. A. (1988). In-session cognitions of a counseling student: A case study. *Counselor Education and Supervision, 28,* 59-70.

Boyd-Franklin, N. (1993). Racism, secret-keeping, and African American families. In E. Imber-Black (Ed.), *Secrets in families and family therapy* (pp. 331-354). New York: Norton.

Braiker, H. B. (1989). The power of self-talk. *Psychology Today, 23*(12), 23-27.

Brewer, M. B. (1991). The social self: On being the same and different at the same time. *Personality and Social Psychology Bulletin, 17,* 475-482.

Brunner, J. (1990). *Acts of meaning.* Cambridge, MA: Harvard University Press.

Butz, M. R. (1997). *Chaos and complexity: Implications for psychological theory and practice.* Washington, DC: Taylor & Francis.

Caplow, T. (1956). A theory of coalitions in the triad. *American Sociological Review, 21,* 489-493.

Caplow, T. (1959). Further development of a theory of coalitions in the triad. *American Journal of Sociology,* 488-493.

Caplow, T. (1968). *Two against one: Coalitions in triads.* Englewood Cliffs, NJ: Prentice Hall.

Capuzzi, D., & Gross, D. R. (1995). *Counseling and psychotherapy: Theories and interventions.* Englewood Cliffs, NJ: Merrill.

Carkhuff, R. R. (1969). *Helping and human relations: Practice and research* (Vol. 2). New York: Holt, Rinehart & Winston.

Carkhuff, R. R. (1972). *The art of helping.* Amherst, MA: Human Resource Development Press.

Chambers, J. C. (1992). *Triad-training: A method for teaching basic counseling skills to chemical dependency counselors.* Unpublished doctoral dissertation, University of South Dakota, Rapid City.

Chen, Y. H., Chen, B. H., & Liao, F. C. (1995). A comparative study on the effects of counselor training by using the Triad Training Model and the Microcounseling Model. *Journal of Teaching and Counseling, 1,* 99-118.

Chertkoff, J. M. (1966). The effects of probability of future success on coalition formation. *Journal of Experimental Social Psychology, 2,* 265-277.

Chertkoff, J. M. (1967). A revision of Caplow's coalition theory. *Journal of Experimental Social Psychology, 3,* 172-177.

Churchman, C. (1968). *The systems approach.* New York: Dell.

Cohen, M. S., & Green, M. F. (1995, August). *Where the voices come from: Imaging of schizophrenic auditory hallucinations.* Paper presented to the Society for Neuroscience, Washington, DC.

Cole, J. (1996). *Beyond prejudice: Teaching tools, a Triad Model approach for the reduction of prejudicial behavior.* Ellensburg, WA: Growing Images.

Cole, S. G. (1961). An examination of the power inversion effects in three-person mixed-motive games. *Journal of Personal and Social Psychology, 11*(1), 50-58.

Corey, G. (1996). *Theory and practice of counseling and psychotherapy.* Pacific Grove, CA: Brooks/Cole.

Corrigan, J., Dell, D. M., Lewis, K. N., & Schmidt, L. D. (1980). *Counseling as a social influence process: A review* [Monograph]. Washington, DC: American Psychological Association.

Corsini, R. J. (1987). Internalization. In R. J. Corsini (Ed.), *Concise encyclopedia of psychology* (p. 610). New York: John Wiley.

Cross, W. E., Jr. (1991). *Shades of black: Diversity in African American identity.* Philadelphia: Temple University Press.

Cross, W. E. (1995). The psychology of Nigresence: Revisiting the Cross model. In J. P. Ponterott, J. M. Casas, L. A. Suzuki, & C. M. Alexander (Eds.), *Handbook of multicultural counseling* (pp. 93-122). Thousand Oaks, CA: Sage.

Cross, W. E., Jr., & Fhagen-Smith, P. (1996). Nigresence and ego identity development. In P. Pedersen, J. Draguns, W. Lonner, & J. Trimble (Eds.), *Counseling across cultures* (4th ed., pp. 108-123). Thousand Oaks, CA: Sage.

Daniels, H. (Ed.). (1996). *An introduction to Vygotsky.* London: Routledge.

Day, H. R. (1972). Interrelationships of Machiavellianism, social desirability, self-evaluation, and self-potency in American and Filipino samples: With a Philippines replication. *Proceedings of the 80th annual convention of the American Psychological Association, Honolulu, HI,* 305-306.

Derlga, V. J., Hendrick, S. S., Winstead, B. A., & Berg, J. H. (1991). *Psychotherapy as a personal relationship.* New York: Guilford.

Diaz, R. M., & Berk, L. E. (Eds.). (1992). *Private speech: From social interaction to self-regulation.* Hillsdale, NJ: Lawrence Erlbaum.

Dixon, D. N. (1986). Client resistance and social influence. In F. J. Dorn (Ed.), *The social influence process in counseling and psychotherapy* (pp. 75-83). Springfield, IL: Charles C Thomas.

Dorn, F. J. (1986). The social influence model: An overview. In F. J. Dorn (Ed.), *The social influence process in counseling and psychotherapy* (pp. 3-15). Springfield, IL: Charles C Thomas.

Elliot, J. E. (1996). Three challenges to conventional thinking about "shoulds." *Journal of Mental Health Counseling, 18*(1), 89-95.

Ellis, A. (1955). New approaches to psychotherapy. *Journal of Clinical Psychology, 11.*

Ellis, A. (1962). *Reason and emotion in psychotherapy.* New York: Lyle Stuart.

Ellis, A. (1987). The evolution of Rational-Emotive Therapy (RET) and Cognitive Behavior Therapy (CBT). In J. K. Zeig (Ed.), *The evolution of psychotherapy.* New York: Brunner/Mazel.

Erikson, E. H. (1968). *Identity: Youth and crisis.* New York: Norton.

Firestone, R. W. (1997a). *Combatting destructive thought processes: Voice therapy and separation theory.* Thousand Oaks, CA: Sage.

Firestone, R. W. (1997b). *Suicide and the inner voice: Risk assessment, treatment, and case management.* Thousand Oaks, CA: Sage.

Fischer, A. R., Jome, L. M., & Atkinson, D. R. (1998). Reconceptualizing multicultural counseling: Universal healing conditions in a culturally specific context. *Counseling Psychologist, 26,* 525-588.

Fiske, S. T., & Taylor, S. E. (1991). *Social cognition* (2nd ed.). New York: McGraw-Hill.

Forsyth, D. R., & Leary, M. R. (1997). Achieving the goals of the Scientist-Practitioner Model: The seven interfaces of social and counseling psychology. *Counseling Psychologist, 25*(2), 180-201.

Frank, J. (1961). *Persuasion and healing.* Baltimore: Johns Hopkins University Press.

Fromm, E. (1962). *Beyond the chains of illusion: An encounter with Marx and Freud.* New York: Touchstone.

Fuqua, D. R., Johnson, A. W., Anderson, M. W., & Newman, J. (1984, September). Cognitive methods in counselor training. *Counselor Education and Supervision,* pp. 85-95.

Fuqua, D. R., Newman, J., Anderson, M. W., & Johnson, A. W. (1986). Preliminary study of internal dialogue in a training setting. *Psychological Reports, 58,* 163-172.

Gamson, W. A. (1961). A theory of coalition formation. *American Sociological Review, 26,* 373-382.

Gao, G., & Ting-Toomey, S. (1998). *Communicating effectively with the Chinese.* Thousand Oaks, CA: Sage.

Gazzaniga, M. (1985). *The social brain: Discovering the networks of the mind.* New York: Basic Books.

Geertz, C. (1975). On the nature of anthropological understanding. *American Scientist, 63,* 329-338.

Gelso, C. J., & Carter, J. A. (1985). The relationship in counseling and psychotherapy: Components, consequences, and theoretical antecedents. *Counseling Psychologist, 13*(2), 155-243.

Giergrist, M. (1995). Inner speech as a cognitive process mediating self consciousness and inhibiting self deception. *Psychological Reports, 76*(1), 257-265.

Gilbert, D. T., Fiske, S. T., & Lindzey, G. (Eds.). (1998). *The handbook of social psychology* (Vol. 2, 4th ed.). Boston: McGraw-Hill.

Glass, C. R., & Arnkoff, D. B. (1994). Validity issues in self statement measures of social phobia and social anxiety. *Behavioral Research and Therapy, 32*(2), 255-267.

Glass, C. R., & Arnkoff, D. B. (1997). Questionnaire methods of cognitive self-statement assessment. *Journal of Consulting & Clinical Psychology, 65*(6), 911-927.

Goldstein, A. P., Heller, K., & Seechrest, L. B. (1966). *Psychotherapy and the psychology of behavior change.* New York: John Wiley.

Goodyear, R., & Robyak, J. (1981). Counseling as an interpersonal influence process: A perspective for counseling practice. *Personnel & Guidance Journal, 60,* 654-657.

Gordon, T. (1972). *Teacher effectiveness training: Teacher notebook.* Pasadena, CA: Effectiveness Training Associates.

Gudykunst, W. B., Gao, G., & Franklyn-Stokes, G. (1997). *Self monitoring for social appropriateness in China and England.* Paper presented at the 4th Asia Regional Conference, International Association for Cross-Cultural Psychology, Kathmandu, Nepal.

Heesacker, M., & Bradley, M. M. (1997). Beyond feelings: Psychotherapy and emotion. *Counseling Psychologist, 25*(2), 201-220.

Heesacker, M., & Carroll, T. A. (1997). Identifying and solving impediments to the social and counseling psychology interface. *Counseling Psychologist, 25*(2), 171-180.

Hermans, H. J. M. (1996). Voicing the self: From information processing to dialogical interchange. *Psychological Bulletin, 119*(1), 31-50.

Hermans, H. J. M., & Kempen, H. J. G. (1993). *The dialogical self: Meaning as movement.* New York: Academic Press.

Hernandez, A. G., & Kerr, B. A. (1985). *Evaluating the Triad Model and traditional cross-cultural counselor training.* Paper presented at the 93rd annual convention of the American Psychological Association, Los Angeles.

Herz-Lazarowitz, R., & Miller, N. (1995). *Interaction in cooperative groups: The theoretical anatomy of group learning.* New York: Cambridge University Press.

Hiebert, B., Uhlemann, M. R., Marshall, A., & Lee, D. Y. (1988). The relationship between self-talk, anxiety, and counseling skill. *Canadian Journal of Counseling, 32*(2), 163-171.

Hinde, R. A. (1997). *Relationships: A dialectical perspective.* London: Taylor & Francis.

Hines, A., & Pedersen, P. (1980). The Cultural Grid: Matching social system variables and cultural perspectives. *Asian Pacific Training and Development Journal, 1,* 5-11.

Hines, P. L., Stockton, R., & Morran, D. K. (1995). Self-talk of group therapists. *Journal of Counseling Psychology, 42,* 242-248.

Hirsch, P., & Stone, G. L. (1983). Cognitive strategies and the client conceptualization process. *Journal of Counseling Psychology, 30,* 566-572.

Ho, D. Y. F. (1991). Relational orientation and methodological individualism. *Bulletin of the Hong Kong Psychological Society, 26-27,* 81-95.

Ho, D. Y. F. (1998). Interpersonal relationships and relationship dominance: An analysis based on methodological relationism. *Asian Journal of Social Psychology, 1*(1).

Hofstader, D. (1986). *Metamagical themes.* New York: Bantam Books.

Hsu, F. L. K. (1971). Psycho-social homeostasis and *jen:* Conceptual tools for advancing psychological anthropology. *American Anthropologist, 73,* 23-44.

Hutchins, D. E., & Vaught, C. C. (1997). *Helping relationships and strategies* (3rd ed.). Pacific Grove, CA: Brooks/Cole.

Ickes, W. (1988). Attributional styles and the self-concept. In L. Y. Abramson, *Social cognition and clinical psychology: A synthesis* (pp. 66-97). New York: Guilford.

Ingram, R. E., Kendall, P. C., Siegle, G., & Guarino, J. (1995). Psychometric properties of the Positive Automatic Thoughts Questionnaire. *Psychological Assessment, 7,* 495-507.

Irvin, R., & Pedersen, P. (1995). The internal dialogue of culturally different client: An application of the Triad Training Model. *Journal of Multicultural Counseling and Development.*

Ivey, A. E. (1971). *Microcounseling: Innovations in interviewing training.* Springfield, IL: Charles C Thomas.

Ivey, A. E. (1994). *Intentional interviewing and counseling* (3rd ed.). Pacific Grove, CA: Brooks/Cole.

Jackson, M. A. (1996). *Stereotype reversal in counselor training.* Dissertation proposal, Stanford University, Stanford, CA.

Jackson, M. A. (1998, April). *Stereotype reversal method in triad multicultural counselor training.* Paper presented at the meeting of the American Educational Research Association, San Diego, CA.

Janis, I. L. (1982). *Counseling on personal decisions: Theory and research on short term helping relationships.* New Haven, CT: Yale University Press.

Johnson, F. (1985). The Western concept of self. In A. J. Marsella, G. DeVos, & F. L. K. Hsu (Eds.), *Culture and self: Asian and Western perspectives* (pp. 91-139). New York: Tavistock.

Jung, C. (1965). *Memories, dreams, reflections.* New York: Random House.

Kagan, N. (1975). Influencing human interaction: Eleven years with IPR. *Canadian Counselor, 9*(2), 74-95.

Kagan, N. I., & Kagan, H. (1990). IPR: A validated model for the 1990s and beyond. *Counseling Psychologist, 18,* 436-440.

Kagan, N., Krathwohl, D. R., Goldberg, D., Campbell, R .J., Schauble, P. G., Greenberg, B. S., Danish, S. J., Resnikoff, A., Bowees, J., & Bondy, S. B. (1967). *Studies in human interaction: Interpersonal Process Recall simulated by videotape* (Research Report No. 20). East Lansing, MI: Educational Publishing Services.

Kagan, N. I., & McQuellon, R. (1981). Interpersonal Process Recall. In R. Corsin (Ed.), *Handbook of innovative psychotherapies* (pp. 443-458). New York: Wiley & Sons.

Kagan, N., & Schauble, P. G. (1969). Affect simulation in Interpersonal Process Recall. *Journal of Counseling Psychology, 16,* 309-313.

Kagan, N. I., & Schneider, J. M. (1975). *Affective sensitivity scale: Form E.* Unpublished workbook to accompany filmed vignettes.

Kagitcibasi, C. (1996). *Family and human development across cultures.* Mahwah, NJ: Lawrence Erlbaum.

Kanfer, F. H. (1984). Self-management in clinical and social interventions. In R. P. McGlynn, J. E. Maddux, C. D. Stoltenberg, & J. H. Harvey (Eds.), *Interfaces in psychology* (pp. 141-165). Lubbock: Texas Tech University.

Kanfer, F. H., & Goldstein, A. P. (1986). *Helping people change.* New York: Pergamon.

Kaufman, R. A. (1968, Winter). A system approach to education: Derivation and definition. *AV Communication Review.*

Kelley, H. H., & Arrowood, A. J. (1969). Coalitions in the triad: Critique and experiment. *Sociometry, 23,* 231-244.

Kelly, A. E. (in press). Client secret keeping in outpatient therapy. *Journal of Counseling Psychology.*

Kelly, G. (1955). *The psychology of personal constructs.* New York: Norton.

Kendall, P., Howard, C., Dennis, L., & Hays, R. C. (1989). Self referent speech and psychopathology: The balance of positive and negative thinking. *Cognitive Therapy and Research, 18,* 588-590.

Kennington, P. A. D. (1999). *Experiencing personal sharing with culturally diverse practicum students.* Unpublished report.

Kim, U., & Berry, J. W. (Eds.). (1993). *Indigenous psychologies: Research and experience in cultural context.* Newbury Park, CA: Sage.

Kimberlin, C. L., & Friesen, D. D. (1980). Sex and conceptual level empathic responses to ambivalent affect. *Counselor Education and Supervision, 19,* 252-258.

Klein, D. L. (1996). Relationship of counselor trainee internal dialogue, self-efficacy, and hypothesis formation to therapeutic performance. *Dissertation Abstracts International Section A: Humanities & Social Sciences, 56*(11-A), 4281.

Kline, W. B. (1988). Training counselor trainees to talk to themselves: A method of focusing attention. *Counselor Education and Supervision, 22*(4), 296-302.

Komorita, S. S., & Ellis, A. L. (1988). Level of aspiration in coalition bargaining. *Journal of Personality and Social Psychology, 54*(3), 421-431.

Kravitz, D. A. (1987). Size of smallest coalition as a source of power in coalition bargaining. *European Journal of Social Psychology, 17*(1), 1-21.

Kreps, G. L., & Kunimoto, E. N. (1994). *Effective communication in multicultural health care settings.* Thousand Oaks, CA: Sage.

Kurpius, D. J., Benjamin, D., & Morran, D. K. (1985). Effects of teaching a cognitive strategy on counselor trainee internal dialogue and clinical hypothesis formulation. *Journal of Counseling Psychology, 32*(2), 263-271.

Langer, S. L., & Wurf, E. (1997). The effects of channel-consistent and channel-inconsistent interpersonal feedback on the formation of metaperceptions. Paper presented at the 105th annual convention of the American Psychological Association, Chicago.

Larson, L., & Daniels, J. A. (1998). Review of the counseling self-efficacy literature. *Counseling Psychologist, 26*(2), 179-218.

Lazarus, A. A. (1997). Friends, images, and appropriate self-talk. *Psychotherapy in Private Practice, 16*(2), 29-32.

Lederman, L. C. (1996). Internal muzak: An examination of intrapersonal relationships. *Interaction & Identity: Information and Behavior, 5,* 197-214.

Lent, R. W., & Maddux, J. E. (1997). Self-efficacy: Building a sociocognitive bridge between social and counseling psychology. *Counseling Psychologist, 25*(2), 240-255.

Liester, M. B. (1996). Inner voices: Distinguishing transcendent and pathological characteristics. *Journal of Transpersonal Psychology, 28*(1), 1-30.

Lifton, R. J. (1993). *The protean self.* New York: Basic Books.

Lonnie, A. (1994). The self as a soliloquy. *Sociological Quarterly, 35,* 521-532.

Loo, C. (1980a). *Bicultural contextualizer model for cultural sensitivity in counseling: Transcript, understanding ethnic identity.* Santa Cruz, CA: Chinatown Research Center and the University of California.

Loo, C. (1980b). *Bicultural contextualizer model for cultural sensitivity in counseling: Transcript, harmful assumptions.* Santa Cruz, CA: Chinatown Research Center and the University of California.

Luria, A. R. (1961). *The role of speech in the regulation of normal and abnormal behavior* (J. Tizard, Ed.). New York: Liveright.

Lutwak, N., & Hennessey, J. J. (1982). Conceptual systems functioning as a mediating factor in the development of counseling skills. *Journal of Counseling Psychology, 29,* 256-259.

Maddux, J. E., Stoltenberg, C. D., Rosenwein, R., & Leary, M. R. (1987). Social processes in clinical and counseling psychology: Introduction and orienting assumptions. In J. E. Maddux, C. D. Stoltenberg, & R. Rosenwein (Eds.), *Social processes in clinical and counseling psychology* (pp. 1-13). New York: Springer-Verlag.

Mahoney, J. E., & Arnkoff, D. B. (1978). *Cognitive and self control therapies.* In S. L. Garfield & A. E. Bergin (Eds.), *Handbook of psychotherapy and behavioral change: An empirical analysis* (2nd ed., pp. 689-722). New York: John Wiley.

Markus, H., & Kitayama, S. (1991). Culture and the self: Implications for cognition, emotion, and motivation. *Psychological Review, 98,* 224-253.

Markus, H., & Nurius, P. (1986). Possible selves. *American Psychologist, 41,* 954-967.

Marsella, A. J., DeVos, G., & Hsu, F. L. K. (1985). *Culture and self: Asian and Western perspectives.* New York: Tavistock.

McCall, G. J., & Simmons, J. L. (1982). *Social psychology: A sociological approach.* New York: Free Press.

McCall, G. J., & Simmons, J. L. (1991). Levels of analysis: The individual, the dyad, and the larger social group. In B. M. Montgomery & S. Duck (Eds.), *Studying interpersonal interaction* (pp. 56-81). New York: Guilford.

McIntosh, P. (1989, July/August). White privilege: Unpacking the invisible knapsack. *Peace and Freedom,* pp. 10-12.

McKay, D. G. (1992). Constraints on theories of inner speech. In D. Reisberg, *Auditory imagery* (pp. 121-149). Hillsdale, NJ: Lawrence Erlbaum.

Mead, G. H. (1934). *Mind, self, and society: From the standpoint of a social behaviorist* (C. W. Morris, Ed.). Chicago: University of Chicago Press.

Mead, G. H. (1982). *The individual and the social self: Unpublished work of George Herbert Mead* (D. L. Miller, Ed.). Chicago: University of Chicago Press.

Meichenbaum, D. (1974). *Cognitive behavior modification.* Morristown, NJ: General Learning Press.

Meichenbaum, D. (1977). *Cognitive behavior modification: An integrative approach.* New York: Plenum.

Meichenbaum, D. (1986). Cognitive behavior modification. In F. H. Kanfer & A. P. Goldstein (Eds.), *Helping people change* (pp. 346-381). New York: Pergamon.

Meichenbaum, D. (1993). The personal journey of a psychotherapist and his mother. In G. G. Brannigan & M. R. Merrens (Eds.), *The undaunted psychologist: Adventures in research* (pp. 189-201). Philadelphia: Temple University Press.

Miller, C. E., & Komorita, S. S. (1986). Changes in outcomes in coalition bargaining. *Journal of Personality and Social Psychology, 51,* 721-729.

Montgomery, R. L., & Haemmerlie, F. M. (1987). Self-perception theory and hetero-social anxiety. In J. E. Maddux, C. D. Stoltenberg, & R. Rosenwein (Eds.), *Social processes in clinical and counseling psychology* (pp. 139-152). New York: Springer-Verlag.

Moore, M. A., Britt, T. W., & Leary, M. R. (1997). Integrating social and counseling psychological perspectives on the self. *Counseling Psychologist, 25*(2), 220-240.

Morin, A. (1993). Self talk and self awareness: On the nature of the relation. *Journal of Mind and Behavior, 14*(3), 223-234.

Morin, A. (1995). Characteristics of an effective internal dialogue in the acquisition of self information. *Imagination, Cognition, and Personality, 15*(1), 45-58.

Morin, A., & James, E. (1990). Inner speech as a mediator of self-awareness, self-consciousness, and self-knowledge: An hypothesis. *New Ideas in Psychology, 8,* 337-356.

Morran, D. K. (1986). Relationship of counselor self-talk and hypothesis formulation to performance level. *Journal of Counseling Psychology, 33,* 395-400.

Morran, D. K., Kurpius, D. J., Brack, C. H. J., & Brack, G. (1995). A cognitive skills model for counselor training and supervision. *Journal of Counseling and Development, 73,* 384-389.

Murgatroyd, W. (1995). *Application of the Triad Model in teaching counseling skills and providing immediate supervision.* Unpublished manuscript, University of New Orleans, LA.

Neck, C. P., Stewart, C., Crag, L., & Manz, C. C. (1995). Thought self leadership as a framework for enhancing the performance of performance appraisers. *Journal of Applied Behavioral Science, 31*(3), 270-302.

Neimeyer, G. J., Fukuyama, M. A., Bingham, R. P., Hall, L. E., & Mussenden, M. E. (1986). Training cross-cultural counselors: A comparison of the pro and anti-counselor Triad Models. *Journal of Counseling and Development, 64,* 437-439.

Neuman, Y., & Schwartz, R. M. (1998). Is self-explanation while solving problems helpful? The case of analogical problem solving. *British Journal of Educational Psychology, 68*(1), 15-25.

Nutt-Williams, E., & Hill, C. E. (1996). The relationship between self-talk and therapy process variables for novice therapists. *Journal of Counseling Psychology, 43,* 170-177.

Oetting, E. R., & Beauvais, F. (1991). Orthogonal cultural identification theory: The cultural identification of minority adolescents. *International Journal of the Addictions, 25,* 655-685.

Ogbonnaya, A. O. (1994). Person as community: An African understanding of the person as an intrapsychic community. *Journal of Black Psychology, 20*(1), 75-87.

O'Quinn, G. M. (1986). A study of the relationship between counselor internal dialogue and counseling performance. *Dissertation Abstracts International, 47,* 180.

Ornstein, R. (1986). *Multimind.* Boston: Houghton Mifflin.

Patterson, L. E. (1988, March). The function of automaticity in counselor information processing. *Counselor Education and Supervision,* pp. 195-202.

Pedersen, A., & Pedersen, P. (1985). The Cultural Grid: A personal cultural orientation. In L. Samovar & R. Porter (Eds.), *Intercultural communication: A reader* (pp. 50-62). Belmont, CA: Wadsworth.

Pedersen, A., & Pedersen, P. (1989a). The Cultural Grid: A complicated and dynamic approach to multicultural counseling. *Counseling Psychology Quarterly, 2,* 133-141.

Pedersen, A., & Pedersen, P. (1989b). The place of age in culture. In L. Adler (Ed.), *Cross-cultural research in human development: Focus on lifespan* (pp. 234-246). Westport, CT: Greenwood.

Pedersen, P. (1966). *Anticipated outcomes of counseling when viewed as an instance of coalition.* Plan B paper for master's thesis, University of Minnesota, Minneapolis.

Pedersen, P. (1968, September). A proposal: That counseling be viewed as an instance of coalition. *Journal of Pastoral Care,* pp. 20-28.

Pedersen, P. (1972a). *Multiple training programs for non-specialists in counseling to work in cross-cultural situations.* A National Institute of Mental Health proposal.

Pedersen, P. (1972b). *A simulated counselor training role play procedure introducing the anti-counselor role of the problem in cross-cultural interaction.* Proposal submitted to the Office of International Programs, University of Minnesota, Minneapolis.

Pedersen, P. (1972c, September). *Simulating the problem role in cross-cultural counseling.* Paper presented at the meeting of the American Psychological Association, Honolulu, HI.

Pedersen, P. (1972d). *Videotaping the problem role in cross-cultural counseling.* Office of Education proposal.

Pedersen, P. (1973a). *A conceptual system describing the counseling relationship as a coalition against the problem.* Paper presented at the meeting of the American Psychological Association, Montreal, Canada.

Pedersen, P. (1973b, September). *A cross-cultural coalition training model for educating mental health professionals to function in multicultural populations.* Paper presented at the 9th International Congress of Ethnological and Anthropological Sciences, Chicago.

Pedersen, P. (1973c). *Development of a design to improve skills of cross-cultural counselors in defining problems and clarifying resistance to intercultural counseling.* Washington, DC: Department of Health, Education, and Welfare.

Pedersen, P. (1974a). Cross-cultural communications training for mental health professionals. *International and Intercultural Communication Annual, 1,* 53-64.

Pedersen, P. (1974b). A summer program for cross-cultural counselor training. *International and Intercultural Communication Annual, 2.*

Pedersen, P. (1975). A two-week international workshop in cross-cultural counseling. *International and Intercultural Communication Annual, 2,* 102-107.

Pedersen, P. (1976a). Counseling clients from other cultures: Two training designs. In *Readings in intercultural communication* (pp. 47-53). Pittsburgh: Intercultural Network.

Pedersen, P. (1976b). The field of cross-cultural counseling. In P. Pedersen, W. Lonner, & J. Draguns (Eds.), *Counseling across cultures.* Honolulu: University of Hawaii.

Pedersen, P. (1976c). A model for training mental health workers in cross-cultural counseling. In J. Westermeyer & B. Maday (Eds.), *Culture and mental health* (pp. 83-99). The Hague, The Netherlands: Mouton.

Pedersen, P. (1977). The Triad Model of cross-cultural counselor training. *Personnel and Guidance Journal, 56,* 94-100.

Pedersen, P. (1979). Cross-cultural Triad Training Model: The case of the counselor. In M. Asante & E. Newmark (Eds.), *Handbook of intercultural communication* (pp. 405-420). Buffalo: State University of New York.

Pedersen, P. (1985). *Handbook of cross-cultural counseling and therapy.* Westport, CT: Greenwood.

Pedersen, P. (1991). Multiculturalism as a fourth force in counseling. *Journal of Counseling and Development, 70*(1), 5-25.

Pedersen, P. (1994). *A handbook for developing multicultural awareness.* Alexandria, VA: American Counseling Association.

Pedersen, P. (1997a). *Culture-centered counseling interventions: A search for accuracy.* Thousand Oaks, CA: Sage.

Pedersen, P. (1997b). Recent trends in cultural theories. *Applied & Preventive Psychology: Current Scientific Perspectives, 6,* 221-231.

Pedersen, P., & Hernandez, D. (1997). *Decisional dialogues in a cultural context: Structured exercises.* Thousand Oaks, CA: Sage.

Pedersen, P., Holwill, C. F., & Shapiro, J. L. (1978). A cross-cultural training procedure for classes in counselor education. *Counselor Education and Supervision, 17*(3), 233-237.

Pedersen, P., & Ivey, A. (1993). *Culture-centered counseling skills.* Westport, CT: Greenwood.

Penn, P., & Frankfurt, M. (1994). Creating a participant text: Writing, multiple voices, narrative multiplicity. *Family Process, 33*(3), 217-231.

Pepinsky, H. B. (1959). *Counseling and psychotherapy as an instance of coalition* [Mimeographed paper]. Columbus: Ohio State University.

Pepinsky, H. B., & DeStefano, J. S. (1982). Interactive discourse in the classroom as organizational behavior. In B. A. Huston (Ed.), *Advances in reading/language research* (pp. 20-36). Greenwich, CT: JAI.

Phillips, A. A. (1990). Inner voices, inner selves: A study of international conversation in narrative. *Dissertation Abstracts International, 50,* 3677.

Quintana, S. M., & Meara, N. M. (1990). Internalization of therapeutic relationships in short term psychotherapy. *Journal of Counseling Psychology, 27,* 123-130.

Rapoport, A., & Chammah, A. M. (1965). *Prisoner's dilemma: A study in conflict and cooperation.* Ann Arbor: University of Michigan Press.

Reandeau, S. G., & Wampold, B. E. (1991). Relationship of power and involvement to working alliance: A multiple case sequential analysis of brief therapy. *Journal of Counseling Psychology, 38*(2), 107-114.

Richardson, B., & Stone, G. L. (1981). Effects of a cognitive adjunct procedure within a microtraining situation. *Journal of Counseling Psychology, 28*(2), 168-175.

Ridley, C. R., Mendoza, D. W., Kanitz, B. E., Angermeier, L., & Zenk, R. (1994). Cultural sensitivity in multicultural counseling: A perceptual schema model. *Journal of Counseling Psychology, 41*(2), 125-136.

Robins, R. W., Gosling, S. D., & Craik, K. H. (1999). An empirical analysis of trends in psychology. *American Psychologist, 54*(2), 117-128.

Robinson, F. P. (1950). *Principles and procedures in student counseling.* Boston: Houghton Mifflin.

Rozecki, T. G. (1994). An investigation of supervisor thought-listed categories of a videotaped counseling session: An extension of counselor self-talk categories. *Dissertation Abstracts International, Section B, 55*(2-B), 605.

Ryan, T. A. (1969, June). Systems techniques for programs of counseling and counselor education. *Educational Technology,* pp. 7-17.

Sampson, E. E. (1988). The debate on individualism: Indigenous psychologies of the individual and their role in personal and societal functioning. *American Psychologist, 43*(1), 15-22.

Sarbin, T. R. (1993). Foreword. In H. J. M. Hermans & H. J. G. Kempen (Eds.), *The dialogical self: Meaning as movement* (pp. xii-xv). New York: Academic Press.

Satir, V. (1964). *Conjoint family therapy.* Palo Alto, CA: Science and Behavior Books.

Schwartz, R. M. (1986). The internal dialogue: On the asymmetry between positive and negative coping thoughts. *Cognitive Therapy and Research, 10,* 591-605.

Schwartz, R. M. (1987). Our multiple selves. *Family therapy networker, 11*(2), 25-31.

Schwartz, R. M., & Garamoni, G. L. (1989). Cognitive balance and psychopathology: Valuation of an information processing model of positive and negative states of mind. *General Psychology Review, 9,* 271-294.

Shapiro, J. L. (1967). An investigation into the word: An adjective checklist. Unpublished manuscript, Hawaii State Hospital, Kaneohe, HI.

Shapiro, J. L. (1970). *An investigation into the effectiveness of sensitivity training procedures.* Unpublished doctoral dissertation, University of Waterloo, Ontario, Canada.

Sheik, A., & Sheik, K. S. (Eds.). (1989). *Eastern and Western approaches to healing: Ancient wisdom and modern knowledge.* New York: John Wiley.

Shorter, J. (1987). The social construction of an "us": Problems of accountability and narratology. In R. Burnett, P. McGhee, & D. Clarke (Eds.), *Accounting for relationships* (pp. 225-247). New York: Methuen.

Siegrist, M. (1995). Inner speech as a cognitive process mediating self conscious and inhibiting self deception. *Psychological Reports, 76*(1), 259-265.

Siegrist, M. (1996). The influence of self-consciousness on the internal consistency of different scales. *Personality and Individual Differences, 20*(1), 115-117.

Singelis, T. M. (1994). The measurement of independent and interdependent self-construals. *Personality and Social Psychology Bulletin, 20,* 580-591.

Spice, M. B. (1982). The thought selection process: A tool worth exploring. *Training and Development Journal, 36*(5), 54-59.

Stanton, W. W., & Morris, M. H. (1987). The identification of coalitions in small groups using multidimensional scaling: A methodology. *Small Group Behavior, 18*(1), 126-137.

Steiner, J. (1986). Private speech among adults. In R. M. Diaz & L. E. Berk (Eds.), *From social interaction to self-regulation* (pp. 285-296). Hillsdale, NJ: Lawrence Erlbaum.

Stern, E. (1987). The race script of the counselor: Concepts from Transactional Analysis. *International Journal for the Advancement of Counseling, 10,* 35-43.

Stevenson, W. B., Pearce, J. L., & Porter, L. W. (1985). The concept of coalition in organization theory and research. *Academy of Management Review, 10*(2), 256-267.

Stoltenberg, C. D., McNeil, B. W., & Elliott, T. R. (1995). Selected translations of social psychology to counseling psychology. *Counseling Psychologist, 23,* 603-610.

Straus, E. W. (1958). Anesthesiology and hallucinations. In R. May, E. Angel, & H. F. Ellenberger (Eds.), *Existence.* New York: Basic Books.

Strohmer, D. C., Moilapen, D. L., & Barry, L. J. (1988). Personal hypothesis testing: The role of consistency and self-schema. *Journal of Counseling Psychology, 35*(1), 56-65.

Strong, S. R. (1968). Counseling: An interpersonal influence process. *Journal of Counseling Psychology, 15,* 215-224.

Strong, S. R. (1978). Social psychological approach to psychotherapy research. In S. L. Garfield & A. E. Bergin (Eds.), *Handbook of psychotherapy and behavior change* (2nd ed., pp. 101-135). New York: John Wiley.

Strong, S. (1995). From social psychology: What? *Counseling Psychologist, 23,* 686-690.

Strong, S. R., Welsh, J. A., Corcoran, J. L., & Hoyt, W. T. (1992). Social psychology and counseling psychology: The history, products, and promise of an interface. *Journal of Counseling Psychology, 39*(2), 139-157.

Strous, M. (1997). *Counsellor inner dialogue as an impediment or facilitation of therapeutic alliance in multiracial counselling.* Research proposal for a dissertation, University of the Witwatersrand, South Africa.

Strous, M., Skuy, M., & Hickson, J. (1993). Perceptions of the Triad Model's efficacy in training family counselors for diverse South African groups. *International Journal for the Advancement of Counseling, 16,* 307-318.

Sue, D. W. (1980). *Evaluation report from DISC: 1978-1979.* Honolulu, HI: East West Center.

Sue, D. W., Carter, R. T., Casas, J. M., Fouad, N. A., Ivey, A. E., Jensen, M., LaFromboise, T., Manese, J. E., Ponterotto, J. G., & Vasquez-Nutall, E. (1998). *Multicultural counseling competencies.* Thousand Oaks, CA: Sage.

Sullivan, H. S. (1953). *The interpersonal theory of psychiatry.* New York: Norton.

Super, D. E. (1995). Values: Their nature, assessment, and practical use. In D. E. Super & B. Sverko, *Life roles, values, and careers: International findings of the work importance study* (pp. 54-62). San Francisco: Jossey-Bass.

Taylor, S. E., Pham, L. B., Rivkin, I. D., & Armor, D. A. (1998). Harnessing the imagination: Mental simulation, self-regulation, and coping. *American Psychologist, 53,* 429-439.

Taylor, S. E., & Schneider, S. K. (1989). Coping and the simulation of events. *Social Cognition, 7,* 174-194.

Thompson, C. E., & Nevile, H. A. (1999). Racism, mental health, and mental health practice. *Counseling Psychologist, 27*(2), 155-223.

Thompson, M., Ellis, R., & Wildavsky, A. (1990). *Cultural theory.* San Francisco: Westview Press.

Thoresen, C. E. (1969). The systems approach and counselor education: Basic features and implications. *Counselor Education and Supervision, 9,* 3-17.

Tomm, K. (1989). Externalizing the problem and internalizing personal agency. *Journal of Strategic and Systemic Therapies, 8*(1), 54-59.

Triandis, H. C. (1977). *Interpersonal behavior.* Monterey, CA: Brooks/Cole.

Tyler, L. (1961). *The work of the counselor.* New York: Appleton-Century-Crofts.

Valsiner, J., & Van der Veer, R. (1988). On the social nature of human cognition: An analysis of the shared intellectual roots of George Herbert Mead and Lev Vygotsky. *Journal for the Theory of Social Behavior, 18*(1), 117-136.

Vinacke, W. E. (1959). Sex roles in a three-person game. *Sociometry, 22,* 343-360.

Vinacke, W. E., & Arkoff, A. (1957). An experimental study of coalitions in the triad. *American Sociological Review, 22,* 406-414.

Vocate, D. R. (1994). *Intrapersonal communication: Different voices, different minds.* Hillsdale, NJ: Lawrence Erlbaum.

Vygotsky, L. S. (1986). *Thought and language* (A. Kozulin, Trans.). Cambridge: MIT Press. (Original work published 1934)

Vygotsky, L. S. (1987). *The collected works of L. S. Vygotsky: Vol. 1. Problems of general psychology* (R. W. Rieber & A. S. Carton, Trans. and Eds.). New York: Plenum.

Vygotsky, L. S. (1993). *The collected works of L. S. Vygotsky: Vol. 2. The fundamentals of defectology* (J. E. Knox & C. B. Stevens, Trans.). New York: Plenum.

Wade, P., & Bernstein, B. L. (1991). Culture sensitivity training and counselor's race: Effects on black female clients' perceptions and attrition. *Journal of Counseling Psychology, 38*(1), 9-15.

Wahba, M. (1972). A coalition formation under conditions of uncertainty. *Journal of Social Psychology, 88*(1), 43-54.

Wile, D. B. (1993). *After the fight: A night in the life of a couple.* New York: Guilford.

Willis, R. H. (1962). Coalitions in the tetrad. *Sociometry, 25,* 358-376.

Wills, F., & Sanders, D. (1997). *Cognitive therapy: Transforming the image.* London: Sage.

Wolff, K. H. (1950). *The sociology of George Simmel.* New York: Free Press.

Wright, R. (1986, March/April). A better mental model. *Sciences,* pp. 8-10.

Young, J. S., & Borders, L. D. (1998). The impact of metaphor on clinical hypothesis formation and perceived supervisor characteristics. *Counselor Education and Supervision, 37*(4), 238-256.

Youngs, D. J. (1996). *Effects of the multicultural Triad Training Model on African American students' perceptions of school counselors.* Submitted in partial fulfillment of the requirements of the degree of doctor of philosophy, Seton Hall University, South Orange, NJ.

Zastrow, C. (1988). What really causes psychotherapy change? *Journal of Independent Social Work, 2*(3), 5-16.

Zifferblatt, S. M. (1972). *Evaluating medical education through operations research.* Paper presented at the 4th International Conference on Medical Education, Copenhagen, Denmark.

Index

Actor-observer bias, 153
Adaptive functioning, 54, 55
Adjective Checklist, 104
Affective Sensitivity Training, 75
Affiliations, and salience, 117, 130-131
African Americans, 105, 113, 153-154. *See also* Blacks
African communitarian context, 51
Age, as salient feature, 121-125
Alienation model, in social psychology of self, 6
Allport, G., x, 48
Alter-ego, 63
Analysis of Values Questionnaire, 107, 109
Anderson, G. B., 104
Anderson, M. W., 58, 66, 71, 86
Anthetic therapy, 60
Anticipating resistance (skill area), 96-97
Anticlient/proclient approach, 149-151
Anticounselor role, 71, 77-80, 89, 90-94
    in prejudice reduction, 154
    in stereotype reversal, 152-154
    research on, 103, 104, 106-114
    transcripts of, 118-131, 138-142
Antiself system, 60, 61
Anxiety, 61-62, 66
Apartheid ideology, 149, 151
Apologizing (microskill), 98
Arbitration (microskill), 99
Armenia, 105
Armor, D. A., 85
Arnkoff, D. B., 62, 87
Arrowood, A. J., 26

Articulating the problem (skill area), 95-96, 103
Artificial intelligence, 43
Assessment:
    self-, using Triad Training Model, 165-177
    workshop, of triad training, 178-180
    See also Evaluation
Assumptions, compared to rules, 56
Asymmetry, in positive/negative thinking, 72-74
Atkinson, D. R., 21
Autocolonialization, 54
Awareness:
    multicultural, 101, 102-105, 117, 131, 162
    self-, 59, 72, 97

Bailey, F. M., 104
Balance, in positive and negative thinking, 72-74
Bandura, A., 8
Banghart, F., 11
Barrett, H., 47
Barry, L. J., 66
Batts, V. A., 87
Baumeister, R., 7
BCC. *See* Bicultural contextualizer
Beauvais, F., 6
Beck, A. T., 56, 67
Behavior:
    attitudes on power, and, 10-11
    expectations and, in Cultural Grid, 12-15, 16-17
    internal dialogue and, 41, 44-45, 46-48, 54-65

intervention and, 29
meanings and, 16-17
measurement of, 36
problem, reality of, and, 30-31
therapy strategies and, 54-65
Belief system, 54, 57
Bender Tolerance of Ambiguity Scale, 104
Benjamin, D., 86
Berg, J. H., 20
Berk, L. E., 42
Bernstein, B. L., 108
Berry, J. W., 51
Bicultural contextualizer (BCC), 144-148
Bicultural model, in social psychology of
    self, 6
Bicultural self-construal patterns, 48-49
Bingham, R. P., 107
Blachowicz, J., x
Blacks, 108, 118, 149-151. See also African
    Americans
Blumer, H., 45
Bolby's Internal Working Model, 47
Bond-Claire, J., 39
Borders, L. D., 19, 67
Boyd-Franklin, N., 87
Brack, C. H. J., 85
Brack, G., 85
Bradley, M. M., 8
Braiker, H. B., x
Brewer, M. B., 9, 40
Britt, T. W., 8
Brunner, J., 48
Buddhist concept of self, 50
Business context, in RDM, 133
Butz, M. R., 45

Caplow, T., 24, 26
Capuzzi, D., 55, 62
Carkhuff, R. R., 11, 103
Carkhuff scales, 103, 104
Carroll, T. A., 3
Carter, J. A., 20
Caucasians, 113, 134, 149
CCCI. See Cross-Cultural Counseling
    Inventory
Challenging (microskill), 98
Chambers, J. C., 110, 111
Chammah, A. M., 27
Change:
    coalition formation and, 20-22, 25, 28-29,
        31-32
    in counseling techniques, fostering of,
        113-114

in counseling triad, over time, 22,
    23(figure), 33-36, 34(figure)
in power influence, 31-32
See also Behavior; Therapy strategies
Changing the topic (microskill), 98
Chaos theory, 45
Chen, B. H., 111
Chen, Y. H., 111
Chertkoff, J. M., 26
Chicanos, 106, 145-148
China, 105, 111
Chinese concept of self, 49-50
Chinese individuals, 105, 111, 118-131
Chinese (Mandarin) language, 111, 118
Churchman, C., 11
Client-counselor coalition. See Coalition
    formation
Clients:
    anti- and pro-, 149-151
    counseling triad changes, and, 23(figure),
        33-36, 34(figure)
    in IPR method, 74-77
    in Triad Training Model, 77-80, 89, 90-94
    in Triad Training Model adaptations,
        145-158
    in Triad Training Model transcripts,
        118-142
    in Triad Training Model variations,
        134-142
    problem metaphor, coalition formation,
        and, 19-38
    regulation of power influence by, 32
    resistance of. See Resistance
    separated from problem, 31
    social power and, 10-11
Co-counselors, 89. See also Counseling
    triads
Coached clients. See Clients, in Triad
    Training Model
Coalition formation, 11-12
    against the problem, 22-38
    alternative models for, 26-27
    assumptions about, 30-36
    goals and, 24, 25, 32
    instability in, 37
    power and, 21, 22-35
    predicting strategy for, 36-37
    problem metaphor and, 21-38
    transactions and, 25
Cognitive models, 33
Cognitive processes, and training, 85-87
Cognitive psychology, xi, 9
Cognitive rational insight (microskill), 95
Cognitive structure schemas, 44-45
Cognitive therapies, 54-58

Cognitive triad, 56
Cohen, M. S., 54
Cole, J., 154, 155, 156, 159
Cole, S. G., 26
Collectivism, 48, 49, 50, 52. *See also* Self, multiple forms in
Colonialization, auto-, 54
Community, person as, 51, 52
Conceptualizing skills, 84, 86
Concerned Listener role, 154-155, 156-157
Concreteness (microskill), 95
Conditional rules, 56
Conflict, 15
Confrontation:
    awareness of (microskill), 96
    identification of (microskill), 96
    multicultural knowledge and, 107, 109
Confucian concept of self, 49, 50
Consciousness, ix-x, 8
Coping:
    behavior change and, 29
    power influence and, 31
    self-talk and, 55, 58
Corcoran, J. L., 4
Corey, G., 55
Corrigan, J., 10
Corsini, R. J., 53
Counseling:
    all as multicultural, 117
    as coalition-forming process, 11-12
    as interaction of contrary forces, 22
    as intrapersonal phenomenon, xiii
    as transaction, 25
    hidden messages revealed for, 53-67
    myths in, 4
    social psychology and, 3-12, 17-18
    social psychology and, common domains of, 3-4
    social psychology and, convergence with, 4-6
    social psychology and, differences between, 5
    social psychology and, terminology for, 27-30
    strategies for, 40-65
    training for. *See* Training
Counseling self-efficacy (CSE), 87
Counseling Technique Self-Report Inventory, 111
Counseling triads:
    analogous to three-person triad, 32
    changes in, over time, 22, 23(figure), 33-36, 34(figure)
    coalition formation and, 24-38
    in family therapy, 89

problem metaphor and, 19-38
    See also Triad Training Model
Counselor-client coalition. *See* Coalition formation
Counselor Effectiveness Scale, 104
Counselor Rating Form, 106, 107
Counselor Technique Evaluation Scale, 111
Counselors:
    counseling triad changes, and, 22, 23(figure), 33-36, 34(figure)
    multiple perspectives needed by, 71
    performance of, 63, 66, 67
    problem metaphor, coalition formation, and, 19-38
    regulation of power influence by, 31, 37
    self-talk in, 62-64
    social power and, 10-11
    training of. *See* Training
    transcripts of, 118-142, 145-148
Crag, L., 66
Craik, K. H., xi
Creativity training, 57
Credibility, 109, 110
Crisis intervention, 61
Cron, E. A., 67
Cross, W. E., Jr., 117, 118
Cross-Cultural Counseling Inventory (CCCI), 106, 107
Cross-cultural training, rationale for, 87-90.
    See also Multicultural context
CSE. *See* Counseling self-efficacy
Cultural accuracy, 95, 176. *See also* Problem articulation
Cultural context:
    awareness and, 102-105
    knowledge and, 106-109
    relational self and, 39, 41, 42, 44, 46, 48-52
    skill and, 109-114
    See also Multicultural context
Cultural contextualizer, 144
Cultural differences, xiii, 71
    training, methods for, and, 74-83
    training, rationale for, and, 87, 88
    training, skill areas in, and, 94-99
    See also Multicultural context
Cultural Grid:
    Interpersonal, 12, 13(figure), 14-15
    Intrapersonal, 12, 13(figure), 16-17
Cultural identity, 117-118
Cultural salience, 117-131, 135
Cultural self, 48-52
Culturally alienated self-construal, 49
Culture:
    broad definition of, 117

message encoding/decoding and, xiii
social psychology of self and, 6, 8, 37
See also Cultural context; Multicultural
   context; Personal-cultural orientation
Culture teachers, 15-17, 164

Daniels, H., 41
Daniels, J. A., 87
Day, H. R., 26
Decoding of messages, xiii
Defensive counselor behavior:
   diminishing of, 97-98, 177
   multicultural knowledge and, 109
Dell, D. M., 10
Deluging, 63
Demographic groups, and salience, 117
Dennis, L., 67
Depression, 56-57, 61, 67
Depression inventory, 56-57
Derlga, V. J., 20
Description (microskill), 97
DeStefano, J. S., 33
Developmental processes, 41-42
DeVos, G., 49
Diaz, R. M., 42
Dialogical self, 45-46, 47. *See also* Internal
   dialogue
Directions (microskill), 96
Directive support continuum, 28
Distracter role, 154-155, 156, 158-159
Dixon, D. N., 11
Dominant majority model, in social
   psychology of self, 6
Dorn, F. J., 10

Eastern concepts of self, 49-50, 51
Ecological power, 10
Education and training. *See* Training
Educational context, in RDM, 132-133
Ego, x, 39, 44
Ego-supportive psychotherapy, 36
Egocentric speech, 42. *See also* Internal
   dialogue
Elliot, J. E., 60
Elliott, T. R., 3
Ellis, A., 21, 28, 40, 54, 67
Ellis, R., 7
Emotions, 8, 57
Encoding of messages, xiii
Equalizing effect, definition of, 30
Erikson, E. H., 39
Errors. *See* Mistakes
Ethnic identity, and BCC, 144-145
Ethnographic groups, and salience, 117

European Americans, 105
Evaluation:
   as a microskill, 97
   of counselor performance, 63, 66, 67
   of internal dialogue effects, 65-67
   of triad training workshops, 178-180
   Triad Training Model and, 101, 102-114,
      165-177
Expectations, in Cultural Grid, 12-15, 16-17
Expected utility, in coalitions, 26-27
Experimental psychologists, and
   self-exploration, 76
Expert power, 10
External speech, 42-43

False consciousness, 54
Family therapy, 63-64, 67, 89, 112, 134
Fhagen-Smith, P., 117, 118
Field theory, 24
Firestone, R. W., 60, 61
Fischer, A. R., 21
Fiske, S. T., ix, 44
Fixed role therapy, 15
Focus (microskills):
   on basic problem, 98
   on group, 97
   on topic, 97
Fong-Beyette, M. L., 67
Forsyth, D. R., 3
Frank, J., 5
Frankfurt, M., 64
Franklyn-Stokes, G., 50
Freud, S., x, 39
Friendly third party, 134
Friesen, D. D., 84
Fromm, E., 60
Fukuyama, M. A., 107
Fuqua, D. R., 58, 66, 71, 86, 87

Game theory, 27, 36-37
Gamson, W. A., 26
Gao, G., 50
Garamoni, G. L., 40, 72, 73, 74
Gazzaniga, M., 43
Geertz, C., 39
Gelso, C. J., 20
Gender, as salient feature, 118-121
Genuineness (microskill), 96
Gestalt therapy, 63
Ghana, 105
Giergrist, M., 3
Gilbert, D. T., ix
Glass, C. R., 62
Global Rating Scale (GRS), 106, 107

Golden section hypothesis, 72, 73
Goldstein, A. P., 5, 57, 58
Goodyear, R., 10
Gordon, T., 103
Gordon scale, 103
Gosling, S. D., xi
Green, M. F., 54
Gross, D. R., 55, 62
GRS. *See* Global Rating Scale
Guarino, J., 62
Gudykunst, W. B., 50

Haemmerlie, F. M., 44
Hall, L. E., 107
Hall, E. T., vii-viii
Hays, R. C., 67
Hearing voices, x, 54, 164. *See also* Hidden
    messages; Internal dialogue; Self-talk
Heesacker, M., 3, 8
Heller, K., 5
Hendrick, S. S., 20
Hennessey, J. J., 84
Hermans, H. J. M., 19, 44, 46, 47
Hernandez, A. G., 106, 107
Hernandez, D., 133
Herz-Lazarowitz, R., 40
Hickson, J., 111
Hidden messages, ix, xiii
    Cultural Grid and, 14-15
    methods for revealing, 53-67
    profound effect of, 53
    training, and implications of, 84-100
    training for access to, 71-83, 87. *See also*
        Triad Training Model
    See also Internal dialogue; Self-talk
Hiebert, B., 63
Hill, C. E., 62, 66
Hinde, R. A., 47
Hines, A., 12
Hines, P. L., 67
Hirsch, P., 9
Hmong Laotian-American, 135-136
Ho, D. Y. F., 50
Hofstader, D., 43
Holwill, C. F., 104
Homosexuality, 128-130
Hostile third party, 134
Howard, C., 67
Hoyt, W. T., 4
Hsu, F. L. K., 49, 50
Human relations training, 103, 104
Humor, sense of (microskill), 97
Hutchins, D. E., 84
Hypothesis formulation skills, 86

"I" and "me," 40-41, 44, 46-47. *See also*
    Internal dialogue
Ickes, W., 58
Id, x, 39, 44
Identity:
    conscious self and, x
    cultural, and salience, 117-118
    ethnic, and BCC, 144-145
    loss of, 47
    relational self, internal dialogue, and, 39,
        40-51
    social psychology and, 9
    therapy strategies, self-talk, and, 64-65
Ideological splits, 118
Imbalance, in positive and negative thinking,
    72-74
Immediacy (microskill), 95
Individualized self, 39, 40, 48, 49, 52
Indochinese refugee, 134-136
Inertia, and behavior change, 29
Influencing skills, 29. *See also* Power; Social
    influence dynamics
Informational power, 10
Ingram, R. E., 62
Inner critic, 60
Inner family, 63-64, 67
Inner speech:
    as self-consciousness mediator, 72
    relational self and, 41-44
    self-instruction and, 55-56, 58
    See also Internal dialogue; Self-talk
Inquirer role, in IPR, 74-77
Interdependent self-construal, 48
Interests, personal-cultural orientation and,
    15, 16
Internal dialogue, x-xi
    assessing the effects of, 65-67
    conceptualizing skills and, 86-87
    developmental processes and, 41-42
    multicultural awareness and, 102
    positive and negative sides of, 71, 72-74,
        77-83
    relational self and, 39-52
    therapy strategies and, 40-65
    training for access to, 71, 74-83, 86-87,
        89. *See also* Triad Training Model
    See also Hidden messages; Self-talk
Internal Working Model (IWM) of self and
    others, 47
International applications:
    of Triad Training Model, 105, 111, 117-131
    of Triad Training Model adaptations,
        149-151
    of Triad Training Model variations,
        134-136

Interpersonal complementarity, 20-21
Interpersonal Cultural Grid, 12, 13(figure),
   14-15
Interpersonal influence continuum, 28
Interpersonal phenomena:
   internal dialogue and, 41, 51, 60, 161
   shift away from, 9
Interpersonal Process Recall (IPR), 74-77,
   104, 154
Interpretation (microskill), 96
Interpreter/translator model, 134-136
Intervention, definition of, 28-29
Intrapersonal Cultural Grid, 12, 13(figure),
   16-17
Intrapersonal phenomena:
   focus of social psychology on, 9
   relational self and, 41-52
   study of, ix-xi, 161
   See also Hidden messages; Internal
      dialogue; Self-talk
Intrapsychic dynamic, x, 20-21
Introspectionists, 76
IPR. See Interpersonal Process Recall
Irvin, R., 108
Ivey, A. E., 11, 12, 28, 29, 104, 110
IWM. See Internal Working Model

Jackson, M. A., 151, 152, 153
James, E., 51
Janis, I. L., 63
Japanese concept of self, 49
Johnson, A. W., 58, 66, 71, 86
Johnson, F., 49
Jome, L. M., 21
Jung, C., x
Juvenile delinquency, 121-125

Kagan, H., 77, 154
Kagan, N., 74, 75, 76, 77, 104, 154
Kagitcibasi, C., 49
Kanfer, F. H., 20, 57, 58
Kaufman, R. A., 11
Kelley, H. H., 26
Kelly, A. E., 53, 56
Kelly, G., 15
Kempen, H. J. G., 44, 46, 47
Kendall, P., 62, 67
Kennington, P. A. D., 105
Kenyans, 108
Kerr, B. A., 106, 107
Kim, U., 51
Kimberlin, C. L., 84
Kitayama, S., 48
Klein, D. L., 84

Kline, W. B., 66
Knowledge, multicultural, 101, 106-109,
   117, 131, 162
Komorita, S. S., 21
Kravitz, D. A., 21
Kreps, G. L., 60
Kuhn, M., 45
Kunimoto, E. N., 60
Kurpius, D. J., 85, 86

Langer, S. L., 61
Language:
   internal dialogue and, 41-42
   multicultural skill and, 109, 110, 111
   See also Internal dialogue; Self-talk
Laotian-American, 135-136
Larson, L., 87
Lazarus, A. A., x
Lead techniques, 36
Leary, M. R., 3, 4, 8
Lederman, L. C., 51, 61
Lee, D. Y., 63
Legitimate power, 10
Lent, R. W., 8
Lesbian lifestyle, 128-130
Lewin, field theory of, 24
Lewis, K. N., 10
Liao, F. C., 111
Liester, M. B., x, 54
Lifton, R. J., 47, 48
Lindzey, G., ix
Listening, effective, 154
Lonnie, A., 45
Loo, C., 144, 145, 147, 148
Luria, A. R., 41
Lutwak, N., 84

Maddux, J. E., 4, 8
Mahoney, J. E., 87
Mainland China, 125-127
Mandarin Chinese language, 111, 118
Manipulation (microskill), 98
Manz, C. C., 66
Markus, H., 44, 48
Marsella, A. J., 49
Marshall, A., 63
Mastery, and behavior change, 29
McCall, G. J., 9, 40, 41
McIntosh, P., 153
McKay, D. G., 40
McNeil, B. W., 3
McQuellon, R., 75, 76
"Me," and internal dialogue, 40-41, 44,
   46-47. See also "Us"; "You"

Mead, G. H., 40, 41, 43, 44, 45, 49
Meara, N. M., 5, 20, 21, 47
Measurement, in internal dialogue, 65, 72
Meichenbaum, D., 40, 54, 55, 67, 86
Metaperception, 61
Metaphorical analysis (microskill), 99
Metaphors:
  problem as, 19-38
  usefulness of, 19, 22, 64
Methodological relationism, 50
Microcounseling, 103, 111
Microskills, multicultural, 95-99, 110
Military context, in RDM, 133
Miller, C. E., 21
Miller, N., 40
Mind, and internal dialogue, 43
Minimum resource theory, of coalition
  formation, 26
Mirroring (microskill), 97
Mistakes:
  allowing trainees to make, 103
  recovery from, 98-99, 177
Modeling, in training, 87
Modular selves, 43, 64
Moilapen, D. L., 66
Montgomery, R. L., 44
Moore, M. A., 8
Morin, A., 51, 59
Morran, D. K., 65, 67, 85, 86
Morris, M. H., 21
Multicultural, all counseling as, 117
Multicultural competencies:
  awareness level of, 101, 102-105, 117,
    131, 162
  knowledge level of, 101, 106-109, 117,
    131, 162
  questions on, 163
  skill level of, 101, 109-114, 117, 131, 162,
    176-177
Multicultural context:
  counselor perspectives and, 71
  self and, 6-7, 16-17
  training in, implementation of, 90-99
  training in, methods for, 74-83
  training in, rationale for, 87-90
  training in, skill areas for, 94-99
  training in, transcripts of, 117-131
  See also Cultural context; Cultural
    differences
Multidimensional model, in social
  psychology of self, 6
Multiple forms, in self, 41, 43, 44, 46-52, 63
Murgatroyd, W., 104, 105
Mussenden, M. E., 107

Narratives, self-, 46-47
Neck, C. P., 66
Needs, and personal-cultural orientation, 15,
  16
Negative thinking, 54-56, 60, 61
  need for, 73
  positive thinking and, 72-74, 77-83, 89,
    105
  training for access to. *See* Anticounselor
    role; Triad Training Model
Neimeyer, G. J., 107
Neurosis, 40
Nevile, H. A., 53
Neuman, Y., 63
Newman, J., 58, 66, 71, 86
Nigrescence theory, 118
Nurius, P., 44
Nutt-Williams, E., 62, 66

Oetting, E. R., 6
Ogbonnaya, A. O., 51
Optimal distinctiveness model, in social
  identity, 9
O'Quinn, G. M., 66
Organizational behavior, 66
Ornstein, R., 43
Orthogonal model, in social psychology of
  self, 6
Outcome psychodrama, 63

Palestine, 105
Paraphrase (microskill), 95
Parental messages, 60, 61
Patterson, L. E., 63
Payoff, definition of, 28
Pearce, J. L., 21
Pedersen, A., 12
Pedersen, P., 12, 15, 22, 77, 88, 89, 102, 104,
  106, 108, 110, 133, 134
Penn, P., 64
Pepinsky, H. B., 25, 33
Perception, meta-, 61
Perceptual field theory, 22, 30, 33
Perceptual schema model, 151
Performance evaluation, of counselors, 63,
  66, 67
Personal constructs theory, 15, 72
Personal-cultural orientation:
  Cultural Grid and, 12-17
  culture teachers and, 15-17
  importance of, 37
  problem metaphor and, 19-38
  See also Cultural context; Multicultural
    context

Personality, x, 44
Pham, L. B., 85
Phillips, A. A., 61
Phobias, social, 61-62
Physical factors, and salience, 135-136
Piaget, J., 42
Pilner, P., 39
Planning (microskill), 98
Plato, 40
Political affiliation, 125-128
Porter, L. W., 21
Positioning (microskill), 99
Positive Automatic Thoughts Questionnaire,
     62
Positive regard (microskill), 96
Positive thinking:
     negative thinking and, 72-74, 77-83, 89,
          105
     training for access to. See Procounselor
          role; Triad Training Model
Power:
     attributes and, 11
     changing equilibrium of, 33-35
     coalition formation and, 21, 22-35
     counseling triad changes and, 22,
          23(figure), 33-36, 34(figure)
     estimation of, 31, 37
     modification of, 31-32, 37
     social influence and, 10-12
Power influence, definition of, 27-28
Prayer, x
Prejudice reduction, 154-159. See also
     Stereotyping
Private events, 7
Private speech, 42, 44, 57. See also Internal
     dialogue; Self-talk
Proactive Approach to Reducing Prejudice,
     154-159
Problem:
     as counseling metaphor, 19-38
     as enemy of coalition, 22, 31
     behavior and, 30-31
     coalition formation and, 22-38
     counseling triad changes and, 22,
          23(figure), 33-36, 34(figure)
     definition of, 27
     reality of, 30-31
     separated from client, 31
Problem articulation (skill area), 95-96, 103
Problem solving, 59, 63, 85
Proclient role, 149-151
Procounselor role, 77-80
     research on, 104, 107-109, 111-114
     transcripts of, 118-131, 136-138, 141-142
Proprium, x

Protean self, 47
Psychodrama, 63
Psychology, changing focus of, ix-x, xi
Psychosis, 39-40
Punishment and reward, 36

Questioning (microskill), 96
Quintana, S. M., 5, 20, 21, 47

Race, 108, 113, 149-154
Racism, 53-54, 87, 151
Rapoport, A., 27
Rational Emotive Behavior Therapy (RET),
     54-55
Rationality, 36, 55
RDM. See Rehearsal Demonstration Model
Reandeau, S. G., 21
Recall. See Interpersonal Process Recall
Receptivity (microskill), 97
Recognizing resistance (skill area), 96-97,
     177
Recovery skill, 98-99, 177
Referent power, 10
Referral (microskill), 99
Reflection of feeling (microskill), 95
Reflective models, 33, 35-36
Rehearsal Demonstration Model (RDM),
     132-133
Relational self, 39-52
Relationships:
     counseling outcomes and, 20
     personal-cultural orientation and, 15
     salience and, 117, 130-131
Resistance:
     anticipation of, 103
     multicultural competencies and, 103, 112
     recognition of, as skill area, 96-97, 177
     social power and, 10, 11
Respect (microskill), 96
RET. See Rational Emotive Behavior
     Therapy
Revised Carkhuff Respect and Genuineness
     Scale, 104
Revised Truax Accurate Empathy Scale, 104
Reward and punishment, 36
Rewards, in coalitions, 24-25
Richardson, B., 86
Ridley, C. R., 151
Risk taking, and training, 87, 98
Rivkin, I. D., 85
Robins, R. W., xi
Robinson, F. P., 36
Robyak, J., 10
Rogers, C., 32, 35

Role plays, 87, 88, 90-94. *See also* Triad
  Training Model
Role reversal (microskill), 98
Rosenwein, R., 4
Rozecki, T. G., 86
Rules, compared to assumptions, 56
Ryan, T. A., 11

Salience, and training, 117-131, 135
Sampson, E. E., 49
Sanders, D., 56, 57
Sarbin, T. R., 46
SASB. *See* Structural Analysis of Social
  Behavior
Satir, V., 89, 134
Saudi Arabia, 105
Schauble, P. G., 76
Schemas, 44-45, 56
Schizophrenics, 54, 55
Schmidt, L. D., 10
Schneider, J. M., 75
Schneider, S. K., 45
Schwartz, R. M., 40, 63, 64, 72, 73, 74
Scripted nature of behavior, 54
Secrets, 53. *See also* Hidden messages
Seechrest, L. B., 5
Self:
  African concept of, 51
  as audience, 7-8
  as crowd of people, 46
  as organizing scheme, x
  as soliloquy, 45
  complexity in social psychology of, 6-7
  cultural, 48-52
  dialogical, 45-46, 47
  Eastern concepts of, 49-50, 51
  in community, 51, 52
  individualized, 39, 40, 48, 49, 52
  multicultural context and, 6-7, 16-17
  multiple forms in, 41, 43, 44, 46-52, 63
  protean, 47
  relational, 39-52
  social power and, 10-12
  social psychology of, 6-12
  Western concepts of, 39, 49
Self-Assessment Survey, 107, 108
Self-awareness, 59, 72, 97
Self-consciousness, 62-63, 67, 72
Self-construal, 48-49
Self-defeating beliefs, 54
Self-disclosure (microskill), 97
Self-efficacy, counseling, 87
Self-information, 59
Self-instruction, 54-55, 57, 86

Self-monitoring, 50
Self-narratives, 46-47
Self-presentation, 7-8
Self-statements, 54-55, 58, 67, 72-73. *See
  also* Internal dialogue; Self-talk
Self-talk:
  ability to control, 60
  balance needed in, 59-60
  quality versus quantity of, 66
  relational self and, 40, 44, 45, 52
  therapy strategies and, 40-65
  training and, 63-64, 65-67, 86-87
  See also Hidden messages; Inner speech;
    Internal dialogue
Sense of humor (microskill), 97
Separation theory, 60-61
Sexual harassment, 118-121
Shapiro Adjective Checklist, 104
Shapiro, J. L., 103, 104
Shares of power, in coalitions, 24-30
Sharing Person role, 154-156, 157-158
Sheik, A., x
Sheik, K. S., x
Shorter, J., 45
Siegle, G., 62
Siegrist, M., 58, 62, 67, 72
Silence (microskill), 98
Simmel, G., 24
Simmons, J. L., 9, 40, 41
Simulations, usefulness of, 85-87, 88. *See
  also* Triad Training Model
Singelis, T. M., 48
Skill, multicultural, 94-99, 101, 109-114,
  117, 131, 162, 176-177. *See also* Training
Skuy, M., 111
Social appropriateness, 50
Social cognitive theory, 8, 61
Social constructionism, 64
Social identity, 9, 40-51. *See also* Identity
Social influence dynamics, 4-5, 10-12
Social phobias, 61-62
Social power, 10-11. *See also* Power
Social psychology:
  counseling and, 3-12, 17-18
  counseling and, common domains of, 3-4
  counseling and, convergence with, 4-6
  counseling and, differences between, 5
  counseling and, terminology for, 27-30
  myths in, 4
  of self, 6-12
  shifting focus of, 9
  social power and, 10-12
Sociocultural context, 37, 117
  relational self and, 44, 46, 48, 52

See also Culture; Multicultural context;
  Personal-cultural orientation
Soliloquy, self as, 45
South Africa, 111-112, 149-151
Speech:
  external, 42-43
  inner, 41-44
  See also Internal dialogue; Self-talk
Spice, M. B., 86
Spiritual factors, and salience, 135-136
Spontaneity (microskill), 97
Stanton, W. W., 21
Status groups, and salience, 117
Steiner, J., 9
Stereotype reversal, 151-154
Stereotyping, 148, 149. *See also* Prejudice
  reduction
Stern, E., 87
Stevenson, W. B., 21
Stewart, C., 66
Stockton, R., 67
Stoker, S. C., 39
Stoltenberg, C. D., 3, 4
Stone, G. L., 9, 86
Stories, and internal dialogue, 46-47
Straight lifestyle, 128, 130
Straus, E. W., 46
Stress-coping insight (microskill), 96
Stress-inoculation training, 57-58
Striving, and behavior change, 29
Strohmer, D. C., 66
Strong, S., 4, 5, 9, 10
Strous, M., 111, 112, 149, 151
Structural Analysis of Social Behavior
  (SASB), 47
Sue, D. W., 101, 102, 104, 109
Suicidal patients, 61
Sullivan, H. S., 46
Summarization (microskill), 95
Super, D. E., 15
Superego, x, 39, 44
Symbolic interactionists, 61
Systems approach, and behavior, 46

Taiwan, 105, 111, 125-127
Taoist concept of self, 50
Taylor, S. E., 44, 45, 85
Termination, of the interview (microskill), 99
TFA (thinking, feeling, acting) framework,
  84
Therapists. *See* Counselors
Therapy strategies, 40-65. *See also*
  Counseling
Think aloud approaches, 66

Third party friendly/hostile variation, 134
Thompson, C. E., 53
Thompson, M., 7
Thoresen, C. E., 11
Thought-listing, 66, 86
Thought self-leadership (TSL), 66
Thought-stopping procedures, 62
Threatened feeling, 97
Three-way dialogue, ix. *See also* Triad
  Training Model
Ting-Toomey, S., 50
Tolerance of Ambiguity Scale, 104
Tomm, K., 64
Topic (microskills):
  changing of, 98
  focus on, 97
Tracking (microskill), 96
Traditional self-construal patterns, 39, 49
Training:
  anticlient/proclient approach to, 149-151
  cognition and, 85-87
  cultural differences and, 71
  cultural differences and, methods for,
    74-83
  cultural differences and, rationale for, 87,
    88
  cultural differences and, skill areas in,
    94-99
  implications of hidden messages for,
    84-100
  internal dialogue and, 63-64, 65-67, 86-87
  international, 105, 111, 117-131
  IPR for, 74-77
  multicultural. *See* Multicultural
    competencies
  positive/negative messages and, 71, 74,
    77-83
  prejudice reduction in, 154-159
  salience-based perspective and, 117-131,
    135
  self-instructional, 54-55, 57-58, 86
  social psychology and, 11, 80
  stereotype reversal in, 151-154
  TFA framework for, 84
  transcripts of, 118-142, 145-148
  Triad Model for. *See* Triad Training Model
Transactions, 25
Transcript applications, 117-143, 145-148
Transitional model, in social psychology of
  self, 6
Transitory self, 45
Translator, 134-136
Triad Training Model:
  adaptations of, 144-160
  advantages of, 79, 80-82, 84, 99

anecdotal reports on, 101, 103, 110-111
basis of, ix
benefits of, xi
conditions needed for, 78
implementation of, designs for, 90-94
implementation of, skill areas in, 94-99
multicultural awareness and, 102-105
multicultural knowledge and, 106-109
multicultural skill and, 110-114
populations used with, 102-103
program evaluation of, 178-180
research findings on, 102-114
research needs for, 114
roles in, 77-80, 89, 103, 104, 106-114
self-assessment using, 165-177
transcript applications of, 117-143
variations in, 132-143
See also Cognitive triad; Counseling
    triads; Simulations; Training
Triandis, H. C., 11, 102
Truax Accurate Empathy Scale, Revised, 104
TSL. *See* Thought self-leadership
Tyler, L., 32

Uhlemann, M. R., 63
Uniqueness theory, in social identity, 9
Unspoken messages, in RDM, 132-133. *See
    also* Hidden messages
"Us," and internal dialogue, 45. *See also*
    "Me"

Valsiner, J., 41
Values, and personal-cultural orientation, 15,
    16, 17
Values conflict, identification of (microskill),
    96
Van der Veer, R., 41
Vaught, C. C., 84

Verbal thinking, 42-43. *See also* Internal
    dialogue
Videotapes, 74, 90-92
Vinacke, W. E., 26
Vocate, D. R., 41, 44
Voice therapy, 60-61
Voices, x, 54, 164. *See also* Hidden
    messages; Internal dialogue; Self-talk
Vygotsky, L. S., 41, 42, 43

Wade, P., 108
Wahba, M., 26
Wampold, B. E., 21
Welsh, J. A., 4
Western concepts of self, 39, 49
Western context, 130, 134-136
White, M., 64, 65
Whites, 113, 134, 149
Wildavsky, A., 7
Wile, D. B., 43
Willis, R. H., 26
Wills, F., 56, 57
Winstead, B. A., 20
Wolff, K. H., 24
Workplace, sexual harassment in, 118-121
Wright, R., 22
Writing therapy, 64
Wundt, W., 76
Wurf, E., 61

"You," and voice therapy, 61. *See also* "Me";
    "Us"
Young, J. S., 19
Youngs, D. J., 113

Zastrow, C., 61
Zero-sum conditions, 36-37

Zifferblatt, S. M., 11

About the Author

Paul B. Pedersen is Professor in the Department of Human Studies at the University of Alabama-Birmingham. He has been a university faculty member at the University of Minnesota, the University of Hawaii, and Syracuse University and for 6 years in Indonesia, Malaysia, and Taiwan. He is a Fellow in Divisions 9, 17, 45, and 52 of the American Psychological Association and an active member of AMCD and ACES in the American Counseling Association. He has published 34 books, 62 chapters, and 92 articles on various aspects of multicultural counseling and communication.